CASTRO AND THE
CUBAN REVOLUTION

**Other Titles in the Greenwood Press Guides
to Historic Events of the Twentieth Century**
Randall M. Miller, Series Editor

The Persian Gulf Crisis
Steve A. Yetiv

World War I
Neil M. Heyman

The Civil Rights Movement
Peter B. Levy

The Holocaust
Jack R. Fischel

The Breakup of Yugoslavia and the War in Bosnia
Carole Rogel

Islamic Fundamentalism
Lawrence Davidson

Frontiers of Space Exploration
Roger D. Launius

The Collapse of Communism in the Soviet Union
William E. Watson

Origins and Development of the Arab-Israeli Conflict
Ann M. Lesch and Dan Tschirgi

The Rise of Fascism in Europe
George P. Blum

The Cold War
Katherine A. S. Sibley

The War in Vietnam
Anthony O. Edmonds

World War II
Loyd E. Lee

The Unification of Germany, 1989–1990
Richard A. Leiby

The Environmental Crisis
Miguel A. Santos

CASTRO AND THE CUBAN REVOLUTION

Thomas M. Leonard

Greenwood Press Guides to
Historic Events of the Twentieth Century
Randall M. Miller, Series Editor

Greenwood Press
Westport, Connecticut • London

Library of Congress Cataloging-in-Publication Data

Leonard, Thomas M., 1937–
    Castro and the Cuban Revolution / Thomas M. Leonard.
        p.   cm.—(Greenwood Press guides to historic events of the
    twentieth century, ISSN 1092–177X)
    Includes bibliographical references (p.   –   ) and index.
    ISBN 0–313–29979–X (alk. paper)
    1. Cuba—History—1959– 2. Cuba—History—Revolution, 1959.
    3. Castro, Fidel, 1927–   . I. Title. II. Series.
    F1788.L388   1999
    972.9106′4—dc21   98–41685

British Library Cataloguing in Publication Data is available.

Copyright © 1999 by Thomas M. Leonard

Library of Congress Catalog Card Number: 98–41685
ISBN: 0–313–29979–X
ISSN: 1092–177X

First published in 1999

Greenwood Press, 88 Post Road West, Westport, CT 06881
An imprint of Greenwood Publishing Group, Inc.
www.greenwood.com

Printed in the United States of America

The paper used in this book complies with the
Permanent Paper Standard issued by the National
Information Standards Organization (Z39.48–1984).

10 9 8 7 6 5 4 3 2 1

Front cover photo: Mikhail Gorbachev and Fidel Castro. AP/Wide World Photos.

For José and "Mimi" Fernández

Contents

A photo essay follows page 66

Series Foreword

As the twenty-first century approaches, it is time to take stock of the political, social, economic, intellectual, and cultural forces and factors that have made the twentieth century the most dramatic period of change in history. To that end, the Greenwood Press Guides to Historic Events of the Twentieth Century presents interpretive histories of the most significant events of the century. Each book in the series combines narrative history and analysis with primary documents and biographical sketches, with an eye to providing both a reference guide to the principal persons, ideas, and experiences defining each historic event, and a reliable, readable overview of that event. Each book further provides analyses and discussions, grounded in both primary and secondary sources, of the causes and consequences, in thought and action, that give meaning to the historic event under review. By assuming a historical perspective, drawing on the latest and best writing on each subject, and offering fresh insights, each book promises to explain how and why a particular event defined the twentieth century. No consensus about the meaning of the twentieth century emerges from the series, but, collectively, the books identify the most salient concerns of the century. In so doing, the series reminds us of the many ways those historic events continue to affect our lives.

Each book follows a similar format designed to encourage readers to consult it both as a reference and a history in its own right. Each volume opens with a chronology of the historic event, followed by a narrative overview, which also serves to introduce and examine briefly the main themes and issues related to that event. The next set of chapters is composed of topical essays, each analyzing closely an issue or problem of interpretation introduced in the opening chapter. A concluding chapter suggesting the long-term implications and meanings of the historic event brings the strands of the preceding chapters together while placing the event in the larger historical context. Each book also includes a section of short biographies of the principal persons related to the event, followed by a section introducing and reprinting key historical documents illustrative of and pertinent to the event. A glossary of selected terms adds to the utility of each book. An annotated bibliography—of significant books, films, and CD-ROMs—and an index conclude each volume.

The editors made no attempt to impose any theoretical model or historical perspective on the individual authors. Rather, in developing the series, an advisory board of noted historians and informed high school history teachers and public and school librarians identified the topics needful of exploration and the scholars eminently qualified to examine those events with intelligence and sensitivity. The common commitment throughout the series is to provide accurate, informative, and readable books, free of jargon and up to date in evidence and analysis.

Each book stands as a complete historical analysis and reference guide to a particular historic event. Each book also has many uses, from understanding contemporary perspectives on critical historical issues, to providing biographical treatments of key figures related to each event, to offering excerpts and complete texts of essential documents about the event, to suggesting and describing books and media materials for further study and presentation of the event, and more. The combination of historical narrative and individual topical chapters addressing significant issues and problems encourages students and teachers to approach each historic event from multiple perspectives and with a critical eye. The arrangement and content of each book thus invite students and teachers, through classroom discussions and position papers, to debate the character and significance of great historic events and to discover for themselves how and why history matters.

The series emphasizes the main currents that have shaped the modern world. Much of that focus necessarily looks at the West, especially Europe and the United States. The political, commercial, and cultural expansion of the West wrought largely, though not wholly, the most fundamental changes of the century. Taken together, however, books in the series reveal the interactions between Western and non-Western peoples and society, and also the tensions between modern and traditional cultures. They also point to the ways in which non-Western peoples have adapted Western ideas and technology and, in turn, influenced Western life and thought. Several books examine such increasingly powerful global forces as the rise of Islamic fundamentalism, the emergence of modern Japan, the Communist revolution in China, and the collapse of communism in eastern Europe and the former Soviet Union. American interests and experiences receive special attention in the series, not only in deference to the primary readership of the books but also in recognition that the United States emerged as the dominant political, economic, social, and cultural force during the twentieth century. By looking at the century through the lens of American events and experiences, it is possible to see why the age has come to be known as "The American Century."

Assessing the history of the twentieth century is a formidable prospect. It has been a period of remarkable transformation. The world broadened and narrowed at the same time. Frontiers shifted from the interiors of Africa and Latin America to the moon and beyond; communication spread from mass circulation newspapers and magazines to radio, television, and now the Internet; skyscrapers reached upward, and suburbs stretched outward; energy switched from steam, to electric, to atomic power. Many changes did not lead to a complete abandonment of established patterns and practices so much as a synthesis of old and new, as, for example, the increased use of (even reliance on) the telephone in the age of the computer. The automobile and the truck, the airplane, and telecommunications closed distances, and people in unprecedented numbers migrated from rural to urban, industrial, and ever more ethnically diverse areas. Tractors and chemical fertilizers made it possible for fewer people to grow more, but the environmental and demographic costs of an exploding global population threatened to outstrip natural resources and human innovation. Disparities in wealth increased, with developed nations prospering and underdeveloped nations starving. Amid the crumbling of former European colonial empires, Western technology, goods, and culture increasingly enveloped the globe, seeping into, and undermining, non-Western cultures—a process that contributed to a surge of religious fundamentalism and ethno-nationalism in the Middle East, Asia, and Africa. As people became more alike, they also became more aware of their differences. Ethnic and religious rivalries grew in intensity everywhere as the century closed.

The political changes during the twentieth century have been no less profound than the social, economic, and cultural ones. Many of the books in the series focus on political events, broadly defined, but no books are confined to politics alone. Political ideas and events have social effects, just as they spring from a complex interplay of nonpolitical forces in culture, society, and economy. Thus, for example, the modern civil rights and woman's rights movements were at once social and political events in cause and consequence. Likewise, the Cold War created the geopolitical framework for dealing with competing ideologies and nations abroad and served as the touchstone for political and cultural identities at home. The books treating political events do so within their social, cultural, and economic contexts.

Several books in the series examine particular wars in depth. Wars are defining moments for people and eras. During the twentieth century war became more widespread and terrible than ever before, encouraging new efforts to end war through strategies and organizations of international cooperation and disarmament while also fueling new ideologies and instruments of mass persuasion that fostered distrust and festered old national rivalries. Two world wars during the century redrew the political map, slaughtered or uprooted two generations of people, and introduced and hastened the development of new technologies and weapons of mass destruction. The First World War spelled the end of the old European order and spurred communist revolution in Russia and fascism in Italy, Germany, and elsewhere. The Second World War killed fascism and inspired the final push for freedom from European colonial rule in Asia and Africa. It also led to the Cold War that suffocated much of the world for almost half a century. Large wars begat small ones, and brutal totalitarian regimes cropped up across the globe. After (and in some ways because of) the fall of communism in eastern Europe and the former Soviet Union, wars of competing cultures, national interests, and political systems persisted in the struggle to make a new world order. Continuing, too, has been the belief that military technology can achieve political ends, whether in the superior American firepower that failed to "win" in Vietnam or in the American "smart bombs" and other military wizardry that "won" in the Persian Gulf.

Another theme evident in the series is that throughout the century nationalism has continued to drive events. Whether in the Balkans in 1914 triggering World War I or in the Balkans in the 1990s threatening the post–Cold War peace—or in many other places—nationalist ambitions and forces would not die. The persistence of nationalism is yet another reminder of the many ways that the past becomes prologue.

We thus offer the series as a modern guide to and interpretation of the historic events of the twentieth century and as an invitation to consider how and why those events have defined not only the past and present but also charted the political, social, intellectual, cultural, and economic routes into the next century.

Randall M. Miller
Saint Joseph's University, Philadelphia

Preface

To many observers Fidel Castro's victory over dictator Fulgencio Batista in 1959 meant the fulfillment of a nationalistic aspiration for Cuba: the elimination of elitist and corrupt government that had served only the interest of the power brokers, native and foreign. For sure, no one in 1959 could predict Cuba's future, not even Castro. Over the next two years, Castro consolidated his power base and launched Cuba on the road to a socialist revolution. In the process, he eliminated Cuba's upper class and their colleague foreign investors (mostly from the United States) and forced the exile of the middle sector. In their place, Castro attempted to create a "New Cuba" in which all contributed according to their capabilities and received according to their needs. It was a great social experiment with every measure taken to ensure mass conformity, but in effect, Cuba became a dictatorship centered around a cult of personality, that of Fidel Castro. On the economic front, Castro ended Cuba's economic dependency upon the United States, only to replace it with the Soviet Union.

The long-term impact of Castro's revolution upon Cuba awaits the judgment of history, but, as events after 1991 indicate, its economic and social programs have failed and the effort to establish political conformity are under serious strain and appear to be cracking.

The literature currently available about Castro and Cuba provide either a long historical narrative of Cuban history, placing the Castro period within that context, or focus primarily upon the years since 1959. The literature is also replete with separate studies about Cuba's economic, social, and cultural development, its foreign policy, and about the Cuban American community.

This work differs from the existing literature on Fidel Castro and the Cuban Revolution. It brings together in one volume the various topics that describe and analyze Castro's revolution. Examined first are the years 1953–1961, during which Castro came to power and consolidated his power base. Next, the historic roots of the Cuban Revolution, from Spanish times through the elitist dictatorships of the twentieth century are presented, followed by the examination of Castro's Cuba since 1961. This approach provides the reader with the comparative "before and after" analysis of the revolution. In the international arena, many observers of the Cuban experience have agreed with Castro that the United States has been Cuba's imperial nemesis, responsible for its economic exploitation and maintaining its elitist rule. Castro has never lost sight of that premise, blaming the United States for all that has gone wrong within Cuba during the past forty years. Given his defiance of Washington, Castro understood that Cuba's new found economic dependence upon the Soviet Union until 1991 forced him to strike a precarious relationship with Moscow while attempting to pursue an independent foreign policy. For the most part, he succeeded remarkably. Finally, an examination of the Cuban American community reveals its rich cultural and political diversity and its influence upon the U.S. understanding of their homeland. This important immigrant group faces new challenges as the century draws to a close. Its anti-Castro leadership that dates to the 1960s is near expiration, being replaced by a younger generation that is more American in its culture and possibly less interested in the events on the island. This change in the Cuban American community comes at a time when the world recognizes that the seventy two-year-old Fidel Castro cannot rule forever.

Supplementing the text are a series of biographic sketches and historical documents. The biographic sketches of Cuba's most important historical figures provide the reader with insights into the political thinking and contributions that each made to the Cuban historical experience. The selected documents are presented in historical sequence, but they also can be divided into four separate themes. For example, an analysis of Cuba's society can be found in the excerpts from Fidel Castro's *History Will Absolve Me*, Che Guevara's 1964 assessment of the Cuban economy, and Fidel Castro's statements in 1970, 1989, and 1990. Perceptions of Cuban society from outside the country can be found in the Central Intelligence Agency's explanation of the 1961 failed Bay of Pigs invasion, the 1992 Human Rights report on Cuba, and in portions of Pope John Paul II's speeches in 1998. U.S. policy toward Cuba is the subject of José Martí, the Platt Amendment, the excerpts of statements by U.S. presidents from John F. Kennedy to William J. Clinton, David Henderson's essay, and Pope John Paul II. Examples of Fidel Castro's effort to make Cuba a significant player in world affairs can be found in his Second Declaration of Havana, 1979 address to the nonaligned nations, and 1990 analysis of revolutionary ideals.

The annotated bibliography provides the reader with references to the most-important works on Cuba and the Revolution. To parallel the text, the bibliography is divided into sections on historic Cuba, the Revolution, Cuba's foreign policy, and the Cuban American community. In addition, separate references are made to biographies, document collections, and reference works. The select listing of media materials is most cogent for the revolutionary period.

A special word of appreciation is extended to Dr. Randall Miller for providing the opportunity to undertake this project. His comments and suggestions proved helpful in making this a more analytical and readable work. I am also appreciative of the support provided by Greenwood Press's Executive Editor, Dr. Barbara Rader and her staff. As always, the assistance given by Kathy Cohen and Bruce Latimer at the University of North Florida's Thomas G. Carpenter Library and by Richard Phillips at the University of Florida's Latin American Collection made life easier in the interminable quest for additional materials. Carol Davis, a most capable student assistant, deserves credit for her assistance in preparing the early drafts of the manuscript. And special thanks go to my wife Yvonne for perennial encouragement, patience, and understanding.

Abbreviations

ACC	Cuban Academy of Sciences
AIC	Independent Colored Party
AJR	Association of Young Rebels
ANAP	National Association of Small Farmers
ANPP	National Assembly for People's Power
CANF	Cuban American National Foundation
CDRs	Committees for the Defense of the Revolution
CIA	Central Intelligence Agency
CNC	National Council for Culture
CNOC	National Confederation of Cuban Workers
CTC	Cuban Confederation of Labor
DEU	Directorate of University Students
FAR	Revolutionary Armed Forces
FEU	University Students' Federation
FMC	Federation of Cuban Women
ICAIC	Cuban Institute of Cinematographic Art and Industry
INAV	National Savings and Housing Institute
INDER	National Institute of Sports, Physical Education and Recreation

INRA	National Institute of Agrarian Reform
JUCEPLAN	Cuban Central Planning Board
MLPA	Popular Movement for the Liberation of Angola
ORI	Integrated Revolutionary Organization
PCC	Cuban Communist Party
PPS	Popular Socialist Party
PRC	Cuban Revolutionary Party
PSP	Popular Socialist Party
PURS	United Party of the Socialist Revolution
SDPE	Economic Management and Planning System
SELA	Latin American Economic System
UJC	Young Communist League
UNEAC	National Union of Cuban Writers and Artists

Chronology of Events

1492 Christopher Columbus reaches the north coast of Cuba to establish Spain's claim to the island.

1733 Havana becomes the undisputed capital of Cuba.

1808 Napoleon invades Spain and places his brother Joseph Bonaparte on the throne, but most Cuban colonists declare their allegiance to the deposed King Ferdinand.

1810–26 As a result of the Latin American independence movements, thousands of Spanish loyalists flock to Cuba, reinforcing the image of the "Ever-Faithful-Island."

1818 A royal decree opens Cuban ports to free international trade.

1848–51 Narciso López conducts three unsuccessful filibustering expeditions to the island.

1854 The U.S. ministers assigned to Spain, Britain, and France issue the Ostend Manifesto recommending that the United States purchase Cuba from Spain.

1868–78 Cuba's first war for independence, the Ten Years' War, is fought. It ends with the Treaty of Zanjón, which promises political reforms and abolition of slavery for Cuba.

1892 In Tampa, Florida, José Martí establishes the Cuban Revolutionary Party committed to win Cuban independence through armed struggle.

1895 The Cuban War for Independence begins on February 24.

1898   U.S. battleship *Maine* is blown up in Havana harbor on February 15, killing the 265 crewmen on board. On April 25, the United States declares war on Spain. The field battles terminate on August 10.

1899   By the Treaty of Paris, Spain relinquishes its control of Cuba, and the three-year formal U.S. military occupation of Cuba begins.

1901   The U.S. Congress enacts the Platt Amendment that places restrictions on Cuban sovereignty. It becomes part of the Cuban constitution.

1902   On May 20, the Republic of Cuba comes into being with the inauguration of President Tomás Estrada Palma.

1903   Cuba and the United States sign three agreements: (a) formalizing the Platt Amendment relationship (prevented Cuba from creating treaties with other foreign powers, gave the United States the right to maintain political order on the island, and allowed the United States to implement a sanitation program on the island); (b) granting Cuban sugar privileged access to the U.S. market; and (c) leasing Guantánamo to the United States for the construction of a naval base.

1906–9   U.S. forces occupy and govern Cuba as a result of the rebellions that followed Estrada Palma's 1906 re-election. José Miguel Gómez serves four-year presidential term after winning the 1908 elections, supervised by U.S. troops.

1907   The *Agrupción de Color* (Independent Colored Party) is founded by Afro-Cubans to protest racism on the island.

1912   U.S. forces intervene to protect properties in Oriente Province, the site of an Afro-Cuban rebellion.

1917   U.S. troops intervene following the "February Rebellion" by Liberals dissatisfied with the presidential election of Conservative Mario G. Menocal.

1920   "Dance of the Millions" takes place between February and May as the price of sugar reaches an all-time high of 22.5¢ per pound, only to collapse to 3¢ per pound by December.

1925   The Cuban Communist Party (PCC) and the National Confederation of Cuban Workers (CNOC) are founded.

1927   University of Havana students establish the *Directorio Estudiantil Universitario* (DEU).

1928   Through unconstitutional means, Gerardo Machado is elected to a second presidential term, which is extended to six years.

1930   The Smoot-Hawley Tariff Act reduces the Cuban share of the U.S. market, further worsening the island's depressed economy.

1933   Three years of political crisis end with the military ouster of President Machado in August and the installation of Carlos Manual de Céspedes. A month later, Fulgencio Batista leads the "Sergeants' Revolt" that overthrows Céspedes and replaces him with a provisional government headed by Ramón Grau Martín.

1934   Batista overthrows President Grau in January and installs Carlos Mendieta as president. In May the United States abrogates the Platt Amendment.

1938   The Communist party is granted legal status.

1940   A new constitution is promulgated, and Fulgencio Batista is elected president.

1944   The Communist party changes its name to the *Partido Socialista Popular* (PSP).

1947   Eduardo Chibás breaks with the *Auténticos* to establish the opposition *Partido del Pueblo Cubano (Orthodoxo)*.

1952   Fulgencio Batista engineers a military coup to oust President Prío Socarrás.

1953   Fidel Castro is sentenced to fifteen years in prison for his leadership role in the unsuccessful attack upon the Moncada army barracks.

1955   After being freed from prison under a general amnesty, Fidel Castro leaves for Mexico to organize the 26th of July Movement for the purpose of overthrowing the Batista regime by force.

1956   In December, Castro returns to Cuba aboard the yacht *Granma* to begin his guerrilla war against the Batista regime.

1957   *New York Times* reporter Herbert Matthews locates Fidel Castro and his guerrilla army in the Escambray Mountains, contradicting Fulgencio Batista's claim that the revolutionary group had been eliminated.

1958   The United States imposes an arms embargo upon the Batista regime. With his army in disarray and confronted with broad-based civilian opposition, Batista flees to the Dominican Republic on New Year's Eve.

1959   On January 8 Castro arrives in Havana and within a month becomes Prime Minister. In May the government enacts its sweeping Agrarian Reform Law.

1960   In May Cuba re-establishes diplomatic relations and concludes a commercial treaty with the Soviet Union. Between June and October, the Cuban government nationalizes numerous U.S. properties. In response, the U.S. government imposes a trade embargo on Cuba.

1961   In January the United States severs diplomatic relations with Cuba. In April the Central Intelligence Agency sponsors the failed Bay of Pigs invasion. In December Fidel Castro proclaims himself to be a Marxist-Leninist.

1962   Cuba is expelled from the Organization of American States. In response, Castro issues the Second Declaration of Havana calling for revolutions across Latin America.

Between October 22 and 28, the United States and the Soviet Union confront each other over the presence of Soviet missiles on the island. The Cuban Missile Crisis ends when the Soviets agree to remove their offensive weapons.

1963   Fidel Castro visits the Soviet Union for the first time.

1965   Castro establishes the new Communist Party of Cuba (PCC). Ernesto "Che" Guevara undertakes a series of trips to Africa and Asia to expand Cuban military contacts.

1967   Guevara is killed in Bolivia, dealing an irreversible blow to Castro's dream for spreading revolution throughout Latin America.

1968   The Cuban government inaugurates its "revolutionary offensive" with the nationalization of the remaining 55,000 private businesses and preparing for a 10-million-ton sugar crop in 1970.

1970   The sugar harvest totals 8.5 million tons, short of the projected goal. The economy goes into a tailspin because of the government's overzealous efforts on sugar at the expense of other sectors.

1972   Cuba becomes the ninth member of COMECON, the Soviet Union's Eastern Bloc economic alliance.

1975   The First Communist Party Congress convenes in Havana. The Family Code is promulgated, establishing a comprehensive set of laws regulating family, marriage, and divorce. Cuban troops enter the Angolan Civil War against Portuguese colonial rule.

1976   A new socialist constitution is promulgated. The central government is reorganized around a Council of Ministers headed by a president.

1977   Cuba and the Untied States establish "Interests Sections" in each other's capitals.

1979   Fidel Castro is elected President of the Nonaligned Movement during its sixth summit conference being held in Havana, but Castro's leadership is weakened later in the year with the Soviet invasion of Afghanistan.

1980   Approximately 125,000 Cubans make their way to the United States during the Mariel boatlift. Castro assumes personal control over the Ministries of Defense, Interior, Public Health, and Culture.

1981   Jorge Mas Canosa founds the Cuban American National Foundation, which achieves significant influence over U.S. policy on Cuba.

1983   Cuban military and construction workers are arrested as a result of the U.S. invasion of Grenada.

1985   The United States inaugurates Radio Martí, and Cuba responds by suspending family visits for Cuban Americans.

1987   Cuba agrees to accept the return of 2,000 "undesirables" who arrived in the United States during the 1980 Mariel boatlift. In return the United States agrees to accept 20,000 new Cuban immigrants annually.

1990   For the first time, Cuba's trade relations with the Soviet Union are conducted on a "hard currency" basis. The Cuban government initiates austerity measures to mark the beginning of its "Special Period."

1991   With the end of Soviet economic assistance, the Fourth Party Congress adopts additional austerity measures. All Cuban troops are withdrawn from Angola.

1992   The United States enacts the Torricelli Bill, which increases trade sanctions against Cuba by prohibiting U.S. subsidiaries in third countries from trading with the island.

1993   The Cuban government legalizes dollar transactions and authorizes limited self-employment. The Caribbean economic community CARICOM reaches a $30 million cooperation agreement with Cuba for tourism, agriculture, and biotechnology. The Russian brigade, sent to Cuba after the 1962 missile crisis, departs the island.

1994–95   Following another mass exodus of Cubans to Florida in the summer of 1994, the United States and Cuba reach a new accord in May 1995 by which the U.S. will accept 20,000 Cubans per year and the Cuban government agrees to control its illegal immigration. Castro visits China and Vietnam to study what free market reforms have been introduced there while retaining one-party political systems. The Cuban government approves the opening of family restaurants.

1996   The Cuban Air Force shoots down two Miami-based exile group planes, allegedly in international waters, which leads to the passage of the U.S. Helms-Burton Bill that further tightens the U.S. embargo on Cuba.

1997   At the conclusion of the Fifth Communist Party Congress in October, there are no indications of Castro relinquishing political power or changing policies. In November the death of CANF president Jorge Mas Canosa leaves a void in the leadership of the Cuban-American community.

1998   In January Pope John Paul II becomes the first Catholic prelate to visit communist Cuba. In public speeches he criticizes Cuba's human rights record and calls upon the United States to lift its embargo.

CASTRO AND THE CUBAN REVOLUTION EXPLAINED

1

Establishing a New Order: The Cuban Revolution, 1959–1961

Fidel Castro's triumphant march into Havana on January 8, 1959, signaled the end to Cuba's old order and the beginning of a new era. Prior to Castro's arrival in Havana, dictator Fulgencio Batista and his closest allies already had fled the island, and shortly thereafter so too did many members of the traditional upper class that had dominated Cuban politics and economy since the nation's independence from Spain in 1898. Within two years, the Cuban middle sector became disillusioned with their new leader, prompting many of them also to leave the island. During the same time period, Castro's policies led to the severance of ties with the United States, Cuba's primary economic partner. From the start, Castro appealed to the masses of the downtrodden that historically had been left out of the nation's economic, social, and political spectrum. The poor became the immediate beneficiaries of Castro's benevolence. But over time, Cuba's economic development stagnated, and the reliance upon the Soviet Union became essential for the nation's economic survival. Politically, the unfulfilled promise of democracy was replaced by a tyrannical and repressive dictatorship dominated by the charismatic Fidel Castro.

Castro's revolution in Cuba was not the first in Latin America, nor would it be the last. Latin America's twentieth-century experience is replete with examples of oligarchical or military dictatorships and with calls to cure the consequences of unequal wealth distribution and social immobility. Prior to Castro, the Mexican Revolution that began with the ouster of Porfirío Díaz in 1911 and the Bolivian experience under Victor Paz Estensarro from 1944 to 1954 illustrate the point. Subsequently, the Sandinista Revolution in Nicaragua (1979–1990) had many parallels to the Cuban experience. Like Fidel Castro in Cuba, the revolutionaries in Mexico, Bolivia, and Nicaragua claimed their desire to end elitist-controlled and corrupt political systems and to provide for greater economic and social opportunities for the downtrodden masses. And with the exception of Paz Estensarro, the other revolutionaries subsequently lost sight of their ideals and sought the institutionalization of their own political power through the Party of Revolutionary Institutions in Mexico, the Sandinista National Liberation Front in Nicaragua, and the Communist party and personal cult of Fidel Castro in Cuba.

In Cuba the ideals of Castro's revolution were not new. During the 1890s José Martí, often described as the father of Cuban independence, not only called for an end to Spanish political and economic domination but also for the improvement in the quality of life for the Cuban masses. In the post–World War II period, Eduardo Chíbas repeated Martí's call for democracy, economic opportunity, and social justice. But it was not to be.

Since its independence from Spain in 1898 until Castro's march into Havana, the Cuban government was controlled by the nation's elite, those wealthy landowners and merchants who used it to serve their own purposes. The elite viewed government employment as an opportunity for self-enrichment, rather than an opportunity to serve in the best interests of the nation. Corruption and nepotism characterized Cuban politics during the first half of the twentieth century as middle and lower socioeconomic groups had no effective voice within the system. Beginning in the 1920s, the white middle sector became a lightning rod for political reform, but it sought entrance into the political arena only for itself. The Afro-Cuban middle sector sought to correct the disparities caused by racial discrimination in the Independent Colored Party in 1911–1912. When political cajoling failed, the Afro-Cubans instigated a rebellion that lasted several months before it was brutally crushed by the Cuban government. Neither the white nor the Afro-Cuban middle sector had any interest in the needs of the working classes.

Labor organizations took root in 1925 with the establishment of the National Confederation of Cuban Workers (CNOC) and the foundation of the country's first communist party. Both groups advocated improvement in working conditions, wages, and human dignity for the working classes but failed to make progress against the elite-dominated political system. The workers groups also attacked U.S. imperialism on the island.

U.S. economic interest in Cuba predated 1898 and only intensified thereafter. The United States became the major market for Cuban sugar, citrus, tobacco, and raw materials and became the chief supplier of goods essential to the Cuban economy—machinery, spare parts, railroad harbor equipment, communications technology, and consumer goods. American companies dominated every aspect of Cuba's economic life. The economic linkage produced a bond, informal at first, between the Cuban white elite and the American business community, and as middle sector job opportunities expanded, it too became invested in the process. Each sector, Cuban and American, sought to maintain the existing political and social structures for its own benefit. They had no interest in meeting the demands of the working classes.

Economic stagnation amid the Great Depression of the late 1920s into the 1930s combined with pent-up anger over economic injustices and political repression to ignite protests in the early 1930s. Student-led protests and demonstrations intensified and attracted elements of the white middle sector to demand an end to the corrupt machine of President Gerardo Machado, who was finally deposed in August 1933. A month later a "Sergeants' Revolt" led by Fulgencio Batista resulted in the so-called "government of one hundred days" led by Ramón Grau San Martín. Grau Martín, a former university professor, immediately promoted measures beneficial to the working class, including an eight-hour workday, a minimum wage, and the legalization of unions. He also moved toward political reorganization to permit the lower classes access to the political arena. These measures threatened the economic, social, and political order that had served the Cuban elite and U.S. interest since 1898. Grau Martín further aggravated the United States by unilaterally abrogating the Platt Amendment, which had governed U.S.-Cuban relations since 1903. The Platt Amendment prevented Cuba from creating treaties with other foreign powers, incurring debts beyond its ability to pay; granted the United States the right to maintain political order on the island; and allowed the United States to implement a sanitation program on the island. In response, Cuba's upper class and the U.S. special envoy on the island, Sumner Welles, maneuvered to oust Grau Martín from office. They found a willing ally in Fulgencio Batista and his colleagues in the middle-rank officer corps whose opportunity for promotion was blocked by the elite-based old-line officers. On January 14, 1934, Grau Martín was deposed and replaced by Carlos Mendieta, but Batista was the power behind the throne. The new government negotiated an end to the Platt Amendment and a new economic treaty with the United States.

For the next eighteen years, Cuban politics returned to the corruption and nepotism that characterized the earlier period, and the primacy of U.S. business enterprise remained intact. In his subsequent attack upon the old order, Fidel Castro would point to the Cuban experiences from 1898 through

1958. He correctly described the bankruptcy of politics, the disparities between upper and lower classes, the discrimination against Afro-Cubans, and the economic omnipresence of the United States.

The immediate causes of the Cuban Revolution are found in the March 10, 1952, coup d'état engineered by Fulgencio Batista against President Carlos Prío Socarrás. Batista publicly justified his action on the grounds that Prío intended to extend his own corrupt presidency, an act certain to result in violence. Batista's underlying motive was equally obvious: to regain power for himself and his close associates who had been excluded from the political process for the preceding eight years. Batista gained immediate popular support by promising free elections for November 1954.

Batista's coup caught Cuba's traditional parties—the Auténticos and Orthodoxos—unprepared, and the subsequent arrest and exile of their leadership made them ineffective. Founded by student leaders from the 1930–1933 period, the Auténtico party was formed in 1934, promising to continue Grau Martín's social justice and civil liberties aspirations. Through the mid-1940s, the Auténticos consistently opposed Batista and his puppet presidents and in 1944 successfully worked for the presidential election of Grau Martín. Unfortunately, he failed to work for the party ideals, instead resorting to the corruption that historically plagued the Cuban presidency. In response to Grau Martín's failure, Eduardo Chibás and other party members split from the party to form the Partido del Pueblo Cubano or Orthodoxo party. Chibás became the party's standard-bearer and unsuccessfully campaigned for the presidency in 1948 on a platform of "honesty vs. money" and the promise to implement social reform.

Early challenges to the *batistianos* (persons who supported Fulgencio Batista) were equally ineffective. The 1954 elections proved farcical. Running unopposed, Batista captured only 40 percent of the vote and moved into the presidential palace. In 1955 the disillusioned moderate forces, hoping to avoid a political crisis, made one last attempt to negotiate a settlement. The Civic Dialogue, as the discussions were known, failed to persuade Batista to hold new elections in which all participants could participate freely. Batista's actions set the stage for confrontation.

In addition to political tensions, Cuba's long-standing socioeconomic disparities worsened in the 1950s. At first glance, Cuba enjoyed widespread economic growth during Batista's administration. Thanks to a sugar boom prompted by World War II and the years immediately thereafter, Cuban entrepreneurs intensified the process of "Cubanizing" the sugar industry. On the eve of World War II, Cuban capital owned 54 sugar mills that produced 22 percent of the total sugar production. By 1952 Cubans owned 113 sugar mills that accounted for 55 percent of the total production. Cuban capital also heavily invested in many foreign-owned mills, and the Cuban-owned cattle industry expanded dramatically. Batista also encouraged expansion of foreign investment, and North American firms capitalized upon the invitation in the production of nickel, cobalt, and other minerals and in the development of tourism. The economic expansion provided the Batista administration with the funds necessary to complete long neglected infrastructure projects and build low-cost housing.

Despite the economic growth, Cuba remained dependent upon the exportation of sugar for its wealth. Sugar was subject to the fluctuations of world sugar prices and the import quotas set by the U.S. Congress, and by the 1950s the nature of the world sugar production had altered so that it no longer could drive Cuba's economic growth. The United States also remained Cuba's major trading partner. In the 1950s, the United States supplied Cuba with approximately 75 percent of its imports and took in nearly 65 percent of its exports.

The postwar economic growth actually exacerbated Cuba's socioeconomic problems. On paper, Cuba enjoyed one of Latin America's highest standards of living during the 1950s, particularly among its middle class. However, because the economy was tied to the U.S. market, North American-made products permeated the Cuban marketplace at U.S. prices. Wages on the island were not high enough for the majority of the Cubans to consume these imported goods. In addition, Cuban wages did not keep pace with the inflationary pressures of the 1950s. As a result, middle-class Cubans experienced a decline in their standard of living in comparison to their U.S. counterparts. At the same time, members of the upper class preferred to invest their wealth abroad because of the volatility of Cuban politics. In the 1950s, urban workers received higher salaries and benefited from social security programs compared to their rural counterparts, but they faced unemployment/underemployment problems, particularly as new workers entered the labor force.

Overall, women and Afro-Cubans did not fare well in the postwar economy. In the 1950s, 65 percent of the working women were employed in the service sector, many at low-wage occupations. To be sure, some women stood as a potentially significant portion of the professional class—in fact, one-third of all Cubans with a college education were women—but women's gains economically remained more promise than reality. Afro-Cubans often lacked even the promise of significant advance as a people. In 1953 the Afro-Cubans made up 27 percent of the population. Occupationally, they were overrepresented in the entertainment and service industries and underrepresented in the commercial and professional sectors. Most were laborers, at the lower end of the wage scale, and they also experienced patterns of discrimination in education, health care, and other government services. Understandably, Afro-Cubans played a major role in labor organizations, particularly in the Cuban Confederation of Labor (CTC).

There also existed a great disparity between urban and rural living conditions. Rural housing, educational opportunities, and health services were scarce and of poor quality. For example, the illiteracy rate in rural areas was four times greater than urban centers. The rural migrants who flocked to the cities during the 1950s faced makeshift housing conditions, indigency, crime, and unemployment. Although Batista's housing and infrastructure projects reached some of the poor, they mostly benefited the middle and upper social groups, largely in and around Havana.

Batista attempted to appeal to the lower socioeconomic groups with his pro-labor policies, and failing that, with bribery, flattery, and intimidation, but he gained little more than a tenuous ally. Batista's decrees made it difficult for landowners to evict tenant farmers, thereby providing the latter with a sense of permanent residency, nurturing lukewarm, if also wary political support for Batista. Despite his efforts, Batista failed to develop a strong political base. He faced a wide array of opponents. Urban and rural labor groups and the middle sector were more influenced by the lack of job opportunities, inflation, and declining social services than by Batista's efforts to build housing, infrastructure, and economic programs for the working classes. Batista also found little support from disgruntled middle- and lower-echelon military officers who faced limited promotion opportunities in an army already top-heavy with officers and riddled with political favoritism and corruption. Batista's most ardent supporters remained the elite native and foreign businessmen.

The middle sector also lamented the administration's corruption and repressive measures. This was most evident in the new surge of literature decrying the republic's moral decay. In addition to the long-standing themes of nationalism, reformism, and anti-Americanism, an idolization of Cuba's independence leaders also surfaced. Antonio Maceo, Maximo Gómez, and particularly José Martí received renewed attention. Martí's speeches and writings of Cuban destiny and the need for vision and self-discipline contrasted with the current dictatorship and prompted young idealists, journalists, and intellectuals to call for change. Batista responded to such criticism with violence and repression, further inciting the protestors.

Soon after the 1954 presidential election, revolutionary groups appeared: the Directorio Revolucionario and the II Frente Nacional del Escambray. But that which received most attention was the 26th of July Movement because of its bold attack upon the Santiago de Cuba military barracks in 1953 and its subsequent revolutionary activities. The Movement was led by Fidel Castro, a young lawyer from Oriente Province. Castro's middle-class background led him to an education at the prestigious Jesuit Belén High School in Havana and later at the University of Havana, where he became interested in politics and the need for social reform. He witnessed the violent demonstrations that followed the 1948 killing of labor leader Jorge Gaitán in Bogotá, Colombia. At the time, Castro did not believe that Gaitán's programs for economic and social reform were communist, as alleged, but rather a legitimate measure to improve the plight of Colombia's poor.

Castro first sought change in Cuba through the political system. He joined the Orthodox party and ascribed to the ideals of party leader Eduardo Chibás. Castro ran as an Orthodox party candidate for the House of Representatives in the aborted 1952 elections. But following Batista's March 1952 coup, Castro determined that the only path to change would be through the violent overthrow of the system. Thereafter, he used the University of Havana campus as a shelter to organize a small group of followers and store ammunition for an attack on the military barracks at Moncada, the army's second largest installation located in Oriente Province. Castro planned his attack for July 26, 1953, during the annual carnival at Santiago in eastern Cuba. With the carnival in full sway, Castro expected the military to have its guard down. The attack was to be accompanied by a publicity campaign designed to give the impression of an army uprising by pro-Orthodox officers, which in turn would paralyze the army. Undercut from his main prop of support, Batista would resign, and the Orthodox party would vault into political power. In reality, Castro failed to consult the party, informing it of his intended actions only a day before the assault on Moncada. The attack ended in disaster. Most of Castro's troops were killed; Castro, his brother Raúl, and a few of their followers momentarily escaped into the mountains, where the army subsequently captured them. But the daring attack catapulted Fidel Castro into the forefront of the anti-Batista forces and convinced many Cubans that only an armed struggle would bring Batista down.

While in prison awaiting trial, Castro wrote *History Will Absolve Me* (1953), from which he read before his sentencing. In it, Castro associated his movement with the ideals of Martí and Chibás; he called for reforms of Cuba's political system, an end to the economic dependency upon the United States, and social justice for all sectors of Cuban society. Castro's

History Will Absolve Me was distributed throughout Cuba, but it did not draw any particular attention at the time. Compared to other contemporary protest literature, Castro's reform proposals appeared rather moderate. Others called for structural changes that would end the sugar monoculture, lift the nation from poverty, and terminate political dictatorship. Castro's thinking on social reform and political revolution would move leftward as he came to appreciate how intractable were the entrenched economic and political elites.

Castro served only eleven months of the fifteen-year sentence he received for the Moncada attack. In a general amnesty, Batista released him from jail and banished him to Mexico. In Mexico City, Castro plotted his return to Cuba and a new strategy for reform there. Meanwhile, in Cuba, the Federation of University Students, led by José A. Echeverría, continued to demonstrate against Batista's regime. To counter the increasing student demonstrations, the military stepped up its repressive measures. Unable to gain the support of Cuba's middle sector and refusing advances from the local communist party, Echeverría and his followers determined that the only way to alter Cuba's political course was to bring Batista down by violent means. Toward that end, Echeverría met secretly in Mexico with the Castro brothers and Ernesto "Che" Guevara, an Argentine doctor and revolutionary, whose travels through Latin America convinced him that only revolution could correct the hemisphere's social and economic disparities. Guevara joined Castro from Guatemala after the U.S. Central Intelligence Agency had overthrown the socialist-leaning president Jacobo Arbenz in 1954.

As a result of the Echeverría-Castro agreement, Castro returned to Cuba. The plan was for Castro and a small band of revolutionaries to land in Oriente Province from the yacht *Granma* on December 2, 1956, while Echeverría's followers conducted diversionary activities in Havana. Alerted to the plan, government authorities squelched the operation. Castro's unit of eighty men was quickly reduced to eighteen, who escaped to the nearby mountains. In Havana, the police rounded up all suspected revolutionaries.

Castro and his followers immediately found themselves isolated in the Sierra Maestra Mountains in southeastern Oriente Province, but there they soon discovered that the patterns of socioeconomic disparity and the instruments of the central government's repression could be used to build a popular resistance movement. The region was home to an estimated 50,000 peasants living in varying degrees of poverty and misery. They worked as low-paid laborers for low-production farmers or squatted on land that belonged to distant landowners and from which they faced constant eviction notices. The government's Rural Guard terrorized the peasants. Angry and desperate, the peasants became many of the earliest recruits for the rebel army, which by May 1957 had overrun key Rural Guard posts at La Plata and El Uvero. News of these insurgent victories brought new recruits to Castro's rebel force. The arbitrariness of the Cuban army's field operations, which became indiscriminate terror by late 1957, provided additional reasons for peasants to support Castro's cause.

To counteract the peasant support for Castro, the Cuban army forced thousands of peasants into hastily constructed camps near Santiago and Bayamo, reminiscent of the Spanish *reconcentrados* constructed in the mid-1890s to isolate the peasants from the rebels. Those not brought into the camps were presumed Castro supporters. Rather than pacify the peasants, the camps served only to swell further the ranks of the *fidelistas* (followers of Fidel Castro). By mid-1957 the Sierra was up in arms.

Throughout 1957 and early 1958, the size of the insurgent force increased, and its field operations expanded. Raúl Castro operated a second front in the north; Juan Almeida opened a third front around Santiago de Cuba; and in April 1958 Camilo Cienfuegos left the Sierra for the Holguín plains, and Che Guevara operated around Turquino peak.

In response to the events in Oriente, the faculty and students at the University of Havana voted to shut down the institution on November 30, 1956. The government used the occasion to close the school until early 1959. The government action did not silence the students but instead propelled them into the country's political dynamics with only one goal: to end the Batista dictatorship. Over the next three years, as the rural insurgency increased, so too did the urban violence. In an attack upon the presidential palace on March 13, 1957, a student group almost succeeded in killing Batista. But the rebels lost before they won. Echeverría was killed in a coordinated attack upon a Havana radio station. The way was open for new rebel leadership that might unite the rural and urban insurgencies.

Thereafter, Castro coordinated the urban underground acts of sabotage and subversions by the 26th of July Civic Resistance. The rebels sought to disrupt the government at every turn and to show the people that the corrupt government could not protect its own interests and by implication had neither legitimacy nor any claim on citizens' loyalty. The rebels exploded bombs, set fires, cut power lines, derailed trains, and kidnapped and killed their political enemies. Batista responded with equal ferocity with the indiscriminate torture and murder of Castro supporters, suspected or real. The violence also led to a series of planned military uprisings against the government. Beginning in April 1956, first-line army officers, then naval officers at Cienfuegos, and later the air force and army medical corps conspired to change governments. Batista not only faced mounting popular opposition but also an increasingly disloyal and unreliable military. The Batista regime became increasingly isolated.

As a result of the rural insurgency and urban violence, the Cuban economy stagnated by 1958, causing a drastic decline in government public works projects and a marked rise in unemployment. Poverty became more visible in Havana and other cities. Petty crime and prostitution climbed. Batista's apparent indifference towards U.S. organized crime control of vice and gambling further intensified the opposition against the regime. At the same time, the guerrillas had exacted a heavy toll. They halted the shipment of foodstuffs into the cities, causing prices to soar. Transportation between Havana and the three eastern provinces had stopped; telephone and telegraph service across the island was paralyzed; large sections of highways and railroads were destroyed; and bridges were put out of service. Matters worsened in February 1958 when the 26th of July Movement launched an attack against sugar mills, tobacco factories, public utilities, railroads, and oil refineries and put the torch to some two million tons of sugar.

Amid the worsening economic conditions, reports of graft, corruption, and Swiss bank accounts opened by Batista and his supporters added to the public outrage and fueled the popular determination to oust the dictator. Even Batista's supporters sought to remove him as a way to cool tensions and, they hoped, appease the various rebel forces, or at least the military. The movement for change was now irreversible, and it favored the bold. In July 1958 the opposition groups organized a meeting in Caracas, Venezuela, where the resultant pact established Fidel Castro as the principal leader of the anti-Batista movement and his as army the main arm of the revolution.

The United States helped with the demise of Batista. In March 1958, just prior to the launching of the government offensive against Castro's guerrilla army, the United States placed an arms embargo on the Cuban government. It had a devastating psychological effect, boosting the rebels' confidence while deflating what little hope Batista's supporters had for outside assistance. The United States also forewarned Batista that it would not extend recognition to his handpicked successor, Rivero Agüro, in the 1958 presidential elections. The United States sought to ease Batista out of office in early December 1958, when it covertly sent William D. Pawley to Havana. Not even U.S. Ambassador to Cuba Earl T. Smith was informed of the mission. Pawley, a Republican businessman long connected to Cuba, was not authorized to represent himself as a representative of the Eisenhower administration, but rather to explain that he came as a private U.S. citizen representing influential friends in the United States. He offered Batista and his family safe haven in Florida, provided Batista form a caretaker government acceptable to Washington, which would then turn on the military assistance spigot in order to prevent a Castro victory. Batista refused. Even had Batista accepted the offer, it might have come too late.

In mid-1958 Batista launched a military offensive against the rebels, but the effort collapsed by the end of the summer. Castro responded with a counteroffensive, and quickly towns and villages in eastern Cuba fell to the advancing guerrilla army. By December the guerrilla army had swelled to 50,000, and Batista's army was in total disarray. With Batista's departure to the Dominican Republic, the remainder of the army troops ceased to fight, giving Colonel Ramón Barquín no other choice but to order an immediate cease-fire, a salute to the "Army of Liberation," and then surrender.

A week later, Fidel Castro arrived in Havana to a euphoric welcome. His charisma would prove to be overwhelming. Fidel and his followers called themselves the "generation of the *centario*," based on the date of José Martí's birth (1853) and the attack on Moncada (1953). The *fidelistas* came to invoke history, they claimed, and therefore would install Cuban democratic government and social justice. The structures of old Cuba were to be abandoned and in its place a new Cuba created.

The government set up at Havana in January 1959 consisted mainly of moderate civilians, with Dr. Manuel Urrutia as president, José Miró Cardona as prime minister, and Castro as commander-in-chief of the armed forces. When it quickly became clear that Castro had no intention of consulting with his colleagues, Miró Cardona resigned in February and Castro became premier. A few months later Urrutia also departed. Other moderate nationalist reformers soon left the government to be replaced by Castro's more radical colleagues. For example, Augusto Martínez Sanchéz replaced Manuel Fernández as Labor Minister, and Che Guevara took over the National Bank from Felipe Pazos. Castro also instituted a style of *personalismo* by which he dispensed favors and made decisions without consulting the provisional government. Castro, personally, became the focal point of the revolution.

Over the next few months, the regime took on its own characteristics. At home, it discouraged and denounced dissident views, used the army for political purposes, and ruled by decree in order to prepare the people for "real democracy." It described its own actions, which included alterations in the rules on property, as efforts to achieve social justice. While it was linked to revolutions in neighboring countries, the regime denounced the United States for interfering in Cuba's internal affairs. Throughout, Castro and his colleagues rejected any suggestion that they were communist-orientated.

While Castro's actions frightened Cuba's middle and upper sectors and policymakers in Washington, his continued call for revolutionary change incited the general populace to demand further political and social reform. The masses supported rapid change, and Castro manipulated such feeling to his advantage in the early months of the revolution.

In the weeks after marching into Havana, the revolutionaries brought many of Batista's more prominent military and civilian leaders before revolutionary tribunals opened to the public and aired on national television. The trials defied any sense of justice and resulted in the summary execution of hundreds of persons. The regime ended the trials only in response to international criticism but continued to confiscate the properties of Batista supporters and collaborators, real or imagined.

Castro's brother, Raúl, used the military and the large civilian militia to rid the country of the *batistianos* and otherwise intimidate the opposition. The traditional Liberals and Conservatives, the *Auténtico* and Orthodox parties, were isolated from government. Anti-government groups organized and conducted urban violence, but to little avail. With the organization of the Committees for the Defense of the Revolution (CDRs) in September 1960, the middle sector lost all room to protest the revolution's direction. Formed as a response to the perceived internal and external threats to the revolution, the CDRs were mass organizations organized by neighborhood blocks, factories, labor unions, and state farms for the primary purpose of watching for and reporting subversive activities. Eventually, the CDRs claimed a membership of 800,000. Furthermore, the general population understood that the military stood behind every Castro action.

Castro and his colleagues did not see their legitimacy dependent upon restoration of the 1940 constitution and the holding of elections. Those who called for new elections were those who had the most to lose from the new government's policies—namely, the Cuban upper and middle sectors and U.S.-owned businesses. They understood that the new Cuba would not protect their interests. This became most evident in May 1959 when Castro announced that the priorities of the new Cuba would focus upon full employment, expanded health care, extended education, and the need to create a new political consciousness among the people. Elections, he argued, would only interfere with these programs.

With the elimination or silencing of the opposition political groups, Castro needed to fill the vacuum with experienced workers and managers loyal to his cause. Under such strictures, the most-qualified people available were members of the communist party. They quickly filled government, commercial, and industrial positions. PSP labor leaders took control of the

CTC. Other mass organizations also came under government control, including the University Students' Federation (FEU), the Federation of Cuban Women (FMC), the Association of Young Rebels (AJR), and the National Association of Small Farmers (ANAP). The latter included small farmers from the old Cane Growers Association and previously unorganized peasant farmers. Supporters of Castro's programs learned that loyalty to the revolution had its rewards, such as government positions, access to government loans for economic activities, and admission to higher education.

Castro's appeal to the lower socioeconomic groups was apparent from the start. Workers, representing all sectors—sugar, railroad, mining, utility—either demonstrated or struck for higher wages, often at the government's encouragement. On many occasions, Castro himself mediated the labor disputes and mandated settlements on behalf of the workers.

Beginning in March 1959 Castro took bolder steps with the Urban Reform Act designed to discourage investments in real estate and construction of private dwellings. The law decreed a 50 percent reduction of rents under $100 monthly, 40 percent reduction of rents between $100 and $200 monthly, and 30 percent for those over $200. The newly acquired National Savings and Housing Institute (INAV) acquired vacant lots upon which it pledged to construct inexpensive public housing. Other measures soon followed. In fact, during the first nine months of 1959 an estimated 1,500 decrees, laws, and edicts were enacted. The government intervened in the telephone company and reduced its rates. Electricity rates were cut drastically. Virtually all labor contracts were renegotiated and wages raised. Cane cutters' wages were increased by a flat 15 percent. Health reforms, educational reforms, and unemployment relief followed in quick order. Property owned by all past government officials, senior army officers, mayors, governors, and members of congress during the 1954–1958 period were confiscated. Through special licensing and higher tariffs, the importation of luxury items was restricted. Although largely symbolic, the action did save Cuba an estimated $70 million in foreign exchange the first year, as the importation of cars and television sets, among other things, plummeted. The new Cuban government also cut its economic dependence on the United States, reducing its trade from $543 million in 1959 to $224 million in 1960.

By far the most sweeping change came with the Agrarian Reform Law in May 1959, which restricted real estate holdings to 1,000 acres, except for sugar, rice, and livestock farms, where the maximum limits were set at 3,333 acres. Estates above these amounts were nationalized with compensation provided at 4.5 percent in 25–year bonds based upon the land values stated in the 1958 tax records, in which all lands had been undervalued. Expropriated lands were reorganized into state cooperatives or distributed into individual holdings of 67 acres, with squatters, sharecroppers, and renters receiving first claim to the land they had been working. The law also created the Agrarian Reform Institute (INRA) designed initially to supervise the reorganization of land systems. Subsequently, INRA became responsible for most programs in rural Cuba: road construction, health facilities, credit enterprises, educational projects, and housing programs.

The search for new markets ended in February 1960 when a Soviet trade delegation headed by Deputy Premier Anastas Mikoyan arrived in Havana to complete a trade pact. As a result, the Soviets agreed to purchase 425,000 tons of sugar immediately and 1,000,000 tons in each of the next four years. In addition, the Soviet Union offered Cuba $100 million in low-interest credits, technical assistance, and crude and refined petroleum. In April 1960 the two nations resumed diplomatic relations, suspended since 1952. With the agreement in hand, in June 1960 an emboldened Castro ordered Standard Oil, Shell, and Texaco to refine Soviet crude oil. On directions from the U.S. State Department, the companies refused, whereupon the Cuban government took them over. In July President Dwight D. Eisenhower retaliated by cutting the Cuban sugar quota to 7,000 tons for the remainder of 1960 and zero after that. Castro was equal to the challenge. In August he nationalized the remaining U.S. properties on the island, including two utilities, thirty-six sugar mills, and branches of American banks. In response, Eisenhower imposed a total economic embargo on Cuba, with the exception of medicines and some foodstuffs. Eisenhower set the cornerstone of U.S. policy toward Cuba for the next two generations: removal of Castro through economic coercion.

The embargo affected Cuba both economically and politically. It thrust the government into managing the economy. By late 1961, approximately 85 percent of the total productive value of the Cuban industry was under state control. The embargo also facilitated the seizure of other Cuban-owned lands. For Cuba's nearly 150,000 managers, clerks, technicians, accountants, and attorneys, the expropriations proved traumatic. Not only were their salaries brought into line with the lower Cuban wage scales, but their jobs were jeopardized if they opposed or did not demonstrate enthusiastic support for the revolution. Also, as a result of nationalization, thousands of Cubans employed in the insurance services, real estate agencies, gambling casinos, and brokers of all types lost their jobs.

Events in Cuba during 1959 and 1960 contributed to an exodus of nearly 200,000 Cubans, mostly to Puerto Rico and the United States. Those adversely affected by Castro's political and economic policies labeled him a

communist. Their opinion was reinforced by the activities of Cuban filibus-
terers who joined exiles from various Caribbean countries to launch a series
of abortive attacks upon the Dominican Republic, Panama, and Haiti. The
disaffected and displaced Cuban "exiles" abroad came to believe that Castro had to be brought down by sabotage before his power base solidified.
Thus, beginning in early 1959, Cuban exiles in the Caribbean and the
United States launched isolated, but futile attacks on the island.

At first, the Eisenhower administration reluctantly welcomed Castro's
victory over Batista. Policymakers in Washington favored the moderate
government that immediately replaced Batista, but soon recognized that it
was powerless. The mock trials, the elimination of political opposition,
along with Castro's increased power and social programs raised questions
in Washington about his communist tendencies. Shortly after his visit to
Washington in April 1959, the Central Intelligence Agency (CIA) began to
devise plans for Castro's ouster and replacement with a more friendly government. The initial acts of sabotage conducted by the Cuban exile community received the agency's tacit approval, but their only impact was to
increase Castro's intransigence.

The U.S. hesitancy turned to belligerency following the Soviet-Cuban
trade agreement in February 1960, Soviet Premier Nikita Khrushchev's
subsequent boast that he would use rockets to defend Cuba, and Castro's
claim that he would convert the Andes Mountains into the Sierra Maestra of
Latin America. Castro's revolution moved onto the Cold War stage. For
U.S. policymakers, Cuba now served as a Soviet pawn in the global struggle
between Washington and Moscow. That communism had gained a foothold
on America's doorstep added to Americans' sense of insecurity as they con-
templated a supposed Soviet supremacy in science in the wake of the Sput-
nik launching and public clamor about a supposed "missile gap." Castro had
to go, lest the region itself be lost to communism.

The tension reached new heights in January 1961 when Castro demanded that the United States reduce its embassy in Havana to eleven persons. Eisenhower seized the opportunity as a pretext to break diplomatic
relations. One of the reasons for Castro's belligerence was the suspicion,
and by late 1960, the knowledge of U.S. preparations for an attack on Cuba.
Eisenhower made the decision in late spring 1960 to force Castro out, and
he approved the CIA's covert operation to remove him with a brigade of
exiles being trained in Guatemala and Nicaragua. When John F. Kennedy
became president in January 1961, he continued the scheme.

The CIA argued that Castro's support base was weak and that a small
landing of exile forces would result in a large uprising within Cuba. In fact,

American intelligence was hopelessly uninformed. U.S. contacts were with the overzealous exiles or the diminished opposition groups within Cuba. When the Cuban exile brigade landed at the Bay of Pigs in April 1961, Castro was prepared to meet the challenge. The invading exiles found themselves stranded as the Cuban Air Force kept the exiles pinned down and destroyed their lone cargo ship off shore. The Cuban army quickly reached the invasion site, where Castro took command. In the cities, the 8,000 CDRs rounded up thousands of suspected counter revolutionaries. There could be no internal uprising. Within three days, nearly 1,500 exile troops surrendered. The invasion was a fiasco that embarrassed the United States and strengthened Castro's hold on the island. The United States could not hide its involvement in the ill-planned attack and appeared weak and unprincipled. Indeed, U.S. prestige suffered throughout the world, especially in Latin America, and the Bay of Pigs invasion convinced Khrushchev that the new president was weak and that Cuba needed more direct Soviet aid. Thus was laid the ground for the later Cuban missile crisis. The United States, in turn, resolved to isolate Cuba further and to launch aid programs, especially the Alliance for Progress, to counter communist appeal in Latin America. And Castro now had the proof of American treachery to justify further stern measures to protect the Cuban revolution. The American attack also allowed Castro to wrap the revolution in the cloak of nationalism and the long-standing desire of Cubans to be free of foreign interference.

Castro used the failed invasion to further tighten his grip upon Cuba. Within weeks of the fiasco, he denounced the constitution and proclaimed that the concept of democracy had been substituted for direct government by the people. He also stressed that his was a socialist regime. On December 2, 1961, he went further. Castro proclaimed: "I am a Marxist-Leninist, and I shall be one until the last day of my life." Cuba set sail on a new course.

2

The Road to Revolution: Cuba to 1953

The inequities of Cuba's society that Fidel Castro assaulted after 1959 can be traced to the island's colonial experience. The economic, political, and social patterns established during the colonial period remained long after Cuba's independence in 1898. At first, the island offered little to Spain. For three hundred years following Christopher Columbus's landing on Cuba in October 1492, the island remained an outpost of the Spanish empire, important only because of its place in the mother country's merchant fleet system that carried goods to and from the New World. That changed in the 1700s when the government at Madrid implemented economic and political reforms that effectively brought greater profits to the *peninsulare* (Spanish born) merchants, who also dominated local politics at the expense of Cuban-born *creoles* (people of pure Spanish blood born in the New World). The most important economic change was the expansion of the sugar industry that opened Cuba to the world market. The flourishing sugar industry brought prosperity to Cuba's western provinces and the port at Havana, but at the expense of the island's eastern sectors.

The sugar industry had a lasting impact upon Cuba's social structure. By the 1860s three distinct social classes emerged based largely upon skin color. The Spanish whites (*peninsulares*) occupied the highest standing on the social ladder followed by their Cuban-born brethern (*creole*). There existed an inexorable reciprocity between them. The *creole* landowner found himself dependent upon the *peninsulare* government officials and merchants for peace and security and to market his products. On the other hand, the government officials depended upon the landowners for their wealth. However, shipping and taxing policies made in Madrid strained this relationship.

The conflict at the top spiraled downward to the middle sector—those people in the professions, salaried personnel, small farmers, and artisans who had limited economic opportunity and lacked political participation in the rigidity of the Spanish system. The middle sector soon found itself on a collision course with the *creole* planter who defended that system. Next came the estimated 232,000 free people of color, who were engaged in virtually every occupational category but denied civil and political rights, admission to the University of Havana, and advanced positions in the Catholic clergy. But they were a feared group because allegedly they could organize a rebellion among the estimated 750,000 black slaves brought to the island between 1763 and 1862 to work on the sugar, tobacco, and coffee plantations where they lived in most wretched conditions.

Preferring the economic and social benefits brought by the Spanish system, the Cuban *creoles* did not seek independence when their fellow Latin Americans revolted against Spanish authority between 1810 and 1826. But the *creoles* did entertain thoughts of annexation to the United States through 1851. Indeed, the *creoles* found compatibility with the southern cotton planter class. Among the most notable annexationists was the filibusterer Narciso López, who launched three unsuccessful raids from the United States against Spanish authority in Cuba between 1848 and 1851.

Cuba's initial thrust at independence came with the outbreak of the Ten Years War. It began in October 1868 as a response to increased Spanish taxes that inflated the cost of U.S. imported goods and virtually locked out Cuban sugar from the North American market. Although Spain made concessions toward home rule in the 1878 Treaty of Zanjón that ended the war, the conflict had set in motion profound economic, social, and political changes that fostered Cuban independence in 1898.

After 1880 Cuba's landholding patterns changed significantly. Planters in eastern Cuba were forced to sell their destroyed properties to eager North Americans at a fraction of their value. *Peninsulares* came to possess most of the former rebel properties confiscated by Spanish authorities. The world demand for Cuban sugar dropped drastically because of the increased production of beet sugar and the development of the sugar cane industry in Hawaii. On top of this, Spain imposed new local taxes to help pay for the Ten Years War. The abolition of slavery, as provided in the Treaty of Zanjón, and the introduction of technology to the sugar mills by the new American owners contributed to the excess supply of an unskilled labor force. By the end of the decade, the Cuban economy was in a tailspin.

In the political arena three distinct groups emerged. In late 1878, the conservative *peninsulares* formed the Union Constitutional party in an effort to maintain their political prominence. The party defended the Spanish colonial system, and the *peninsulares* wielded power beyond their numbers, even though they were a minority of the population. In contrast stood the Liberal, or Autonomist party, comprised of the *creole* elite and much of the middle sector. The Autonomists sought reform within the colonial system, which meant home rule within the empire, a place in government for themselves, and close economic ties to the United States. These political groups represented the historic conflict among Cuba's white upper class.

The third group proved to be more important. Comprised of exiles who fled to the United States after the Ten Years War, it advocated *Cuba Libre*, a free and independent Cuba. Its most ardent spokesman was José Martí, a poet, writer, and effective critic of Spain's influence over Cuba. Martí called for a united opposition front encompassing all social sectors from planters to the black freedmen. He argued that shared political power and a redistribution of wealth would provide for a more prosperous Cuba. Martí pushed for Cuba's political separation not only from Spain but also from its economic dependence upon the United States. Martí's program threatened Cuba's established order. In April 1892 Martí founded the Cuban Revolutionary Party, which he envisioned as the organization of unification for all sectors of Cuban society.

Despite the stagnant economy and political tension, sustained overt conflict did not come to Cuba until February 1895. At first, it appeared as if any conflict would be short-lived. Conspiracies in Havana and Matanzas —engineered by exiles in the United States, José Martí, Maximo Gómez, and Antonio Maceo—had been uncovered and quickly crushed; likewise the government put down rebel groups in Las Villas and Camagüey. Only in Oriente did the uprising take hold and last for most of the year, but *peninsulare* and *creoles* alike thought it nothing more than a provincial affair in a historically rebellious province. By the fall of 1896, however, Cuba faced open warfare. The Oriente insurgents, mostly Afro-Cuban peasants led by Gómez and Maceo, marched out of the eastern mountains, across the central plains, and into the western valleys. The established order was threatened by the rebel army's burning of the cane fields and its recruitment of thousands of volunteers representing the lower classes demanding not only a free Cuba but social justice for all. The war for independence threatened to expand into a social revolution. The Spanish response was swift and brutal. Its army was expanded to 200,000 troops under General Valeriano Weyler, who determined that in order to destroy the rebel army, he had to first destroy the rural communities that supported it. To accomplish his goal, in the fall of 1896, he ordered the destruction of peasant farms, tools of toil, and livestock, and the relocation of the peasants into specially designed fortified towns (*reconcentrados*). Although the countryside became a wasteland and thousands of peasants died in the *reconcentrados*, Weyler failed to destroy the ever-growing insurgent army. By the end of 1897, everyone understood that the Spanish could not win.

Amid the turmoil, the *creole* Autonomists understood that Cuba's social fabric would unravel in the face of an insurgent victory. Recognizing that the Spaniards could no longer protect them, in 1896 the Autonomists petitioned the U.S. government to resolve the crisis. Some even sought a U.S. protectorate over the island. Cuba's white community sought the preservation of the old order.

Economic, strategic, and humanitarian reasons determined U.S. policy towards Cuba. Beginning in the 1790s, New England merchants conducted clandestine trade with Havana and Santiago, but the lure of sugar in the nineteenth century cemented ties between the mainland and the island. Cuba became nearly totally dependent upon the United States for the sale of its sugar and as the supplier of manufactured and consumer goods. On the eve of the war for Cuban independence, U.S. private investment on the island reached nearly $50 million. But as a Spanish colony, decisions affecting this economic relationship were made in Spain, not Cuba. U.S. policymakers understood Cuba's strategic importance. Its close proximity to the U.S. mainland and its location on the windward passage could well serve an American enemy to threaten the security of the United States. Thus, throughout the nineteenth century, the United States retained a sense of security as long as Cuba remained in the hands of a weak Spanish government. By the mid-1890s, conditions changed. An independent Cuba might open the door not only to new European investors to rival the Americans on the island, but also to European navies, a potential threat to U.S. security. Also by the mid-1890s, a large sector of influential U.S. opinion makers envisioned a transisthmian canal under American control, and to them, European naval presence threatened its security. Accordingly, naval strategists cast covetous eyes on Cuba and the Spanish possession of Puerto Rico, located between the Mona and Virgin passageways to the Caribbean Sea.

Humanitarian considerations were added to the economic and strategic concerns after General Weyler established the *reconcentrados*. The camps' squalid conditions and the inhumane treatment imposed upon its residents were driven home to the American public by the sensationalist New York press. Although this "yellow journalism" often exaggerated the extent of the Spanish cruelty, its impact upon public opinion was profound. Americans, outraged over reports of atrocities and suffering on Cuba, demanded American intervention to ease Spain's grip.

Despite these pressures, until February 1898 official U.S. policy sought a compromise solution that would provide the Cubans with some measure of home rule. On February 9, the *New York Journal* printed the contents of a private letter from the Spanish Minister in Washington Dupuy de Lome to a friend at home. In it, de Lome criticized both U.S. policy and President William McKinley. Six days later, on February 15, the U.S. battleship *Maine* was mysteriously blown up in Havana harbor. Although responsibility has never been firmly fixed, the Americans were quick to blame the Spanish. Thereafter, public and political pressure drove President McKinley to ask Congress to declare war on April 11, 1898. Congress complied.

What had been a war for Cuban independence now became the Spanish-American War. It was, as one American journalist described it, a "Splendid Little War," lasting only three months before the Spanish asked for peace in August 1898. The war became a North American one. The Americans not only liberated Cuba but also the Philippine Islands in the Pacific, and a few days before the battles ended, American troops occupied Puerto Rico. American troops defeated the Spanish and accepted its flag in surrender, not the Cuban liberators led by Maximo Gómez. The North Americans, not the Cuban *independentistas* (those who fought for Cuba's independence from Spain), negotiated the Treaty of Paris in 1898 that provided for the Spanish departure from the island and Cuban independence. The war also produced an American hero, soon to become president, Theodore Roosevelt.

The war also turned Cuba into a wasteland. Visible signs permeated the landscape: homes, roofless and in ruins, were uninhabited; roads, bridges, and railroads had fallen into disuse and disrepair; mines closed; commerce was at a standstill and manufacturing suspended. With livestock scattered, herds declined to a minuscule part of their prewar numbers. The once lush countryside appeared as scorched earth and singed brush. Towns and villages stood in rubble.

Given the presence of an occupying army and the distraught economic environment, José Martí's vision of an economically and politically independent Cuba failed to materialize. In this vacuum, Cuba fell victim to U.S. presence and elitist *creole* rule.

By congressional mandate (the Teller Amendment), the United States could not annex Cuba, but still it remained committed to the establishment of a stable government capable of maintaining order and observing international obligations. Conditioned since the 1830s by a condescending attitude about Latin Americans, U.S. policymakers concluded that years of Spanish rule made all Latins incapable of self-government and residents of stagnant societies based upon people of color. Cuba was no exception, and nothing during the U.S. military occupation from 1898 to 1902 changed that perception. This view was shared by the Cuban *creoles* and the *peninsulares* who remained on the island. Both groups flocked around the newly arrived North Americans. Together, they sought to establish a local government, but the results of the 1900 municipal elections and 1901 election of a constituent assembly spoiled their plans. Another method had to be found.

The answer came with the so-called Platt Amendment, named after Connecticut Senator Orville Platt, which the United States insisted the Cubans had to attach to their 1902 constitution as a condition for Cuban independence. The Platt Amendment forbade Cuba from entering into agreements with foreign countries that threatened U.S. interests or indebting itself to a foreign power beyond current revenues. Equally significant was the U.S. right to intervene to maintain Cuban independence, life, and property. The Republic of Cuba came into being on May 20, 1902, when the U.S. military government turned the island over to the newly elected administration of Tomás Estrada Palma. To the Cuban *independentistas*, however, their homeland had become an American economic colony and protectorate, not an independent nation.

Cuban politics remained a privilege of the white elite. Estrada Palma's Conservative party represented those white men of comfortable social origins, some with Automomist antecedents. The opposition Liberal party leadership came from the officers and enlisted men in the Liberation army, many of modest social origins. Ideology meant little; *personalismo* prevailed, a factor that contributed to political instability and resulted in three different occupations by the U.S. Marines between 1906 and 1922 under the terms of the Platt Amendment. In this political ambience, the *Agrupción Independiente de Color* (Independent Color Association), which later became a political party, made no headway in correcting the discrimination against blacks.

Politics served the double purpose of providing social status and economic prosperity for the Cuban *creoles*. Control of the presidency meant the appointment of officials, the issuing of licenses and permits, the awarding of public service contracts. Each activity was subject to graft and corruption. Self-enrichment for the party officials, not public service for the good of the country, characterized Cuban government at every level after independence. The frequent indictments of corrupt officials were washed away by general amnesties or presidential pardons. One of the most visible forms of corruption came with the National Lottery established in 1909. It provided the incumbent administration with approximately $250,000 and national legislators with $54,000 of monthly discretionary income.

Beginning with the occupation period, the North Americans came to dominate the Cuban economy. They purchased tobacco and sugar properties, sugar mills, railroads, factories, public utilities, and whatever else became available. In 1902, U.S. capital on the island totaled $100 million, nearly double what it had been in 1895. By 1929, U.S. capital investment in Cuba reached $1.5 billion. The economic link was further tightened by the 1902 reciprocity treaty that granted a preference to Cuban sugar entering the United States and also opened the Cuban floodgates to U.S. manufactures. So intertwined were the two economies, the policies of the U.S. Federal Reserve Bank at Atlanta directly affected the Cuban finances and economy.

Sugar remained the backbone of Cuba's export economy. Sugar exports reached 3.7 million tons in 1920 and accounted for 92 percent of the total value of Cuban exports. The year 1920 was known as the "Dance of the Millions" as sugar prices reached 22.5¢ per pound on the world market and brought undreamed of prosperity to the island. In the process, the North Americans modernized the sugar operations, displacing unskilled labor and sending it to the cities in search of limited job opportunities The few jobs that existed went to the whites, both longtime residents and the newer immigrants who came after the war. The old white class preferred its own over the Afro-Cuban.

The high-water mark of U.S. intervention came in 1920 when Conservative Alfredo Zayas assumed the presidency following corrupt elections that stirred revolutionary plots. At the same time, the price of sugar plunged to 3.8¢ per pound, triggering a deep recession. Into this situation President Warren G. Harding dispatched General Enoch G. Crowder. He demanded that Zayas reform the government, end the special sinecures and national lottery, and replace corrupt judges with honest ones. Confronted with a bankrupt treasury, Zayas succumbed in order to receive a badly needed $50 million loan from J. P. Morgan and Company. No sooner had Crowder returned home than Zayas fired the North American appointees and replaced them with his family and friends. Corruption continued in almost every government division. Zayas succeeded because the traditional opposition groups remained disparate and disorganized.

In the 1920s winds of political change swept the island and converged with the corrupt 1928 presidential election won by the incumbent, Gerardo Machado. Several new political groups appeared, each demanding a place in the political arena to protect its particular interests, and an end both to corrupt government and U.S. interference in Cuba's internal affairs. Foremost was a new generation of entrepreneurs engaged in construction, real estate, retailing, the production of small consumer goods, and the management of small sugar plantations and mills. These entrepreneurs formed associations to press their demands for more-favorable trade relations with the United States, currency stability, and fiscal and tax reform. A second vocal group included university students. Led by Julio Antonio Mella, in 1922, they organized the National Student Congress to demand the dismissal of incompetent faculty, student participation in university governance, and government support for education. Intellectuals joined in the fray, extolling everything Cuban. One of the most outspoken was Rubén Martínez Villena.

During the 1920s, labor emerged as a potentially important political force. Working women, although still confined largely to the service industries (e.g., as teachers, servants) and to low-wage production (as launderers, seamstresses, dressmakers, and cigar workers), formed several associations. The most significant was the Partido Nacional Sufragistas, which demanded political enfranchisement. And for the first time, in 1919, Cuban males overtook foreign laborers in all major occupational categories, and they eventually coalesced in the Confederación Nacional Obrera de Cuba (CNOC), which represented over 200,000 workers from 128 separate unions. The workers also formed the Radical Socialist Party in 1920. Together, these groups called for improvement in wages, working conditions, an eight-hour work day, an array of social benefits, and government regulation of key industries.

The sense of national protest was best expressed by the National Association of Veterans and Patriots, founded in 1923. These nineteenth-century war veterans presented a twelve-point plan that embraced the goals of the separate groups and quickly captured the imagination of Cubans across the social spectrum.

President Zayas understood the extent of the opposition but chose to ban their public meetings and arrest their leadership who did not first go into exile.

The veteran Liberal politician Gerardo Machado also understood the extent of political unrest when he won the 1924 presidential election. His "Platform of Regeneration" addressed the varied demands, including honest government and the termination of the Platt Amendment. During the first two years of his administration Machado committed the government to a policy of industrial development and economic diversification through a public works program and a protective tariff for the fledgling Cuban industries. Despite a temporary economic upswing, Cuba remained dependent upon the export of sugar. When world sugar prices dropped to a low of 2.4¢ per pound in 1928 and the global depression struck a year later, the Cuban economy again spiraled downward.

In the midst of the economic crisis, Machado was re-elected in 1928 through intimidation, coercion, and bribery that only served to intensify the opposition. As the economic crisis worsened, opposition to the administration intensified. The various groups formed earlier in the decade were now joined by more-radical ones: Directorio Estudiantil Universitario (DEU), the ABC Revolutionary Society, and the newly organized Communist party (PCC). Added to the mix were thousands of "baby boomers" born after independence who just now entered the work force but could not find jobs. As the protests and demonstrations increased, Machado reacted with arbitrary arrests, torture, and other brutalities, including the practice of seizing suspects who then "disappeared" after arrest. By 1931 the country was in open warfare.

To protect the political peace and U.S. investments, President Franklin D. Roosevelt sent Ambassador Sumner Welles to Cuba in May 1933 to mediate the crisis. Welles failed to persuade Machado to depart, but Welles's threat to form a coalition government more acceptable to Washington prompted the Cuban army to oust Machado on August 12, 1933. Subsequently, one Cuban officer claimed that the sole purpose of the coup was to prevent U.S. intervention.

Carlos Manuel de Céspedes was chosen to be the new president by virtue of his lack of political affiliation. Céspedes, without a mandate and, in fact, without a party, could not provide effective leadership. Nor could he control the continuing demonstrations and violence brought on by the hard economic times, exacerbated by the 1929 U.S. Smoot-Hawley Tariff, which further limited the access of Cuban sugar to the U.S. market.

Into the turmoil stepped a group of disenchanted army sergeants, corporals, and enlisted men who demanded improved pay, promotion opportunities, and adequate housing. Supported by the more militant civilian opposition groups, the "Sergeants' Revolt" of September 5, 1933, ousted Céspedes and replaced him with a junta—the Pentarchy—centered around Ramón Grau San Martín. Many thought that Grau Martín, a former university professor who suffered imprisonment and exile for opposing Machado in 1926, would be able to unite the various factions, but he did not. Rather, he was committed to fulfilling José Martí's dreams of the 1890s: a democratic Cuba based upon political liberty and the promotion of social justice.

For Grau Martín, the revolution at hand was socialistic, anti-imperialistic, and, above all, nationalistic.

Grau Martín acted quickly. On September 10, 1933, he unilaterally suspended the Platt Amendment and ten days later decreed eight-hour work days for Cuban laborers. Subsequently the government prohibited the importation of Haitian and Jamaican workers and decreed that 50 percent of all employees in any company be Cuban. Grau Martín also proclaimed land distribution and reduced interest on loans to spur sugar production by small farmers. Women received the right to vote. These social actions struck at both the domestic and foreign capitalist interests. Both the parties of the old Cuba and those new to the political arena protested these actions. The more radical PCC and CNOC said that Grau Martín had not gone far enough. Ambassador Welles requested that Washington intervene in order to maintain political order and to protect U.S. property, but Roosevelt and Secretary of State Cordell Hull demurred because they feared any such action in Cuba would undercut the Good Neighbor Policy they were hoping to promote at the upcoming Buenos Aires Conference. Devoid of support, Grau Martín looked to the old officer corps, but they refused to support him. Throughout, Welles continued to intrigue on his own account. He eventually convinced Fulgencio Batista, the leader of the "Sergeants Revolt," that he should change the government, unless he wanted to risk his own future in case of U.S. intervention.

Understanding his political isolation, Grau Martín departed for Mexico on January 15, 1934. Two days later, Batista and his sergeants placed Carlos Mendieta in the presidential palace. Within five days, the United States recognized the new government.

In the years following, the generation of 1930 learned the harsh realities of Cuban politics. The university students, who played a significant role in the events leading to Grau Martín's presidency, became disillusioned and fractured. Some found solace in pursuing their own careers or shared in the spoils of government office. Most, however, turned to one of two new groups: the Auténtico party and the Jóven Cuba. The Auténticos took their name from Martí's Revolutionary Cubano and became a repository for the revolutionary cause. The party selected the exiled Grau Martín as its leader and put forth a nationalistic platform calling for civil liberties, social justice, and greater economic benefits for all Cubans.

Jóven Cuba, in contrast, called for the violent overthrow of the Mendieta administration and joined with disenchanted workers in carrying out daily acts of terrorism and violence. In fact, opposition to the government culminated in a general strike in March 1935. Fearing that the movement might

topple the government, Batista used the army to break the strike and suppress the opposition. Student and labor leaders were arrested, tortured, and
assassinated and their associations dissolved, except for the communist-
dominated CNOC. The ever-opportunistic communists reorganized themselves into the *Partido Unión Revolucionaria* (PUR) and made peace with
Batista. In 1939 the communists reorganized CNOC into the Confederación de Trabajadores de Cuba (CTC), which boasted a membership of
350,000. It would become a major player in Cuban politics.

With his opponents destroyed or co-opted, Batista ruled for the rest of the
decade either through puppet presidents or shadow governments: José A.
Barnet (1935–1936), Miguel Mariano Gómez (1936), and Federico Laredo
Bru (1936–1940). Through these presidents, Batista attempted to broaden
his political base by reaching out to Cuba's poorer classes with state-
sponsored health programs, the establishment of consumers' cooperatives,
a reorganization of the tax system, a modest agrarian reform program, and
government control of rents and utility rates. The military undertook rural
civic action programs in education, agriculture, hygiene, and nutrition. Batista also officially terminated the Platt Amendment, save the proviso that
gave the United States use of Guantánamo Bay. For all this, he gained support from urban and rural workers.

With his political position firmly in place, Batista engineered the writing
of a new constitution in 1940. The new document embodied the ideals of the
generation of 1930, including universal suffrage and guarantees for civil
liberty and workers rights.

Supported by a coalition of political parties, including the communists,
Batista swept to the presidency in 1940 over his old nemesis Grau Martín.
Batista rewarded many of his supporters with appointments to government
positions, including two key communist leaders, Juan Marinello and Carlos
Rafael Rodríguez. The latter subsequently collaborated with Fidel Castro.

Batista's four-year term coincided with World War II, which proved to be
a mixed blessing. Thanks to the Jones-Costigan Act and the Reciprocal
Trade Agreement, both concluded in 1934, the Cuban economy resumed
its dependency upon the U.S. market. The wartime demand for Cuban
sugar increased that prosperity and enabled the government to undertake
new public works programs. But other economic sectors did not fare as
well. The shortage of ocean shipping cut deeply into the fruit and vegetable
production and the cigar and tourist industries, and consumer goods were in
short supply.

As the war drew to its close in 1944 and 1945, political discontent increased, but neither *Auténtico* Presidents Grau Martín (1944–1948) nor

Carlos Prío Socarrás (1948–1952) met the expectations of the Cuban elec-
torate. Both men lost their idealism of public service and returned to using
government as a personal trough. Embezzlement, graft, corruption, and
malfeasance of public office permeated every branch of national, provincial, and municipal government. Cronyism and nepotism contributed to the
employment of 11 percent of the working population in government posts
by 1950. Government funds were used irrationally.

During the same time period, organized violence took on a new dimension. The three most prominent opposition groups were the ARG (*Acción
Revolucionaria Guiteras*), the MSR (*Movimiento Socialista Revolucionario*) and the UIR (*Unión Insurreccional Revolucionaria*). These *pisteleros*
(armed gunmen), as they were popularly known, found safe haven and allies
on the University of Havana campus. There, many student leaders joined
the gangs to press their own agendas, which included obtaining government
appointments to passing courses without attending class.

The continued political corruption and renewed urban violence forced
Auténtico Senator Eduardo Chibás, a prominent student leader in 1933, to
break with the party and organize the *Partido del Pueblo Cubano*, or Orthodox party, in 1947. In claiming to uphold the ideals of Martí and the "Generation of 1930"—economic reform, political freedom, social justice, and
public honesty—Chibás caught the popular imagination. By 1950 the Orthodox party became a formidable political force. Through his weekly radio
program, Chibás awakened the consciousness of the old-generation politicians and the new generation of university students determined to bring
honesty and morality to Cuba's political arena. The party also benefited
from the demise of the Communist party (PSP), which fell into disfavor because of its longtime association with Batista and because of the anticom-
munist attitude of the Cold War.

Among the students taken in by Chibás's call for reform was Fidel Castro. A student at the Jesuit Belén High School in Havana during the early
1940s, Castro was captivated by his Falangist leaning instructors and their
call for *Hispanidad* (identification with Spanish heritage). Accordingly,
Latin America's independence had been frustrated by the lack of social reforms and the imposition of Anglo-Saxon values. Castro also seemed to be
impressed with the totalitarian model as a means to organize society. As a
university student, Castro participated in gang activities. Although he never
became a student leader, Castro earned a reputation for personal ambition
and forceful and fine oratory. In 1947 Castro joined an abortive expedition
to eliminate Dominican Republic dictator Rafael Leóndas Trujillo, and a
year later he participated in the riots at Bogotá that followed the assassina-

tion of Colombian Jorge Eliecer Gaitán, a prominent labor spokesman. Both incidents earned him a reputation as a revolutionary and, for some, an agent of international communism. Castro returned to Cuba in 1948, where he resumed his loyalty to the reforms advocated by Eduardo Chibás. He became active in the Orthodox party and became its candidate to the House of Representatives in the fateful 1952 elections.

Cuban politics took another fateful turn in late August 1951 when Chibás committed suicide at the end of a routine radio broadcast. The reason for his suicide remains in question, but it stimulated an emotional response from the Cuban people. He stood as the model against the current state of national politics, where elected politicians did not owe allegiance to their constituencies or their nation but only to their own appetite for power and wealth.

The vacuum created by Chibás's death led directly to Batista's carefully executed coup d'état in the early morning of March 10, 1952. To forestall any protests, the telecommunications were seized, offices of opposition parties and the University of Havana closed, constitutional guarantees suspended, and congress dissolved. Most people were not unhappy with the unseating of the *Auténticos*, which along with the Orthodox party and other groups futilely protested the violation of the 1940 constitution. There was no immediate threatening outcry because Batista promised free elections in 1953.

As Batista settled into power and the elections appeared to be nothing more than a promise, challenges to the *batistato* (Batista's dictatorial regime) increased. Despite their failure, in the long run one challenge would prove significant. On July 26, 1953, the young Orthodox Fidel Castro led a nearly suicidal attack upon the second largest army installation of Moncada in Santiago. Although the attack failed, its brazenness established Castro's leadership of the anti-Batista camp and reaffirmed armed struggle as the principal means of the opposition. The attack indicated that a new generation of Cubans as prepared to take up the banners of Martí and Chibás.

3

Fulfilling the Revolution: Castro's Cuba since 1961

Following Fidel Castro's commitment to Marxism-Leninism in December 1961, Cuba experienced four distinct phases of development: (a) the 1960s, during which Castro consolidated his power and attempted to diversify the economy; (b) the 1970s, during which Cuba appeared to benefit from political and economic reforms; (c) the 1980s, during which stagnation characterized the Revolutionary process; and (d) the 1990s, during which the collapse of the Soviet Union brought new challenges to Cuban communism.

In January 1959 Castro and his cadre of close advisors remained but one element of the factions that ousted Batista. To eliminate his political rivals, Castro silenced all political parties, save the communist Popular Socialist Party (PSP) and the established popular tribunals. Set up in neighborhoods, factories, and in the rural areas, these courts imposed penalties, from incarceration to execution, on enemies of the revolution. The lack of concern for legal correctness and fairness characterized this revolutionary justice even after the popular tribunals were incorporated into the restructured legal system in 1973. In addition, the government imposed tight restrictions on the media and the intellectual community, and the Committees for the Defense of the Revolution (CDRs) reported on any critical discussion of government policies. As a result, by the early 1970s an estimated 20,000 political prisoners languished in Cuba's squalid prisons. Cubans learned to follow the proper code of revolutionary conduct or suffer the consequences.

Initially, Castro needed the old-line PSP leadership to provide administrative skills and linkage to the Soviet Union, but he also needed to eliminate those party members who potentially served as focal points of opposition to the revolution. Toward that end, in 1961 he fused the PSP with his 26th of July Movement into the Integrated Revolutionary Organization (ORI). After strengthening his grip over the organization in 1962, he purged PSP leader Aníbal Escalante and his close colleagues for lacking revolutionary zeal. A year later, Castro replaced the ORI with the United Party of the Socialist Revolution (PURS), and again, several old-line communists were attacked. Among them was Marcos Rodríguez, a former member of the urban underground, who found himself on trial for collaborating with Batista's police force in 1957. Castro then went on to proclaim the new Cuban Communist Party (PCC) in 1965. Escalante, however, continued to feud with Castro over the revolution's direction until 1968 when he and his followers were punished for deserting the revolutionary cause.

As a result of his political maneuvering, Castro served not only as prime minister and commander-in-chief of the armed forces, but also as secretary of the PCC and top member of the Politburo. His brother Raúl was second in command. The interlocking leadership roles of the Castro brothers remained a characteristic of Cuban life into the 1990s. Castro controlled membership in the PCC. One gained party membership, and subsequently government appointments and military rank, only by invitation and professions of loyalty to Castro and commitment to his revolution. By the end of the 1960s, an estimated 55,000 Cubans out of a population of nearly 8 million claimed party membership.

To further enhance his position, Castro implemented popular programs to gain mass support. The 1961 "Campaign Against Illiteracy" set the tone. Some 300,000 people were mobilized to provide the estimated 1 million illiterates with basic reading and writing skills and in the process promote national solidarity and a belief in the revolution and its leaders. Because the revolutionary leaders saw education as a means to raise social consciousness and develop a commitment to the revolution, the state assumed responsibility for education from kindergarten through the university. Religious and private education were abolished. Throughout the 1960s the government spent an estimated 275 million pesos on education, four times the pre-1959 levels. As a result, the number of schools and students more than doubled in a decade. Although the education programs expanded Castro's base of support, critics pointed to its ideological content at the sacrifice of critical thinking. Indeed, even a friend of the revolution, Jacobo Timmerman, noted in his book observing life in Castro's Cuba that Cuba's vaunted educational reforms left no room for free thinking and, worse, the country had no books to read.

Castro also moved quickly to incorporate "outsiders," such as women, into the revolution. The Federation of Cuban Women (FMC), founded in 1960, sought to liberate women through revolutionary programs, not gender-based activism. The FMC became an instrument for the government to communicate its objectives to the populace and to report women's needs to the government. The two-way communications resulted in the Maternity Law, the Family Code, the Protection and Hygiene Law, and the Social Security Law. The FMC formed health brigades to conduct programs in infant care, environmental hygiene, uterine cancer diagnosis, and health education. By 1986 the FMC established 838 child care centers throughout Cuba. With education now more accessible, women accounted for 50 percent of the university students and comprised 35 percent of the work force by the early 1980s. Still, critics pointed out that females remained underrepresented in key administrative, managerial, and government positions.

Castro turned sports into a revolutionary tool. Although baseball had long been considered Cuba's national pastime, Cubans otherwise did not pursue sporting activities with great vigor. In 1961 the revolutionary government established the National Institute of Sports, Physical Education and Recreation (INDER) and established its headquarters in Sport City, a Havana suburb. INDER was empowered to develop a national sports program that would have positive lifelong effects on the population. To Castro, athletes not only contributed to the nation's health but also taught the valuable lesson of collectively working together and advancing Cuba's international prestige. By 1975 INDER reported that 3.5 million Cubans actively engaged in various sporting activities. At the same time, Cuba began to achieve success in the Pan American Games and subsequently in the Olympics. Castro found particular pleasure when his athletes and teams captured gold medals in baseball, boxing, and track and field at the expense of the United States.

Intellectual life did not escape revolutionary control. In an early declaration that "for the revolution everything is acceptable and against it nothing," Fidel Castro demarcated the boundaries that would govern what was and was not permissible intellectual behavior. This statement exposes the government's fear of the intelligentsia because they constituted the only group predicated upon free thinking and because the revolutionary leadership and much of the bureaucracy could not and did not trust them. The first step to force intellectual conformity came on March 23, 1959, with the establishment of the Cuban Institute of Cinematographic Art and Industry (ICAIC) designed to create a new, revolutionary film and art industry and eliminate foreign-produced motion pictures that conveyed messages contrary to the revolution's ideals. Cuban-produced movies would have to have ideological messages and didactical purposes to mesh with aesthetic considerations.

In 1961, through the National Council of Culture, the state gained control over publishing, and through the Union of Cuban Artists and Writers, all authors and artists were brought under government control. Others worked in research, writing, or publishing divisions of such organizations such as UNEAC, Casa de las Américas, the National Library, the Academy of Sciences, or the National Council of Culture. In effect, Castro came to determine the limits of freedom; only the true revolutionary intellectual or artist would be supported. Those whose work did not conform to revolutionary dogma or attempted to protest government strictures, including those whose loyalty to the revolution was even doubted, found themselves without government support to pursue their work and lost access to government social services, food rations, and in the most "flagrant" cases, their jobs. By the mid-1960s ICAIC and Casa de las Américas had gained international reputations for their artistic productions and literary writings, albeit with appropriate Cuban interpretations. However, with Castro's total commitment to economic socialism in 1968, the government further clamped down on the intellectual community, effectively contributing to the stagnation of ideas in the arts and literature. Thereafter, until the national crisis of 1991, the quality of Cuban arts and literature languished. Only then did the government admit to the need for re-examining the loss of freedom of expression in the written and visual arts. It had no choice; by then many of Cuba's artists and writers had found their way into the many dissident groups existing clandestinely under Castro's regime.

Beginning in 1961, Castro's overriding consideration was to transform the Cuban economy by expanding non-sugar exports, achieving self-sufficiency in food production, and developing an industrialization plan based upon the import-substitution model, all to be achieved while continuing sufficient sugar production to maintain full employment during the transition. Economic success would make it easier to force conformity through the other social and intellectual institutions. Failure would mean that the populace had reason for protest and political change.

Based upon the assumption that Moscow would not want communism to fail within the U.S. sphere of influence, the Cuban leadership anticipated unlimited economic assistance from the Soviet Union and its eastern European bloc allies. With this confidence, the Cuban Central Planning Board (JUCEPLAN) anticipated economic annual growth to reach 10–15 percent for the 1962–1965 period.

The plan quickly failed. For the first time in Cuban history, food rationing began in 1962. Scarcities of all consumer goods multiplied thereafter. The program was in disarray. Persistent delays and bottlenecks plagued the internal distribution system, and the industrialization plans failed to materialize. Rather than look to the shortcomings of their own idealism and inexperience and the weaknesses of centralized planning, the Cuban leadership placed responsibility elsewhere, particularly at the doorstep of the U.S. embargo, which prevented the arrival of badly needed spare parts and other materials. But there was more. The anticipated Soviet bloc assistance did not materialize. The emigration of Cuban and American technicians, skilled workers, and managers proved costly. Cuban workers appeared unmotivated and unprepared to meet the challenges before them. Although sugar production actually declined, it still accounted for nearly 85 percent of Cuba's exports. Cuba's trade deficit climbed to $327 million by 1963, of which $197 million was with the Soviet Union alone.

The failed economic policies caused a debate among the revolution's leadership beginning in 1964. From the start of the revolution in 1961, Castro accepted the advice of his close friend Che Guevara, a Marxist idealist but not an economist. As Minister of Industries, which included sugar, Guevara had implemented a highly central planned approach and relied upon moral incentives for the workers to produce for the good of the revolution. It failed, particularly in the sugar industry—a fact Guevara admitted in a speech in Algiers in July 1963. In the leadership debates that followed, Guevara's idealism lost out to the pragmatists, those who believed in quasi-capitalist methods that provided material rewards for workers. Guevara's decline in importance was first registered on July 3, 1963, when he lost direct tutelage of the sugar industry, which now would have its own ministry. At the same time, President Osvaldo Dorticós replaced Regino Boti at the Ministry of Economy and was also named head of the Central Planning Council. Guevara understood that he had lost the power of economic planning. Henceforth, emphasis was placed upon the exportation of all agricultural goods in order to earn the foreign exchange needed for the acquisition of machinery and equipment. Industrial planning shifted to the development of those sectors that utilized Cuban natural resources most efficiently. The new economic plan also resulted in the nationalization of the remaining 55,000 small businesses, such as restaurants, repair shops, and retail stores. Castro took a greater interest in the economy and even devised a number of "micro plans."

The Cuban government also needed popular support for the new programs. To accomplish this objective, Castro re-emphasized Guevara's ideal of creating a "new man," one who would put aside personal gain for the collective good. Rather than pay incentives, increased productivity was acknowledged with badges, medallions, and other awards, frequently distributed by Castro himself. Castro hoped that his personal appeal and popularity would be sufficient to overcome people's natural instinct for personal material gain.

As a result of the changes in economic policy and the alignment of Cuba with the Soviet Union in January 1964 during Castro's second visit to Moscow, Guevara had been relatively marginalized from the daily running of the economy. Castro attempted to pacify Guevara by making him head of the Cuban delegation to the United Nations Conference on Trade and Development in Geneva in March 1964 and naming him Cuba's representative to the anniversary of the Russian Revolution in November. By the year's end, Guevara felt isolated and alone, yet he remained true to his commitment not to attack Fidel Castro. The feeling was mutual; Fidel had a special relationship with and fondness for Guevara.

Guevara's wanderlust and desire for a new adventure led him away from Cuba and into revolutionary ventures in South America. He turned to Bolivia as the place to initiate a new social revolution. The country's large indigenous population (Inca Indians and their descendants) lived on the margins of the national economy and were not represented in the national government. Just what role Castro had in pushing Guevara towards Bolivia is not clear. Although Cuba provided a training ground and supplies for the mission, there is evidence Castro attempted to dissuade Guevara from the undertaking.

Guevara departed for Bolivia in the fall of 1966 and began his military actions there in March 1967. In the Bolivian Andes Mountains, however, he never attracted the local Indians to his cause. They did not accept the foreigner, nor did they view the world through the same Marxist lens that Guevara did. The Bolivian military, aided by the United States Central Intelligence Agency, pursued Guevara with a vengeance. Guevara's time finally ran out; he was captured and executed by the Bolivian military in the remote Andes on October 9, 1967.

As for Castro, once Guevara arrived in Bolivia, he failed to provide him with the necessary support for victory, nor did he make any effort to rescue Guevara when the opportunity presented itself in July and August 1967—facts that led Guevara to conclude in his diary that he had been betrayed by the Cuban leader. Subsequently, Castro claimed that the Russians had tied his hands, and that the Bolivian communists, hopelessly split among themselves, refused to cooperate. In reality, Castro could not afford widening the revolutionary spectrum in Latin America, and if he attempted to do so, U.S. President Lyndon B. Johnson would stand as a staunch obstacle with the threat to destroy the Cuban Revolution itself. For the same reasons, Castro claimed he could not rescue Guevara from his fate. And what would he have done with the rescued martyr? On the other hand, Guevara may have expected too much. Reportedly, those closest to Castro observed that the Cuban leader was saddened by the loss of his companion of a thousand battles, but that he had resigned himself to the inevitable outcome of the Bolivian adventure.

Economic hard times plagued Cuba in October 1967, and Castro used the occasion of Guevara's death to try to instill a fresh sense of purpose and order into the Cuban Revolution. He publicly extolled the virtues of Che's Marxist idealism and bravery for taking up the cause of Bolivia's downtrodden. It had little impact. Thirty years later, in 1997, when Guevara's remains were exhumed from their place below an isolated Andean airstrip and returned home for a hero's burial, Castro again applauded the Argentine revolutionary. By this time, however, Guevara had become an icon to many left-leaning people throughout the world. Young people especially admired him. In the United States, T-shirts with an image of Che emblazoned on their fronts sold briskly at rock concerts and in suburban shopping malls—an ironic turn of capitalists cashing in on an anticapitalist revolutionary. His ideals for social change and his challenge to the established order overshadowed the bloody side of his revolutionary pursuits. His writings were reprinted, and he became the subject of new and analytical biographies and of documentaries and movies.

Meanwhile, during the mid-1960s, as the gap between Castro and Guevara widened and the latter went off to Bolivia, the Cuban economy continued to falter. By the time of Guevara's death in 1967, the reforms introduced in 1964 began to show signs of total failure due to mismanagement and bureaucratic snafus. Production of sugar, tobacco, vegetables, dairy products, poultry, beef, and pork dropped steadily during that time. Worker absenteeism and low productivity crippled the manufacturing sector.

The combination of economic need and a new moral crusading led Castro to call for the production of a 10–million-ton crop of sugar in 1970. Castro described it as "the harvest to end all harvests" so that Cuba would have the capital to make future economic development viable and usher in an era of social comforts for everyone. An estimated 1.2 million workers, including Castro, from all sectors of society joined the 300,000 cane cutters for the *zafra* (sugar harvest season). Although a record 8.5 million tons of sugar were harvested, the failure to reach the stated goal had disastrous effects upon the Cuban economy and psyche. Other economic sectors had been ignored in order to reach the sugar objective. The concomitant loss of foodstuffs and consumer goods meant only several more years of sacrifice.

To the surprise of many observers, Castro used the July 26, 1970, speech to admit failure. He even offered to resign. In the speech, Castro blamed the economic failure upon excessive centralization and bureaucratization of decision making by the PCC and state authorities at the expense of the mass organizations and the workers. Castro's confession and resignation offer were not bold moves in 1970 because his political opposition had been eliminated and the institutional means to replace him did not exist. Still, 1970 is a high-water mark in the course of the revolution. Government reorganization and a sense of democratization followed.

Three new ministries and an executive committee of the Council of Ministers were established. The Finance Ministry was reorganized. The communist party held its first congress in 1975, which resulted in a new constitution that provided for a presidential form of government. National and municipal assemblies were established. The latter gave the appearance of popular participation in government with the power to elect delegates to the national assembly and to appoint judges to local courts. Each municipal assembly also was given authority over schools, health services, cinema, sports facilities, and transportation enterprises within its boundaries; and it assumed responsibility over local enterprises including retail operations, consumer services, and factories producing for local consumption. Although membership in the communist party also expanded to 202,807 in 1975 and to 487,000 by the mid-1980s, the PCC was restricted to the coordination and supervision of administrative functions.

At the same time, mass organizations, such as the FMC, CDRs, and ANAP expanded their roles in the formulation and implementation of policy. Reorganization of the CTC increased membership to 867,000 within 26,000 new local unions. The organizations were directed to address local social problems with a new sense of volunteerism.

These changes were little more than cosmetic. Castro remained the dominant figure as the "maximum leader." The tightly knit leadership built around Fidel Castro and his brother Raúl remained intact and continued to control policies and functions in Cuban society. There still was no room for dissent; opposition was silenced in defense of the revolution. The masses continued to receive indoctrination of Marxism-Leninism in formal classes at the workplace and in the neighborhood. Loyalty to the revolution was paramount. Castro remained a master manipulator of public opinion and in the propagation of partial truths, which in the controlled media gave the appearance of reality.

In the process of reorganization, Castro focused upon the military's role in defending the revolution, not only abroad but at home. Headed by Raúl Castro, Cuba's Revolutionary Armed Forces received generous allotments of the national budget and became a modern and effective fighting unit. Its officers, many trained in the Soviet Union and eastern Europe, became highly skilled technicians and government administrators. The Armed Forces' loyalty to the maintenance of the regime was never in doubt.

The changes in economic policy that followed Castro's 1970 confession were equally important. Material incentives replaced moral rewards. Workers were paid according to productivity goals. Those who exceeded the established norms received percentage wage increases, and exemplary workers received preferential access to consumer goods such as automobiles, television sets, refrigerators, and washing machines. The government also moved against absenteeism. The 1971 antiloafing law, incorporated into the 1976 constitution, required that all men between 18 and 60 perform productive labor. To be sure, health care, education, and old-age pensions remained free; rents were still fixed at 10 percent of income; and many food items remained rationed. But service fees were restored for the use of telephones, local bus transportation, and sporting events, and day-care fees were adjusted according to income. The additional income productive and favored workers earned generated a new purchasing power that, in turn, created a stimulus for consumer goods. Consumers soon found cameras, phonographs, appliances, bicycles, furniture, clothing, kitchenware, jewelry, cosmetics, and perfumes available, but at higher prices than when rationed.

External pressures also forced Castro's Cuba to institute economic reforms. Frustrated at the waste of its direct economic assistance, which included balance of payments credits, and subsidies for sugar, petroleum, and nickel (estimated at $12.5 billion for the 1970s), the Soviet Union demanded economic reform. Moscow insisted upon the implementation of the Economic Management and Planning System (SDPE) that introduced limited market reforms and expanded autonomy for state enterprises. One of SDPE's most successful efforts came with the establishment of farmers' free markets, where foodstuffs were sold at prices dictated by supply and demand. The government also improved its efficiency. Planning techniques and data collection improved, and a cost accounting system was introduced. The government gave new attention to the training of technicians, economists, systems analysts, and business administrators. In addition, during the 1970s the Soviets provided several thousand technicians for construction, of a variety of industrial enterprises, including modern sugar mills, fertilizer plants, and an electric plant. Cubans also studied engineering, computer science, agriculture, construction and food processing in the Soviet Union.

The reorganization efforts had a salutary affect upon the Cuban economy. Productivity and exports expanded. Cuban textiles, shoes, construction materials, metals, and pharmaceuticals found their way into the world market. World sugar prices increased, which helped offset the decline in sugar production after 1970. In fact, the economy grew at a 5.7 percent annual rate between 1971 and 1980. Still, sugar remained Cuba's primary export, accounting for 65 percent of the total share in 1985, and the Soviet Union continued to underwrite the economy through debt postponement and extended credits. As late as 1986, a new agreement between Moscow and Havana provided for $3 billion in annual credits through 1990. Also, by 1986 the Soviets accounted for 64 percent of Cuba's exports and 62 percent of its imports. In economic terms, the Cuban Revolution had traded a colonial client status with the United States for one with the Soviet Union. But the new arrangement offered promises of national autonomy and, over time, at least limited development.

The combination of sustained economic growth and political stability, supported by the Soviets, enabled the Castro government to meet many of its egalitarian goals: redistribution of land, rent reduction, and the rationing of scarce goods. Private beaches, clubs, and schools were eliminated, and resorts and luxury hotels opened to all Cubans. The 1963 social security law extended illness benefits to all workers and retirement to the totally incapacitated. Wages increased, especially in the agricultural sector.

By the late 1980s, Cuba pointed to notable achievements in education, nutrition, and health services. In education, a variety of programs brought the nation's literacy rate to 96 percent, a figure higher than many other Latin American countries. Primary and secondary school enrollments increased markedly to 3.3 million children in the mid-1980s. University enrollments expanded greatly beyond the pre-1959 levels, and the focus of education changed from the humanities, social sciences, and law, which prepared one for government positions, to the sciences, engineering, architecture, and agriculture.

In the health field, the government's rationing system set a target of 1,900 calories per capita daily intake in the early 1960s, but improved food production led to higher consumption. The United Nations reported that Cuba had reached a daily per capita daily intake of 2,705 calories by the early 1980s, above the generally recognized minimum of 2,500 calories. Not all of this could be attributed to the government programs. Workers also paid a small fare for lunches at the workplace, and gray and black markets offered food items otherwise unavailable. Gray markets enabled families to swap goods among themselves, and the black market provided goods at above controlled market prices.

Health services expanded rapidly in the 1970s. A decade later, Cuba counted one doctor for every 490 residents. The number of nurses, X-ray and laboratory technicians, anesthetists, and rehabilitation specialists also markedly increased. By the 1980s, the number of hospitals and clinics, both general and in specialty fields, expanded significantly and spread across the breadth of the country. The island's hospitals and clinics also performed experimental and lifesaving surgery that attracted patients from around the world. Equally impressive figures were found in dental hygiene. The U.S. embargo severely limited Cuba's access to medicines, and it took a long time for Cuba to recover, but in the 1980s the nation produced 83 percent of its own pharmaceuticals. As a result of this effort, Cuba counted a significant decrease in infant mortality rates and death by communicable disease, but joined the ranks of industrialized nations in which the principal causes of death were heart disease, cancer, and stroke.

The advances in education, nutrition, and health were not matched in personal comforts. A severe housing shortage existed despite the exodus of nearly 1 million Cubans between 1959 and the Mariel boatlift of 1980. The housing shortage that existed at the time of the revolution was exacerbated by an exploding birth rate that nearly doubled the population to 10 million by 1980. The diversion of construction materials to other projects such as hospitals, schools, and roads also contributed to the problem. Despite the public attention given to the construction of vast projects like Ciudad José Martí in Santiago, which was designed to house 50,000 residents, and Alamar East outside of Havana for 100,000, housing units still lagged by one million by 1980. The crisis worsened as older homes fell into disrepair for want of both capital and materials for improvements. Across the island, the government simply lacked the resources to keep them in a proper state of repair. So bad was the situation that a total of 25,000 houses collapsed in 1979 alone.

Other inequities also surfaced. With the return of material incentives in the 1970s, wage disparities reappeared, but at a greater rate than in the 1960s. In addition, the workers who successfully earned bonuses like refrigerators and televisions in the 1970s enjoyed a higher standard of living than the less successful. At a higher level, government officials, union leaders, and high-level technicians came to enjoy valued goods and services, including automobiles, better housing, and vacations abroad. These inequities became more pronounced in the 1980s.

On a personal level, men refused to accept the changing role of women and engage in household chores. The government attempted to legislate new social arrangements. The 1974 Family Code law mandated that men share in household maintenance responsibilities. In practice, the older "macho" culture persisted as men refused to yield to egalitarian imperatives from the government in matters of home and sexual relations. Women still found themselves discriminated against at home and in the workplace in the late 1980s. Professional advancement remained limited.

By the mid-1980s, the concentration of political power in the Castro clique, the privileges granted to communist party members, and the failure of the revolution to achieve its lofty social and economic objectives contributed to a measure of discontent across the island. The economic and social injustices prompted Castro to declare the nation's recommitment to the revolution in 1986. The "Rectification Program," as it became known, reemphasized the primacy of the communist party and Castro's pre-eminent role in the decision-making process. The few market reforms in place were rescinded, and a new emphasis on the collective good returned. Volunteerism again became the model for achieving new state-mandated goals.

Under rapidly changing world conditions over the next three years Castro exhorted the Cuban people to recommit themselves to the revolution. Indeed, as socialism went into reform or retreat elsewhere, Castro emphasized the significance of Cuba's role as the standard-bearer for a vigorous socialism. The reaffirmation of socialist values and the success of socialism in Cuba, Castro argued, would light the way for socialism everywhere. National pride, hitched to socialist ideas, became the engine of *fidelismo* (Castro's personal philosophy) in the 1980s and 1990s.

The most significant global changes of that time period occurred in the Soviet Union. The *perestroika* (restructuring of economic and political institutions) and *glasnost* (freedom of expression) reforms introduced by Mikhail Gorbachev not only led to the collapse of the Soviet Union and ended its stranglehold over eastern Europe, much to the dismay of Gorbachev, but also recast its special relationship with Cuba. The new world order meant that Cuba would have to pay its own way. The loss of privileged market access and economic subsidies from the Soviets proved disastrous to the Cuban economy. In 1991 Gorbachev ordered the withdrawal from Cuba of the 3,000 Russian troops stationed there and later announced that future arms transfers would be on a commercial basis. Such actions signaled an end to the guarantee of Cuba's security.

The loss of its major trading partner threatened to undo all the progress Cuba made during thirty years of revolution. Soviet oil and oil by-products, which the Soviets had made available to Cuba at prices below the world market and which accounted for nearly all the island's energy needs, decreased by 90 percent in 1993. Other key Soviet imports declined drastically: fertilizers, by 80 percent; animal feed supplies, by 70 percent. Imports of capital grade consumer goods, grains, foodstuffs, raw materials, and spare parts ceased altogether. Commercial relations with the Soviets declined from $8.7 billion in 1989 to $7.6 million in 1993, and trade with eastern Europe nearly ended. In addition, eastern European merchant fleets refused to carry goods to or from Cuba unless paid for in hard currency. The world market even militated against Cuba: World oil prices rose while sugar prices fell.

The United States did not help the situation. The 1992 Cuba Democracy Act prohibited U.S. companies operating in third countries from trading with Cuba and prohibited ships trading with Cuba from visiting U.S. ports for six months after it left the island. Subsequently, new restrictions were placed upon Cuban Americans who visited the island and brought consumer goods, medicines, and cash to their relatives.

The end of the Cold War brought Castro's experiment to near death. Scarcities of food, medicine, and consumer goods spread. The continuing decline in industrial and agricultural production caused by fuel, spare parts, and shipping shortages added to a vicious cycle. The consequences proved staggering. By 1993 an estimated 50 percent of the industrial plants suspended operations. Factory closings, production declines, and transportation difficulties led to the displacement of nearly 20 percent of the population. Publication of books dropped by 50 percent. Work animals replaced machines in agriculture as the sugar crop dropped from 8.1 million tons in 1991 to 4.2 million tons in 1993.

The social consequences of economic scarcity were devastating. At times, rationing failed to provide sufficient food for a two-week period; nearly three hundred medicines disappeared from circulation. World attention was drawn to the island in 1993 when some 50,000 Cubans suffered optic neuropathy due to a deficiency of Vitamin B complex. Abortions increased; for every ten live births, there were an equal number of abortions. By the end of 1992 nearly 40 percent of bus and train schedules had been suspended, and taxi service all but disappeared. In 1994 nearly 700,00 bicycles had been distributed. Imposed blackouts shut down refrigeration and cooking facilities for hours at a time.

Government reactions were almost predictable. Castro denounced the Soviet abandonment of communism and asserted that Cuba would go it alone, that it had a responsibility to demonstrate to the world that socialism could succeed. Once again Castro summoned the Cuban people to greater heroism and courage. Across the country, on streets and highways, in schools and at workplaces, billboards and posters alluded to Antonio Maceo's refusal to surrender at Baraguá to the Treaty of Zanjón in 1878. The nation was called upon to endure a new period of austerity. Castro proclaimed this to be a "Special Period" (*período especial*) that necessitated new rationing schedules. Foods of all kinds became increasingly scarce, prompting the organization of urban workers into agricultural brigades in an effort to increase food production.

In addition to the reminiscences of the past, new strategies had to be devised. Foreign investment was attracted through joint ventures, profit-sharing, profit repatriation, and tax exemption. As a result, Australian, British, Canadian, Chilean, Mexican, and Spanish firms expanded into telecommunications, pharmaceuticals, construction, transportation, food processing, textiles, and mining. By the mid-1990s, the number of foreign firms operating in Cuba increased fourfold since 1987 to five hundred firms. Cuba also expanded its commercial relations and sources of foreign exchange by concluding agreements with China, North Korea, Vietnam, Italy, and Jordan. They agreed to purchase Cuban sugar and tobacco, and in exchange Cuba agreed to purchase their pasta, grain, chemical fertilizers, detergents, and medicines. The governments of Brazil, Chile, and Mexico extended credit lines.

The most-extensive changes came in the tourist industry, which became a prime source of badly needed hard currency. Spanish, Germans, and Austrians engaged in joint ventures with the Cuban government to build and operate facilities at Varadero, Camagüey, and Cayo Coco. Niche markets were developed in "eco," medical, and scientific tourism. Nightclubs opened to provide evening entertainment.

Tourism proved to be a double-edged sword. While the expanded tourist industry brought in the badly needed hard currency, it created animosity among the Cubans as foodstuffs, gasoline, and medicines were readily available to the dollar-spending tourists. The beaches, nightclubs, and consumer goods were out of reach for the average Cuban; the Cuban peso had no value in the tourist zones, as hard currency, especially the U.S. dollar, was accepted as legal tender. Prostitution flourished, and the government appeared to ignore the problem. Teachers, office workers, engineers, architects, and the like took jobs as servants, taxi drivers, bellhops, porters, busboys, and waiters to get tourist dollars. The mass infusion of dollars also contributed to an inflationary spiral. On the booming black market, the exchange rate leaped from 10 pesos per dollar to 100.

The "dollarization" of the economy created new problems. While the government sought long-term solutions, it improvised with short-term measures. In September 1993 the Council of State ended the state monopoly on employment, production, and distribution by authorizing self-employment in more than fifty trades and services. Under the law, automobile mechanics, taxi drivers, photographers, hairdressers, carpenters, cooks, and computer programmers, among others, were authorized to operate businesses and offer their services to the public at large at competitive prices. Artisans also were allowed to sell their works directly to the public for pesos or dollars. By mid-decade nearly 20,000 individuals had obtained self-employment licenses. In September 1994 the government authorized farmers to sell their surplus production on the open market after the quota for state markets was met. By the end of the year, nearly 150 farmers markets appeared across the island. Homeowners opened small restaurants on their premises and rented rooms to travelers.

There also were political changes in the early 1990s. The Fourth Party Congress in 1991 provided for the direct secret ballot elections of members. Membership in the Central Committee underwent substantial change, with new persons constituting 60 percent of the total 225 members. The Council of State also underwent a 50 percent personnel turnover. In 1992 the National Assembly ratified party recommendations to provide for direct popular vote to elect provincial delegates and assembly deputies. But Castro remained the ultimate decision-maker.

Most astonishing to many Cuban watchers was the government's announcement of a papal visit to Cuba in January 1998. After all, the Roman Catholic Church had come under attack early in the revolutionary process. Its schools were closed, foreign nuns and priests expelled, and practicing Catholics harassed by government officials. The state was declared atheistic in 1962 and remained so until 1992. But in the "new Cuba" of the 1990s small doses of capitalism and Christianity gained official sanction. In December 1997, Christmas became an official holiday again, twenty-eight years after Castro abolished it. Other religions—Protestant, Jewish, and the Afro-Cuban Santeria—also were permitted greater latitude and openness—and perhaps ominously for a political system that had outlawed religion for over a generation. The Cuban youth visibly expressed their religious beliefs.

Fidel Castro's reasons for inviting Pope John Paul II were more important to his foreign policy than to Cuba's domestic situation (see Chapter 4). Still, the pope's visit increased the risk of encouraging opposition to the Castro regime. Castro understood that the papal visit to Pope John Paul II's native Poland in 1979 had ushered in a period of political discontent that led to the end of communist rule there. Whereas Polish communist leaders had erred, Castro claimed, the Cuban Revolution had not, and the public confidence he expressed in his own system was bolstered by his call for all Cubans to attend the papal Masses. Pope John Paul II's four-day visit, January 21–25, proved a festive occasion. Large crowds greeted him enthusiastically. His four public Masses were well attended, during which there were only isolated cases of public dissent against the Castro regime. The pontiff, however, did not disappoint those who anticipated his call for change within Cuba. He admonished the lack of family values; criticized government-sanctioned abortion; challenged the youth to serve as the beacon of future progress; chastised the lack of human rights; called for greater political dialogue; and in a private meeting with Castro, presented a list of political prisoners he wished to be released. Pope John Paul II continued the pressure in a public address at the Vatican after his return from Cuba. He compared this trip to his 1979 visit to Poland.

In the weeks immediately following the pontiff's visit, observers of Cuban society noticed an air of optimism, particularly a greater expression of freedom in the idle gossip at the sidewalk restaurants that dot Havana's busy streets. Castro even promised the release of some two hundred political prisoners. But the flurry of optimism quickly faded. In reality, fewer than one hundred of the political prisoners were released, and new arrests were made of those who spoke out against the revolution. And in a decision that surprised none, on February 24, 1998, Cuba's National Assembly elected Fidel Castro as president of the thirty-one-member Council of State for five more years and reconfirmed his brother Raúl as First Vice President. Nor did the Cuban population directly benefit from the estimated $15–$20 million windfall generated by the papal visit through exorbitant hotel, food, and transportation charges, and souvenir buying. The funds went to state-run industries.

Despite statistical data from 1995 to 1997 that the Cuban economy had improved, Cuba's official 1998 portrait is one of stability, of slow but real progress after the economy all but collapsed between 1989 and 1994. Tourism and mining are booming, and foreign investment is flowing into the energy sector, telecommunications, shipyards, and other industries. The Internet has reached Havana, direct dial telephone service to the United

States from major hotels is opening, and there are even two fast-food restaurants, Burgi and Rapido.

Yet, the hardships increased for the Cuban people. The United Nations reported that hunger and child malnutrition reappeared on the island. A poll carried out surreptiously by academics from Mexico's University of Guadalajara in January 1998 showed that 76 percent of Cubans believed that life had gotten tougher, not better, during the previous year. Petty crimes and burglaries increased, and reports of cattle rustling surfaced. During the same time period, Cubans became more open in their criticism of the regime. By the mid-1990s, an estimated fifty dissident groups appeared across the island. Antigovernment demonstrations erupted in Cojímar and Regla in 1993 and in Havana in 1994. In the spring and summer of 1997, a series of bombings ripped through Havana's tourist hotels. The government denounced the protests and reacted harshly with harassment and arrests. So concerned was the government with public protest, in a national television address prior to Pope John Paul II's visit, Castro cautioned against public demonstrations.

The ever-worsening economic and social conditions, along with the continued political repression, prompted a new wave of emigration. Recognizing that it could relieve the discontent by permitting migration, the Cuban government eased travel restrictions. In the early 1990s, an estimated 13,000 Cubans gained permanent U.S. residency by entering on visitors visas, and countless others came through third countries. But it was the rafters (*balseros*) who drew most attention. Between 1990 and 1993 approximately 10,000 émigrés came across the Florida Straits in anything that floated. It became a deluge in August 1994 after Fidel Castro announced that his government would no longer interdict or hinder the departure of Cubans wishing to leave for the United States. Before the crisis ended in late September 1994, another 21,000 Cubans escaped the island to seek refuge in the United States.

Like a soap opera, the drama continued when, in February 1996, the Cuban Air Force shot down two aircraft flown by a Miami exile group for allegedly violating Cuban airspace. The shoot down was accompanied by a further crackdown on dissident groups. In response, the U.S. Congress approved the Cuban Liberty and Democratic Solidarity Act (popularly known as the Helms-Burton Bill) that further tightened U.S. trade restrictions. Washington continued to pursue Castro's downfall by economic strangulation.

Through it all, Fidel Castro continued to hold considerable authority and personal popularity. At the Fifth Communist Party Congress in October

1997, Castro clearly indicated that as long as he remained healthy and alive and capable of discharging responsibilities, there would be no change in Cuba. He continued to implore the Cuban people to work for *patria* (fatherland), that Cuba would continue the struggle for its independence despite the crumbling of the communist world around him. As in 1962, Castro placed blame upon the United States for the plight of his people. "*Socialismo o muerte*" (socialism or death) remained the credo.

4

Castro's Search for Prestige: Cuba and the World since 1961

For two years after his arrival in Havana in January 1959, Fidel Castro pursued domestic policies that challenged the United States imperial presence in Cuba. Since 1898, when the United States meddled in Cuba's independence, it continued to support corrupt governments and its businesses exploited the island. To break the chains of dependence appeared to Castro and Cubans as a fulfillment of José Martí's ideals. To policymakers in Washington, however, Castro increasingly appeared more like a communist who needed to be removed from power. Over the next thirty-eight years, the governments in neither Havana nor Washington wavered from these starting points.

Castro also understood that he needed economic support from elsewhere to replace that provided by the North Americans. He found that support in the Soviet Union, but at a price he did not want to pay. Cuba became economically dependent upon the Soviets and their eastern European allies. The dependency did not prevent Castro, however, from pursuing an independent foreign policy, first in Latin America and then on a global scale. As a result, until 1991, when the Soviet Union collapsed and its economic assistance terminated, relations between Havana and Moscow were often strained.

In 1959 and 1960 the Eisenhower administration sought to end Castro's economic nationalization policies through ever-increasing trade restrictions, culminating in a trade embargo and the closing of the U.S. embassy in January 1961. When Castro did not succumb to economic strangulation, the

Central Intelligence Agency (CIA) thought it could remove him by supporting guerrilla groups within Cuba. When that failed to bring success, the CIA turned to an exile-supported invasion that, the agency argued, would ignite an internal uprising against Castro. President John F. Kennedy inherited the invasion plan from the Eisenhower administration, but not until February 1961 did he approve the CIA plan to organize a provisional government among the exile Cuban community in Miami under the leadership of Dr. José Miró Cardona, Castro's first premier. Only a week before the actual invasion in April 1961 did Kennedy approve the actual Bay of Pigs operation.

The Cuban exile community did not reflect the socioeconomic mix of the island's society, but rather that of the upper and middle classes, who were divided among themselves. The exile groups did not represent the lower-class Cubans, both rural and urban, particularly the Afro-Cuban. And with opposition groups within Cuba effectively silenced by the government, the possibility of an internal uprising was remote.

This division was apparent among the Cubans trained for the invasion by the CIA in Guatemala and Nicaragua. Rather than former *batistianos*, the recruits represented varied professions and politics. Some wanted to restore the gambling and vacation paradise of pre-Castro Havana; others sought a true democracy; yet another faction consisted of those who had become disenchanted with Castro's policies. Whatever the divisions among them as to why they sought Castro's overthrow, the recruits did come to agree that the CIA-run operation was less organized and less informed than they orginally supposed. In their training camps, the Cuban mercenaries soon discovered that the Americans were training them for a conventional military operation, not a guerrilla conflict. They understood that a brigade of 1,500 men was no match for Castro's standing army. Nor did the Cubans see much advantage of training on volcanic terrain dissimilar to the Cuban landscape where they would be fighting. But the CIA operatives tolerated no criticism, and the recruits let their anti-Castro passions overcome their misgivings about the poor training and tactical support offered by the CIA. The invasion went on as scheduled.

When Brigade 2506 landed at the Bay of Pigs in the morning hours of April 17, 1961, it was doomed to failure. The invasion failed for several reasons. Castro and the rest of the world knew an attack was coming because the CIA training of Cuban exiles in Guatemala made national news in the United States beginning in January 1961. This gave Castro time to prepare. The invasion itself was poorly planned. The wetland terrain at the Bay of Pigs, for example, did not provide the natural cover to protect the invading forces, a fact that became glaringly apparent on invasion morning. In preparation of the brigade's landing, Cuban exile pilots, flying unmarked U.S. World War II vintage airplanes, in surprise attacks were supposed to eliminate Castro's aged Air Force on the ground. In the initial assault on April 16, one of the exile planes was hit by Cuban ground fire and the pilot, rather than return to Nicaragua, landed in Miami where he announced what had just happened. Kennedy, mistakingly thinking he still could keep the U.S. role secret, called off a second attack on the remaining six Cuban military aircraft. His decision proved costly to the Cuban invaders.

The Cuban exile brigade was left stranded as the remnants of the Cuban Air Force pinned them down and destroyed their lone cargo ship off shore. The Cuban army quickly reached the invasion site, where Castro took command. In Havana and other cities, Castro's security forces and 8,000 CDRs rounded up thousands of suspected antigovernment persons, and possibly thwarted a CIA-approved, Mafia-conducted assassination attempt on Castro. There could be no internal uprising. In Washington, Kennedy resisted all pressure to offer any overt assistance. Isolated on the ground and devoid of American support, within three days, nearly 1,500 exile troops surrendered.

When the brief battle ended, Castro ordered the execution of only the *batistianos*; the remaining 1,100 invaders were imprisoned for over a year until the United States paid nearly $53 million in medicine and foodstuffs for their release. For Castro, the Bay of Pigs proved a godsent gift. It enabled him to consolidate his position on the island and to enhance his image in the non-aligned world and among many quarters in the Western Hemisphere.

Although the failed invasion proved a dreadful embarrassment for the United States, President Kennedy did not drift from the policy of isolating Castro with the ultimate objective of his removal. In January 1962, on the diplomatic front, Kennedy engineered the eviction of Cuba from the Organization of American States (OAS) because of its Marxist-Leninist government. All Latin American nations, except Mexico, complied in severing diplomatic and trade relations with Cuba. Kennedy harassed Castro in other ways. In April 1962 a U.S. military exercise, involving some 40,000 troops in another amphibious landing on Puerto Rico, sent a strong signal that Kennedy had intentions of ordering an invasion of Cuba. He also approved the CIA's "Operation Mongoose," a program designed to disrupt the Cuban economy and to discredit Castro personally. Some of the more bizarre suggestions to embarrass Castro publicly included having a cigar blow up in his face while making a national television address and putting a potent powder in his drink that would cause his beard to fall out. By 1962 approximately two hundred anti-Castro organizations operated within the United States, unmolested by U.S. authorities, if not actually supplied by American sources. Some of these anti-Castro groups actually launched attacks upon the island nation, burning cane fields, destroying sugar mills, blowing up oil storage tanks, and the like. At the same time, the CIA recruited dissidents within Cuba to plot Castro's assassination. As Kennedy increased the pressure to oust Castro from power, the Cuban dictator tightened the link to Moscow.

Cuba moved to the center stage of the Cold War in October 1962. Early that summer Soviet Premier Nikita Khrushchev decided to place missiles on the island, both to challenge the U.S. sphere of influence and to counter-balance U.S. missiles at the Soviet doorstep in Europe. In late August 1962, a U.S. U-2 spy plane photographed the construction of missile sites in Cuba, expected to be operational shortly. The stage was set for a confrontation between Washington and Moscow that brought the world to the brink of nuclear disaster for thirteen days in mid-October 1962.

On October 22, President Kennedy announced via a national television address a quarantine on the introduction of Soviet offensive missiles into Cuba. Critics quickly asserted that this was an act of war and would prompt a Soviet retaliation. The vagaries of international law aside, the young president stated that the Soviet action violated a basic principle of U.S. policy toward Cuba that dated to the early nineteenth century: No foreign interlopers were to be permitted on the island.

Kennedy deployed U.S. Naval ships to intercept Soviet ships bound for Cuba, authorizing his officers to board and search them for such weapons. In fact, two Soviet ships were stopped and allowed to pass. At the same time, preparations for an invasion of the island went forward. Unbeknownst to the U.S. policymakers at the time, an estimated 13,000 Soviet combat troops had been brought to Cuba disguised as technicians, construction workers, and the like, and Soviet commanders on the ground had tactical nuclear weapons with the authority to use them if necessary. The world stood closer to a nuclear holocaust than it realized.

The crisis eased on October 26 when a flotilla of missile-carrying Soviet ships (actually U.S.-made "liberty ships" provided to the Soviets during World War II under the Lend-Lease Program) stopped dead in its tracks shortly after entering the Atlantic Ocean from the Mediterranean Sea. That same day, Kennedy received two messages from Khrushchev. The first took the "soft" line that Russia would remove its missiles from Cuba in return for the United States ending its quarantine of Cuba and assurances that the United States would not invade Cuba. The second, more harsh in its tone, accused the United States of creating the crisis and demanded that it take its missiles out of Turkey in return for Russian missiles coming out of Cuba. These events prompted the president's brother and attorney general, Robert F. Kennedy, to remark: "We are eyeball to eyeball, and I think the other side just blinked."

In the negotiations that followed, Khrushchev agreed to remove the Soviet missiles from Cuba in return for the withdrawal of U.S. missiles from Turkey and a Kennedy promise not to invade the island. However, because Castro would not permit it, the withdrawal of the Soviet missiles was not done under United Nations supervision as the agreement called for, which made Kennedy's noninvasion pledge a moot point. Because Khrushchev dealt directly with Kennedy throughout the crisis without consulting Castro, the infuriated Cuban leader understood his tenuous relationship with Moscow.

The meaning of the Khrushchev-Kennedy understanding surfaced in 1970 after the United States discovered the ongoing construction of a submarine base at Cienfuegos. Secretary of State Henry Kissinger discovered that no written agreement had been concluded in 1962. Furthermore, he asserted, that because the United Nations never verified the understanding, the U.S. noninvasion pledge was voided. According to Kissinger, the Soviets confirmed his interpretation but reaffirmed the pledge not to introduce operational ballistic missiles into Cuba or to construct a naval base on the island.

Still, in the mid-1960s, Cuba remained a focal point of Cold War tensions. Shortly after the missile crisis, Khrushchev promised to defend the island against an external attack, and following Castro's visit to Moscow in April 1963, Khrushchev increased Soviet economic assistance to Cuba. At the same time, Kennedy approved a new round of sabotage to the cane fields, industrial sites, and sugar mills, and the CIA plotted Castro's assassination, including the use of poison. Beneath the posturing though, Cuba and the United States sought accommodation. French journalist Jean Daniel acted as an intermediary between Castro and Kennedy and, in fact, was meeting in Havana on November 22, 1963, the day of Kennedy's assassination.

New President Lyndon B. Johnson decided to put the tenuous private talks on ice. For the next decade, with few exceptions, Cuban-American relations remained frozen. Johnson continued the policy of isolating Cuba from the hemispheric family and pursued a stiff attitude toward Castro. The latter was best illustrated by an incident on February 2, 1964, when two Cuban fishing boats deliberately entered U.S. territorial waters in the Florida Keys. In response to the U.S. seizure of the ships and crewmen, Castro momentarily turned off the water supply to the U.S. naval base at Guantánamo Bay. When Castro offered to turn the water spigot back on, Johnson refused. The base became self-sufficient as water tankers brought the precious liquid in from Florida until the completion of a desalination plant at Guantánamo. Johnson also ordered a reduction in the number of Cubans working at the base. In all, some 2,000 Cubans lost their jobs.

For the next decade, 1965–1975, the war in Vietnam, the battle for civil rights at home, and the Watergate scandals that led to the resignation of President Richard M. Nixon preoccupied Americans. They lost interest in Latin America in general, and even Cuba slipped from national consciousness, except in the Cuban exile community in South Florida and the CIA offices.

Castro's adventurism in Latin America during the 1960s further strained relations with the Soviets. In the Second Declaration of Havana on February 4, 1962, Castro challenged all revolutionaries to fan the fires of liberation and in so doing irked Moscow's conservative leaders who replaced Khrushchev and jockeyed for détente with the West in the early 1970s. Castro's adventurism in Bolivia, Colombia, Guatemala, Peru, and Venezuela were at odds with the orthodox communist parties in those countries, which adhered to the Soviet policy of working within existing political systems. Military governments in those countries repressed communists, both traditional and *fidelista*. The death of Che Guevara at the hands of the Bolivian military in 1967, coupled with the domestic economic failures, caused Castro to temper his hemispheric ambitions and secure his place with the Soviet Union.

Clearly, by the end of the 1960s, Cuba stood alone, isolated by the United States, ostracized by all of Latin America save Mexico, and increasingly frowned upon by the Soviet Union. By contrast, ten years later, Cuba enjoyed an international stature out of all proportions to its size and economic strength. Some analysts contend that Castro achieved this status as a result of Soviet economic support and encouragement. Others argue that Castro gambled that the Soviets could not afford to cut him off without suffering a tremendous loss of international prestige, particularly in the underdeveloped world.

The economic pragmatism that necessitated Castro's rapprochement with the Soviets played out in the international arena. For example, when Castro visited Chile in November 1971 as the guest of the Marxist elected President Salvador Allende, he openly admitted that the road to socialism could take many forms, including the ballot box. Castro also strongly defended the Soviet Union as a nonimperialist country before the 1972 meeting of the Nonaligned Movement at Algiers. In 1974, apparently pleased with the change in Cuban policy, Leonid Brezhnev, the first secretary general of the Soviet Communist party to visit Cuba, clearly indicated that the Kremlin was promoting Cuba as a model for developing nations to follow. Though Brezhnev undoubtedly meant that Cuba was now in the Soviet fold, Castro took it to mean that he could again pursue an independent foreign policy.

Even after the Chilean military ousted Allende in 1973, Castro pursued a more temperate policy in Latin America until 1979. By 1975 he successfully established diplomatic relations with ten Latin American countries. Cuba also gained membership in a number of Latin American economic organizations, the most important being the Latin American Economic System (SELA). Castro saw these associations as a vehicle to wean the Latin Americans away from their special relationships with the United States and move them toward the Nonaligned Movement.

Castro also openly identified with Michael Manley in Jamaica and General Omar Torrijos in Panama. Manley, following his 1976 re-election, showed interest in Cuba's socialistic model. To encourage Manley, Castro promised an abundance of assistance from construction workers, doctors, teachers, and technicians, to busses, tractors for sugar development, and prefabricated housing. Castro singled out Torrijos as an example of how to stand against U.S. imperialism without provoking a response. Still he did not believe that Latin America was on the verge of a socialist revolution as had occurred in Cuba.

Castro looked beyond Latin America. His incipient globalism began in the spring and summer of 1972 when he undertook two separate international trips during which he visited ten African and eastern European nations, and to the Fourth Nonaligned summit conference in Algiers. There, in addition to defending the Soviets as nonimperialist, Castro sought to unite the underdeveloped world in a struggle against the world's industrialized nations for improved economic relations. He also focused attention on the national wars for liberation raging in Africa and subsequently sent new advisory and training missions to Sierre Leone, South Yemen, Equatorial Guinea, and Somalia. Cuban combat units appeared in Syria during the 1973 Yom Kippur War, but their role has never been fully revealed. He also unsuccessfully encouraged the OPEC nations to recycle their petro-dollars to needy Third World countries. All these activities elevated Castro's place among the nonaligned nations and set the stage for a new prominence for Cuba that came with the Angolan civil war.

In October 1975 Castro sent an estimated 20,000 troops to help repel a South African invasion designed to defeat the Popular Movement for the Liberation of Angola (MLPA), a left-wing organization loosely aligned with the Soviet Union. The Cubans had close contacts with the MLPA since Guevara trained Congolese guerrillas in 1965. Castro identified with the MLPA on several grounds, including Cuba's black racial heritage and the MLPA's willingness to follow the Cuban model with a state-controlled economy and political centralization. Although the evidence suggests that the Soviets did not authorize the sending of the Cubans, the movement strengthened the relationship between Moscow and Havana. If Castro acted independently in Angola, he could not negate the charges that he interfered in Ethiopia and Somalia in 1978 at the behest of the Soviets, who had long-standing interests on the Horn of Africa. Some 15,000 Cuban troops, with massive Soviet supplies, drove the Somalians from the Ogadden Desert in February 1978. Most African states at the United Nations and the Organization of African Unity praised the Cuban intervention in Somalia, but these same states criticized Castro's Ethiopian venture, which reaffirmed the African image of the Soviets as imperialists.

In addition to its military adventurism, Cuba undertook a modest program of developmental assistance. Focusing upon labor, not capital aid, over 8,000 Cuban doctors, agronomists, teachers, and other specialists toiled in selected African, Caribbean, and South Asian (Laos and Vietnam) countries as part of a Cuban aid policy intended to provide humanitarian and nation-building assistance while showcasing Cuban achievement under socialism. Conducted as low-budget missions, with the host country paying for living expenses and logistical support, Cuba earned much needed goodwill. The peak of Castro's place in the Nonaligned Movement came in September 1979 when he hosted the organization's sixth summit in Havana and was selected to head the organization for the next four years.

Perhaps Castro was influenced by the larger détente policy pursued by the Soviets, or by the pragmatists who wanted closer U.S. economic links, but either way, United States-Cuban relations warmed slightly for seven years after 1972. The rapprochement began with the 1973 antihijacking agreement and continued with high-level secret discussions in New York and Washington between November 1974 and November 1975. President Gerald Ford terminated those conversations with the Cuban invasion of Angola. However, in 1977 new president Jimmy Carter signaled his desire to improve relations with Cuba. In 1978, as a result of discussions, several agreements were signed dealing with fishing and territorial rights in the Florida Straits and the establishment of diplomatic "interest sections" in each others' capital. The latter was viewed by many as a step towards normalization of relations. Castro also made goodwill gestures, including the release of nearly 3,600 political prisoners and the relaxation of travel restrictions to the island.

Discussions of full diplomatic relations stalemated on issues that dated to 1959. Carter refused Castro's insistence that the United States lift its embargo, and Castro refused to rescind his demand that the United States abandon Guantánamo Bay and agree to compensate the owners of properties nationalized during the revolution. In addition, Castro refused Carter's demand that Cuban troops abandon Angola.

Events in 1979 and 1980 (discussed next) confirmed Washington hardliners' suspicion that Castro's adventurism would not end and that he could only be viewed within the East-West context. As a result, the Carter administration concluded that the Soviets were again probing in the Caribbean. Carter signaled a change in U.S. policy in a speech before the OAS on October 1, 1979, when he called for an expansion of U.S. security interests in the region.

Two events in the Caribbean in 1979 caused Carter to alter his policy and prompted Castro to express greater optimism about the future of the Caribbean region. In March 1979, Maurice Bishop ousted the rightist government on the island of Grenada, and in July the Sandinista National Liberation Front (FSLN) toppled the Somoza regime in Nicaragua. Although Castro played no role in the Bishop coup, he quickly demonstrated his solidarity with the new government by providing arms, security advisors, doctors, and a fishing trawler to Grenada. Cuba also agreed to pay one-half the cost of a new $50 million airport to be built by Cubans. In Nicaragua, where the Cubans provided support to the FSLN in its fight against Somoza, Cuba now supplied the Sandinistas with fifty military advisors and 2,000 civilian workers (mostly doctors and teachers) to assist in rebuilding the country's shattered economy. FSLN leader Daniel Ortega visited Cuba during that year and, along with Michael Manley in Jamaica, denounced the United States as imperialistic.

Castro tried to reassure the hemisphere that he was not attempting to export his brand of socialism, but he did not find a receptive audience. Most Latin Americans, like policymakers in Washington, understood that Castro designed his hemispheric policy to create a radical left/progressive nationalist and anti-American coalition. This also was consistent with Castro's long-term objective of trying to create an alternative to his dependency upon one superpower.

Just as events in the Caribbean raised questions about Castro's hemispheric intentions, the Soviet invasion of Afghanistan in December 1979 contributed to the decline of Cuban influence in the Third World Movement. The Soviets intervened to maintain a communist government over that of a local insurgent movement. The action verified a common opinion among Third World nations—that the Soviet Union, like the United States, was imperialistic. The Cubans, dependent upon Soviet economic assistance, unsuccessfully attempted to walk a tightrope throughout the affair. When the United Nations General Assembly took up the matter in January 1980, Cuba's ambassador to the UN, Raúl Roa, opposed a resolution condemning the Soviet action, not because Cuba was instructed to do so by the Kremlin, but because Cuba viewed the resolution as a United States ploy to reassert its global policeman role by heating up the Cold War. Roa went so far as to assert that the United States manipulated the events in Afghanistan. His efforts failed to convince anyone. The General Assembly approved the resolution condemning the Soviets, and Cuba's negative vote tainted its nonaligned credentials and reaffirmed its position as a surrogate of the Soviets. Castro's failed effort to serve as mediator of the conflict further tarnished the Cuban image as broker in North-South issues. The entire affair ended Cuba's hope of becoming a member of the United Nations Security Council in 1980. In a contest for that vacancy with Colombia, which was backed by the United States, Cuba's image as a Soviet surrogate proved costly and led to the compromise selection of Mexico.

Castro's adventurism tarnished his image in the international arena, and the Mariel boatlift in the spring of 1980 tarnished the image of his socialist revolution. The exodus of nearly 125,000 Cubans from the island bespoke of the revolution's economic failure and political repression.

With its prestige sinking, Cuba lost influence in the Nonaligned Movement, which now sought more-moderate leaders. Still, Castro was not deterred from seeking new opportunities in Latin America. Although Castro had no master plan and was tempered by the emergence of moderate leaders among the Caribbean governments, he benefited from his support of the Argentines in the 1982 Falklands/Malvinas war against Great Britain and his call for a cartel among the Latin American debtor nations to gain a moratorium, if not outright cancellation, of their international debt obligations. By 1987 Cuba restored diplomatic relations with most of the hemisphere, and trade and credits were flowing from Argentina, Brazil, Mexico, and Venezuela. European nations, particularly Spain, increased their economic contacts with Cuba.

At the same time that Castro improved his standing with Latin American nations, he found himself increasingly at odds with the United States. And by the end of the decade he was less confident about the link to the Soviet Union. After 1981, Castro's support of the Bishop regime in Grenada and revolutionaries in Central America ran afoul of the Reagan administration, which came to Washington with a hard-line Cold War mentality.

In Grenada, Cuba became engaged in a literacy campaign, the upgrading of health services, the development of a sophisticated fishing industry, and the improvement of roads. But the most contentious issue was the construction of a 10,000–foot runway that would be capable of handling the Soviet Union's largest military aircraft. To the Reagan administration, it meant a threat to U.S. regional security interests. Reagan used the political turmoil that followed Bishop's assassination in October 1983 to launch an invasion of the island, which brought U.S. and Cuban forces into direct confrontation. The brief conflict revealed the competency of the Cuban fighters, and it also served notice to the communist groups on the Central American isthmus that the United States would brook no socialist advances in the region.

In addition to continued support for the Sandinistas in Nicaragua, Cuban assistance reached the guerrilla groups in El Salvador and Guatemala. Reagan quickly determined that U.S. security was at stake. After threatening to "go to the source," meaning Cuba, the Reagan administration conducted a proxy war against the FSLN in Nicaragua, spent millions of dollars shoring up the regime in El Salvador, and turned Honduras into an armed camp, all to rid the isthmus of an alleged Soviet conspired plot, fronted by Cuba. In the end, the Central Americans found their own path to peace, but the conflict fundamentally altered the U.S.-Cuban-Soviet triangular relationship.

Throughout the 1980s the Reagan and Bush administrations insisted that the Soviets curtail their military assistance to Cuba, which in turn would force Castro to weaken his commitment to leftist groups on the isthmus. The Soviets refused and charged that such efforts interfered with its internal policy-making process. On the other hand, the Soviets supported the Cuban (and FSLN) call for the United States to withdraw its military presence from the entire circum-Caribbean region, including Guantánamo Bay. Washington refused on security grounds.

The triangular relationship over Central America had wider implications. By the mid-1980s, Soviet Premier Mikhail Gorbachev clearly understood that the highly centralized state-run Soviet system did not serve his own country well. Gorbachev was always a communist. His argument was never with socialism; rather, it was with old-line, heavy-handed state-run programs. Those programs had failed to meet the Soviet Union's domestic needs, which, in turn, limited Moscow's foreign policy options. Therefore, he attempted to persuade Reagan and Bush to live with Castro and lift the long-standing U.S. embargo. Apparently aware of the Soviet economic shortcomings, Bush, at both the Washington summit in June 1990 and at Moscow in July 1991, unsuccessfully attempted to link Soviet aid to Cuba with the Central American crisis. Even after Gorbachev's ouster in August 1991, the Soviet Foreign Ministry reaffirmed its commitment to Cuba. The promise soon proved to be empty.

The Cuban-Soviet relationship, which had never been close, began to drift apart in the mid-1980s when Mikhail Gorbachev introduced his *glasnost* and *perestroika* reforms. Gorbachev signaled Castro about changes in the relationship during his state visit to Havana in April 1989. Speaking before the national assembly, Gorbachev said that it was essential to keep pace with the times rather than continue down the path of stagnation. Socialism needed "a new face," to adjust, he told the Cubans, and that the Soviet economic relationship would have to reflect the new realities. Publicly, Castro was unmoved. He remained committed to his brand of socialism and reminded Gorbachev of his country's historic commitment to the island. Subsequently, the Soviet economic ministries were directed to devise plans that would put economic relations with Cuba on a more equitable basis. The chasm between the two widened.

Castro, however, sensed the seriousness of the strained relationship, and he reacted with a childlike petulance. He directed that English replace Russian as the required foreign language of study in schools. In ordering the change, Castro pointed out that there were no literary masterpieces nor major scientific journals in Russian. And for the Cubans who received their university degrees in the Soviet Union there were fewer government jobs. At the same time, his advisors pointed out that, over the years Cuba may have taken cheap Soviet oil, raw materials, basic industrial machinery and equipment, foodstuffs, consumer goods, and military aid, but for the more sophisticated needs that supplied its pharmaceutical factories, hospitals, and biotechnological center, Cuba shopped in Germany and Japan. Cuba earned the hard currency to do so by reselling refined Soviet crude oil and its biotechnological and pharmaceutical products to the Western Europeans and Latin Americans.

With the collapse of the Soviet Union in August and September 1991, editorials in the Cuban communist party newspaper *Granma* indicated Castro's commitment to stay the communist course. Events in Moscow were described as a tragedy, and the Cuban party claimed that no matter what followed, Cuba would not deviate from the path it was on. The editorials also asserted that the Soviets sold out Cuba to the North Americans and in so doing compromised Cuban security and gave the United States a green light to carry out its long-standing plans of aggression against the island. Cuba was no longer important to Moscow in its relationship with Washington.

In a terse statement on December 26, 1991, the Cuban Foreign Ministry noted only the formation of the Commonwealth of Independent States and that Cuba recognized ten as independent republics. The Union of Soviet Socialist Republics no longer existed. Cuba could only hope that the ties developed during the previous thirty years would continue.

All Soviet aid came to end with the trade agreements that terminated on December 31, 1991. The Soviet Union no longer could prop up the Cuban economy. No other country could replace the Soviet Union as the provider of oil, machinery, equipment, and spare parts essential to the Cuban economy's operation, much less provide other commodities and consumer goods to sustain the Cuban people. And the eighty-four projects of Soviet-Cuban cooperation now stood still.

The end of the Soviet connection to Cuba immediately spurred the ongoing debate within the United States on how best to deal with Castro. The hard-liners wanted to toughen U.S. policy in order to hasten Castro's fall from power. In contrast, moderates advocated steps towards the normalization of relations with Cuba as the best way to bring democracy to the island. For the moment, the hard-liners won, thanks to election-year politics. Just prior to the 1992 presidential elections, Representative Robert Torricelli (D.), representing the heavily Cuban American populated Hudson County, New Jersey, proposed legislation to tighten the economic noose around the island. Neither Torricelli's colleagues, nor President George Bush, supported the measure. The proposal remained dormant until the Democratic party's presidential candidate Bill Clinton told a fundraising dinner in Miami, sponsored by the Cuban American National Foundation, that he would sign the bill if elected. Not to be outdone, Bush reversed himself and endorsed the legislation. Both presidential contenders wanted to please the Cuban community in Miami, a critical voting bloc in the electorally rich swing state of Florida. Congress obliged, and the bill became law.

The Cuban Democracy Act, the official name for Torricelli's proposal, prohibited trade with Cuba by U.S. subsidiaries in third countries and blocked access to U.S. ports for ships that made recent stops at Cuban ports. Once in the White House, however, Clinton did not vigorously pursue its application. He did not want to increase tensions with other countries (particularly Canada and members of the European Union) who viewed the ban on subsidiary trade as an infringement upon their sovereignty. Clinton shifted grounds again, two years later in August 1994, in response to the mass exodus of Cubans. He imposed restrictions on remittances and travel to the island that were designed to deny the Cuban economy approximately $50 million annually.

As Clinton vacillated between the hard-liners and the moderates, the Republican electoral takeover of the Congress in November 1994 added a new dimension to the argument. Hard-liners came to control foreign policy. Long-time Castro nemesis Jesse Helms (R., N.C.) became chair of the Senate Foreign Relations Committee, and Dan Burton (R., Ind.) headed the Western Hemispheric Subcommittee of the House International Relations Committee. Their Cuban Liberty and Democratic Solidarity Act, better known as the Helms-Burton Bill, was designed to tighten further the economic sanctions. It also granted owners of properties nationalized by the Cuban government since 1959 to sue (in U.S. courts) any foreign persons or companies that invested in those holdings; denied U.S. visas to citizens of foreign countries who engaged in the sale or use of confiscated U.S. properties; banned the importation into the U.S. of any foreign-made products that included Cuban sugar; banned foreign ships from U.S. ports that had stopped in Cuba during 180 previous days; promised to withhold funds from the International Monetary Fund, World Bank, or any other such agency by the amount equal to the credits it might advance to Cuba; and threatened to reduce aid to Russia and the former Soviet states by the amount equal to any military or intelligence assistance they provided to Cuba. Neither the president nor the majority of Congress favored the bill.

Only after the shooting down in February 1996 of two civilian airplanes, operated by a Cuban American group in Miami, allegedly in international waters off the Florida Straits, did Congress pass and Clinton sign the Helms-Burton Bill. Immediately, a worldwide furor erupted. Europeans, Canadians, and Latin Americans charged that the legislation was an illegal intrusion into their sovereignty. When the Europeans threatened to take their case to the World Trade Organization in 1997, Clinton suspended the application of the legislation. At the same time, the U.S. business community argued that Americans were losing opportunities in Cuba to foreign firms. In fact, executives of nearly 175 U.S. Fortune 500 companies had visited Cuba in anticipation of potential opportunities for their firms.

Overlooked were the bill's provisions that the United States would provide up to $8 million to assist with the democratization of the island through reforming government institutions and assisting with elections. In addition, Clinton dispatched Stuart Eisenstat to Europe to explain the U.S. position and to win support for U.S. policy. By late 1997, Eisenstat's mission was credited with some success. The European Union adopted a binding resolution to pressure Castro to improve his human rights record as a condition for future economic assistance. But Castro proved equal to the challenge. He dispatched diplomats throughout the Caribbean and Latin America to denounce the continuing U.S. embargo and to assert that they could be the next victims of U.S. aggression. Obviously, Castro had not lost sight of his historic nemesis.

Castro also used the January 21–25, 1998 visit of Pope John Paul II to the island (see Chapter 3) as a vehicle to enhance Cuba's opening in the world community at the expense of the United States. Castro was pleased with the Pope's call for an end to the thirty-six-year-old U.S. embargo and his plea for assistance to the poor of Cuba. The impact was registered in the United States immediately after the papal visit. Longtime Castro opponent, Senator Jesse Helms, with input from the Cuban American National Foundation, crafted a $100 million federally supported food and medical supply aid program for needy Cubans, possibly using the Roman Catholic Church as the distributor on the island. Promptly, the Clinton administration gave its blessing, as did former special presidential advisor on Cuba Richard A. Nuccio, Senator Christopher Dodd (D., Conn.), Rep. Esteban Torres (D., Cal.), and the U.S. Catholic Conference of Bishops. Obviously, such a program would empower the Catholic Church and potentially strengthen its position vis-à-vis the regime. Castro understood this too. He rejected the proposal as a "dirty maneuver and rude" response to the papal appeal for an end to the U.S. embargo. "Cuba is not asking for humanitarian aid," Castro continued, "it is asking for an end to the embargo."

The Clinton administration persisted, and in late March, Secretary of State Madeline Albright announced a proposed shift in U.S. policy that would enable the Cuban Americans once again to board direct flights to Havana once a year and send $300 every three months to relatives on the island. The U.S. government also proposed to ease restrictions and paperwork on the shipment of food and medical supplies to Cuba. Again, the Catholic bishops and several leading Democratic politicians applauded the change. But members of the so-called Cuba lobby, such as Helms and U.S. Representatives Ileana Ros-Lehtinen (R., Fla.) and Lincoln Diaz-Balart (R., Fla.) blasted the proposed program as an end run around Congress and promised to resist any legislative package designed by Albright. By late spring 1998, the administration could count only 26 supporters in the Senate and 112 in the House of Representatives.

The papal visit influenced the Dominican Republic, Guatemala, and Honduras to re-establish diplomatic relations with Cuba by late spring 1998 and also prompted the Argentine and Brazilian governments to consider doing the same. At the Second Summit of the Americas held in Santiago, Chile, on April 19–20, 1998, the representatives from Canada, Barbados, and Mexico hinted that they might soon seek Cuba's readmission to the United Nations. Immediately after the summit, Canadian Prime Minister Jean Chretien visited Cuba. And in a startling blow to U.S. policy on Cuba, two days after the Santiago Summit ended, the United Nations Human Rights Commission in Geneva, Switzerland, rejected a U.S. proposal to continue monitoring reported abuses on the island. In Havana, gleeful Cuban officials credited John Paul II's visit in January with helping to bring improvement to Cuba's standing in the international community. In Washington, the State Department characterized the United Nations action as unconscionable, and a member of the Cuba lobby, Rep. Robert Menendez (D., N.J.) criticized the Clinton administration for permitting such an action.

Pope John Paul II's visit to Cuba had contributed to a major diplomatic triumph for Fidel Castro. The forces within and outside of the United States seeking to force an end to the U.S. embargo made major strides toward their objective. As the century closed, relations with the United States remained the touchstone for Cuban independence and, for many in the United States, the Cuban revolution remained the "cancer" that had to be eradicated if U.S. security were to be assured and regional stability achieved.

José Martí. Date unknown. Courtesy of OAS Archives.

A Cuban cane field. Courtesy of U.S. National Archives.

Women volunteer school teachers armed with machine guns march in a parade that featured a great display of Soviet-Bloc arms. Courtesy of UPI/CORBIS-BETTMANN

Mikhail Gorbachev and Fidel Castro hold their clasped hands high facing toward a crowd of spectators. Courtesy of AP/Wide World Photos

Fulgencio Batista. Circa 1940. Courtesy of OAS Archives

5

Angry Exiles: Cuban Americans

On the eve of Fidel Castro's triumphant march into Havana in January 1959, an estimated 125,000 Cubans lived in the United States. They shared many characteristics with those Cubans who had migrated before them. Most came to the United States primarily for political reasons, planning to return home quickly, as the political landscape changed. The majority of these émigrés represented the middle- and working-class sectors of Cuban society. Florida was the choice of residence because of its climate and proximity to Cuba. The Cubans in the United States did not want to be very far from "home."

As early as the 1820s, Cubans disgruntled with Spanish governance of the island began arriving in the United States. By 1870 approximately 5,300 people of Cuban descent resided in the United States, mostly in cities along the Gulf and Atlantic coasts. And thanks to the continuing political turmoil caused by the Ten Years War (1868–1878), the number climbed to 7,000 by 1880. By 1890 Key West and Tampa, Florida, earned the title of "Little Havanas."

The early migrants were mostly white upper- and middle-class *creoles* who sought independence from Spain and annexation to the United States. Identifying with the U.S. antebellum southern slave society, these *creoles* feared that independence without annexation would bring the end of slavery on the island and, with it, an end to their social position and way of life. This group supported the filibustering of Narciso López from 1848 to 1851.

Following the termination of the Ten Years War in 1878, a new wave of Cuban businessmen came to the United States to seek the fortunes not attainable on the island. Among the most notable was cigarmaker Vicente Martínez Ybor, whose forty-acre tract adjacent to present-day Tampa still bears his name and Cuban culture. The war also resulted in the migration of blue-collar workers, who in the mid-1880s accounted for 80 percent of the Cuban émigré community, and of these, 20 percent were black or mulatto. The latter groups experienced the same racial discrimination in Florida as they did in Cuba, from both the native southerners and the Cuban *creoles*. Given its social diversity, by the 1890s, the Cuban community also was badly divided politically between conservative separatists and revolutionaries.

Into this vacuum stepped José Martí, whose Cuban Revolutionary Party (PRC) sought a broad-based and internally inspired uprising in Cuba. He called for a revolution that benefited all Cubans, not just the white elite. He spoke out against any notion of a class struggle and the undemocratic legacies of Spanish colonialism. He advocated land distribution to the poor and the need for government protection of the workers against the corporate elite. Martí also warned the Cubans always to be prepared to fend off the United States, which was ever anxious to exploit the island's resources and people.

Thousands of Cubans residing in the United States answered the call to arms in February 1895. They joined revolutionary leaders Martí, Antonio Maceo, and Calixto García in the war for Cuban independence against Spain from 1895 to 1898, and like the three leaders, many of the Cuban émigrés lost their lives in the name of *patria*. Martí's dream of a more egalitarian society was not achieved, however, thanks to the U.S. intervention in 1898. The North Americans shared the Cuban elite's concern that a social revolution would bring, among other things, the Afro-Cuban to the forefront of society. Only the Spanish political and military authorities departed the island; otherwise, much of Cuba's economic and political prewar status quo remained.

From 1900 until Castro's revolution, Cubans continued their sporadic migration to the United States. An estimated 40,000 came in the decade after Cuban independence, but the number drastically dropped with World War I, the anti-immigrant attitude in the United States during the 1920s, and the economic adversity brought on by the Great Depression. Another spurt accompanied the terrorism of the Batista regime from 1952 to 1959. In Miami alone, the Cuban community grew by nearly 30,000 people during that time, and the Cuban communities in New York City, northern New Jersey, New Orleans, and other major cities also increased.

The economic, racial, political and religious divisions within the Cuban American "community" became more pronounced over time. The "community" became a kaleidoscope of rich and poor, black and white, Catholic and Protestant, and it divided politically along conservative, liberal, and radical lines. These divisions were overlooked by the North Americans because of the popularity of Cuban culture. Dances like the rumba, the congo, the mambo, and the cha-cha-cha swept ballrooms during the 1920s and 1930s. Though Afro-Cuban music mixed with jazz, many Cuban musicians achieved success in their own right, such as Xavier Cugat, José Curbelo, and Miguelito Valdéz. The most recognizable was Desi Arnaz, Jr., who left Cuba in 1934 and made his way to Hollywood, where he married actress Lucille Ball. The two teamed in several movies and the long-running television sitcom *I Love Lucy*. Sports enthusiasts recall boxers Kid Gavilán and Kid Chocolate, whose careers prospered in the 1940s and 1950s, and after the integration of Major League baseball in 1947, Cuban baseball stars like Minnie Minoso, Cookie Rojas, Orlando Cepeda, and Bert Campaneris became household names in the United States.

In the meantime, the wealthy and middle-class Cuban *creoles* quickly melded into the larger U.S. society. For the wealthy, their stays were usually of short duration. If not escaping political turmoil on the island, they came to call on business clients, to seek sophisticated medical treatment, to vacation, and to shop. They sent their children to U.S. schools and colleges, and many of them married North Americans, after which many of them infrequently returned to the island. Whatever their stay, the wealthy *creoles* in the United States identified with their white counterparts on the island. The stateside visits also informed their thinking about their identity and interests. They no longer wished to be successful by Latin American standards but rather by North American ones. Also, many of the wealthier class converted to one of several Protestant faiths, so that by the 1950s the number of Protestant churches among Cubans in the United States outnumbered those of the Catholic.

In the first half of the twentieth century a substantial number of middle-class Cuban *creoles* also migrated to the United States for economic, not political, reasons. Unable to find jobs in the agro-commercial industries on the island, highly educated teachers, lawyers, accountants, physicians, dentists, engineers, librarians, professors, pharmacists, journalists, nurses, technologists, architects, and scientists found prosperity across the Florida Straits. They made their homes in the United States and adapted to its culture, but like the wealthy *creoles*, identified with their counterparts on the island.

For the Afro-Cuban and the poor white Cuban worker, life in the United States only replicated that on the island. The former group resented the racism, and the latter hated the ethnocentrism, and they both despised the self-serving conservative wealthy and middle-class *creoles*. Many of the Afro-Cubans and poor white Cubans who came to the United States returned to the island and made their way into the communist party. For those who remained in south Florida, many supported the *fidelista* movement of the 1950s. They organized clubs and raised money to purchase arms and supplies for Castro's guerrilla army. Castro found many recruits among them during a 1955 visit to south Florida.

On January 1, 1959, the day that Fulgencio Batista departed Cuba, another 500 of his supporters fled to the United States. By the end of June, 26,000 more followed. A second wave of 83,500 Cuban immigrants arrived in the United States during 1960; and they kept coming, nearly a quarter of a million by October 1962.

The first Cuban arrivals came from the upper class that had been closely associated with the Batista regime. The later arrivals represented the middle sector—government technicians, medical personnel, professionals, and managers of many of the nationalized industries. Stripped of their wealth before departing, these embittered Cubans sought quick revenge against Castro. Many of them organized into paramilitary groups—Omega 7 and Alpha 66, for example—in south Florida from where they conducted commando raids against the Cuban coastal cities. An estimated 12,000 of them found employment with the United States Central Intelligence Agency (CIA) to carry out covert actions around the globe, including Cuba, and some were enlisted in plots to assassinate Castro. But it was Brigade 2506, comprised of nearly 1,400 Cuban exiles under the command of José Pérez San Román, that drew most attention for its failed invasion at the Bay of Pigs in April 1961. Not until 1964 did the CIA move to shut down the exile groups and curtail its own attacks upon Castro.

United States policy toward the Cuban exiles evolved in response to the number of new arrivals. Both the Eisenhower and Kennedy administrations accepted the Cubans with open arms on humanitarian grounds and also understood that the loss of upper- and middle-class talent would have adverse economic repercussions upon Castro's regime. For example, in 1960 the Eisenhower administration designed the "Save the Children Program," which provided foster care for Cuban children sent unaccompanied to the United States to avoid communist indoctrination. Until the program ended in April 1961, following the Bay of Pigs invasion, 14,068 Cuban children arrived in the United States. As the exodus increased, in January 1961, the Eisenhower administration provided visa waivers on an emergency basis. Thereafter, Cubans claiming to be escapees from communist tyranny qualified to enter the U.S. under the visa waiver program. In the summer of 1961, when Castro demanded advance cash payments for exit visas and air flights, Kennedy persuaded the U.S. Congress to appropriate $350,000. Subsequently, Congress exempted Cubans from the 120,000 Western Hemisphere quota established in the 1965 immigration law, and Richard Nixon granted special status to those 30,000 Cubans residing in Spain who wished to relocate to the United States.

Although Castro professed pleasure at ridding the country of dissidents and opponents to the revolution, he understood that the brain drain had serious repercussions. To halt the out-migration, he used the October 1962 missile crisis to terminate the officially sanctioned immigration program. Still, through 1965, another 35,000 Cubans came to the United States.

Without warning, on September 28, 1965, before a huge crowd in Havana's *Plaza de Revolución*, Castro announced that those with relatives in the United States could leave the island. Within days, Cuban exiles in Miami made their way with small boats to the port of Camarico to pick up their relatives. An estimated 5,000 came to the United States in this manner, and the movement prompted the United States and Cuba to reach an understanding that provided for the monthly airlifting of 3,000 to 4,000 Cuban refugees to the United States at Washington's expense. Cuba did not, however, open its doors to free emigration. Men of military age (14–27) and those with critical job skills were not to leave the island until a replacement could be found. Also, those Cubans who registered for the program risked losing their jobs and property and being assigned to field work. Until Castro abruptly terminated the program in April 1973, another 260,000 Cubans took advantage of the "Freedom Flights." Despite the flights' termination, Cubans kept coming to the United States, either through third countries or by raft and boat across the Florida Straits. By the end of the decade, an estimated 800,000 Cubans resided in the United States.

The relocation costs were extremely high. Between 1961 and 1976 alone, the U.S. government spent nearly $1 billion on Cuban relief programs that included English-language training, job training, low-cost college tuition loans, certification of professionals, food distribution, and housing subsidies. By 1979 the relocation program proved somewhat successful in moving Cubans to New York City/northern New Jersey, California, and Illinois, but still over 50 percent of the Cuban immigrants had settled in the Miami/Fort Lauderdale, Florida, corridor. There also was a change in the makeup of the Cuban immigrants. Whereas the Cubans who arrived in the United States during the early 1960s were largely upper-class whites with highly marketable job skills, the majority of those who arrived beginning in the late 1960s were semiskilled and unskilled workers. Approximately 17 percent of the latter were either Afro-Cubans or mulattos. Whatever their economic, social, and cultural status, both groups still represented an important economic drain on Cuba, shared a close link with the United States, and believed that their stateside stay would be short lived.

As the Cubans assimilated into North American society, the national press became enamored with their success as professionals and entrepreneurs and made much of the Cubans' quest for education and their ability to assist each other in the drive for upward social and economic mobility. A closer look revealed a more varied picture, as it also showed that Cuban "success" was resented by native-born Americans, especially during slow economic times. Miami is a case in point. There, longtime African American residents resented the extent of special aid programs available to the Cubans while blacks lived in poverty. Local blacks also considered the Cubans a threat to the black community's service jobs, particularly in the tourist industry. Recognizing a potential powder keg, some U.S. policymakers privately expressed relief with the termination of the "Freedom Flights" in 1973.

There were other important changes in the characteristics of the Cuban American community that contributed to its further division. A good number of extreme rightists remained active, and they rejected any discussion of accommodation with Castro. Some groups, such as Alpha 66 and Omega 7, continued their own operations against the island: others claimed responsibility for bombings and attacks upon leftist Latin Americans visiting the United States. In significant contrast, a large political center emerged by the 1970s, comprised mostly of second-generation Cuban Americans who had adapted to U.S. culture. Recognizing the emerging heterogeneity of the Cuban community abroad, Castro invited their leaders to a conference in November 1978, which resulted in Castro releasing political prisoners. Ironically, while 12,000 of the ex-political prisoners were welcomed in south Florida, the right-wing groups there condemned the Cuban Americans who participated in the November conference. Despite the widening gap within the Cuban community, it enjoyed widespread popularity across the United States.

That perception soon changed, and inadvertently Castro contributed to it. In December 1979 Castro announced that Cuban Americans could come to the island for one-week family visits. Through early 1980, nearly 100,000 Cubans flew to Havana from the United States despite exorbitant airfares, hotel costs, and fees for legal documents. They brought with them as gifts a cornucopia of consumer goods—designer clothes, jewelry, stereos, televisions, sporting goods equipment, toys, household items. This bountiful display of Cuban prosperity in the United States became living proof that life on the island was indeed dreary, whereas life in the United States brought material success. Castro also opened "dollar stores" for the visitors to purchase every imaginable item for their families. They did, spending an estimated $100 million. Castro's decision created a new kind of discontent among the Cubans, for whom such goods were beyond their reach, and with it a desire to emigrate. Castro also understood that the Cuban American community served as a source of badly needed hard currency, so why not let people emigrate.

The impetus for the next wave of emigration came on April 1, 1980, when six Cubans in a bus crashed through the gates onto the grounds of the Peruvian embassy in Havana. They quickly received political asylum. Castro's response followed previous patterns. After Radio Havana encouraged all asylum seekers to go to the Peruvian embassy, approximately 10,000 Cubans took up residence on the embassy compound over the next three days. U.S. journalists and government officials attributed the crisis to the failures of Castro's tyranny. For Castro, he again had the opportunity to cleanse the country of dissidents. Therefore, he announced on April 21, 1980, that the port of Mariel would be open to boats from Florida to provide for the exit of those wishing to leave Cuba. Reminiscent of the 1968 Camarioca experience, a "Freedom Flotilla" headed for Cuba. The "Mariel Boatlift," as the exodus came to be known, carried approximately 125,000 Cubans to south Florida before it ended in September 1980. And like his predecessors, President Jimmy Carter opened the door to the escapees of Cuban communism. Overlooked at the time were the changes in U.S. immigration policy.

Conditions in the United States had vastly changed since 1968. By the terms of the March 1980 Refugee Act, a yearly quota of 19,500 Cubans could legally migrate to the United States, and then, only if they could prove that they escaped political, racial, religious, or other persecutions. The *Marielitos* clearly fled from economic hardship, but not all of them from other persecutions. At the same time, Carter faced a flood of Haitian immigrants, whose escape from political tyranny and economic hardship was unquestioned. To grant the Cubans special status and not the Haitians was immoral argued those who wanted the United States to accept the Haitians. To solve the problem momentarily, Carter granted both groups a new status, "Cuban-Haitian entrant," which entitled the new arrivals to remain in the United States and adjust their status to that of permanent resident alien after two years. In the meantime, they were eligible for supplemental income and emergency assistance benefits.

The *Marielitos* faced an uncertain future once in the United States. Unwelcomed by south Florida's white Cuban American community because the majority of the new arrivals were Afro-Cubans and practiced Santeria, they also had few job skills and often were described as social misfits and criminals. Granted, 26,000 of the *Marielitos* had prison records, but most were for political crimes. An estimated 4,000 to 5,000 were identified as hard-core criminals, and many of them ended up in federal prisons in Georgia and Louisiana. And, as in the past, Miami's African American community viewed the new immigrants as competitors for jobs and again resented the largesse of federal assistance programs for them. The *Marielitos'* arrival in Miami also prompted a reaction from the Anglo community, which feared its own loss of political and economic influence in the area. The Anglos successfully pushed for a 1980 referendum demanding that all government meetings, documents, and the like be in English. At the same time, the general nationwide backlash against Asian and Latin American immigration only enhanced the *Marielitos'* already tarnished image.

Although 80 percent of the *Marielitos* remained in south Florida, in the decade that followed they repeated their predecessors' pattern. They learned English, earned high school and college degrees, found jobs or built businesses. Not until 1987 did the governments in Havana and Washington reach an accord that provided for the deportation to Cuba of "excludables," those hard-core criminals and mental patients who had arrived with the *Marielitos*. In return, the United States agreed to take in 27,000 Cuban immigrants annually.

By the mid-1980s the Cuban community in south Florida had become a permanent fixture. Cuban culture permeated the area, particularly in Miami. Calle Ocho, a main street in Miami's large Cuban sector, is home to shops, restaurants, and bars that reflect Cuban clothing and cuisine, and provide the space and ambience to discuss everything Cuban. Cuban holidays are celebrated here. Beyond servicing the regional community, Cuban businessmen have become key players in state, regional, and international economic activities. Cubans also have emerged as a dominant force in local and state politics. Some cultural observers describe Miami as "Havana North," which provides the Americans the opportunity to understand Cuban culture. At the same time, however, south Florida has provided second- and third-generation Cubans the opportunity to adapt to American culture—its sports, music, dress, education, and transiency—everything non-Cuban.

Throughout the 1980s, the vast majority of the Cuban Americans still harbored anti-Castro feelings. They found allies in U.S. citrus and sugar growers who, for self-serving reasons, opposed normalization of relations with Cuba. Added to the mix was President Ronald Reagan, whose strident anticommunism sought the downfall of Castro just when Cuban global adventurism increased. With Reagan, militant anti-Castro groups such as the Cuban American National Foundation (CANF) headed by Jorge Mas Canosa found a sympathetic ear.[1]

To tighten the economic noose around Cuba, the Reagan administration ordered the suspension of tourist travel to Cuba, which had reached an estimated 40,000 American visits per year. Under the new guidelines, only diplomats, journalists, scholars, and individuals on family visits could go to Cuba directly from the United States. Reagan also limited to $1,200 a year the amount of money a Cuban American could send to a relative on the island. When the United States Information Agency (USIA) established Radio Martí in May 1985 to broadcast anti-Castro stories into Cuba from Florida, CANF played an important role in the station's programming. Four years later, President George Bush approved a plan to have the Voice of America establish TV-Martí to beam anticommunist programs into Cuba, and again, CANF had significant influence in the programming. The embittered Castro vehemently protested the broadcasts as an intrusion into his nation's sovereignty and successfully blocked the TV signal.

Although few legal immigrants arrived in the United States following the 1987 immigration agreement, the rapid decline in the Cuban economy in the late 1980s and early 1990s raised new fears of a mass exodus. In anticipation of a large-scale Cuban immigration flow to the state, Florida governor Bob Martínez established the Free Cuba Committee to study the potential impact a new Cuban influx might have on Florida. Nothing happened. The Florida Straits remained quiescent until 1994.

Events and incidents reminiscent of those leading to the 1980 Mariel boatlift again played out in Havana from May to August 1994. Nearly 150 Cubans sought political asylum in foreign consulates, and at least four Cuban government boats were hijacked to bring émigrés to the United States. On August 5, the Cuban government suppressed a small riot in Havana. The economic ravages caused by the loss of Soviet economic assistance and the continuing U.S. embargo contributed to these incidents. In response, Castro took to the airwaves. In language similar to that used in 1965 to signal Camarioca and 1980 to signal Mariel, Castro charged that rumors of another Florida boatlift were responsible for the Cuban street actions. If that were the case, he continued, the Cuban government would discontinue its policy of stopping people from trying to emigrate illegally. And as before, the number of escapees, described as *balseros* (rafters), reached record proportions: 2,886 on August 23 alone, and 21,300 for the entire month. Like their predecessors, the *balseros* believed that they would be welcomed in Miami and that the U.S. government would again be generous. Their perceptions proved wrong.

Determined not to confront another Mariel, President Clinton conferred with Florida governor Lawton Chiles, CANF leader Jorge Mas Canosa, and other Florida civic and political leaders. As a result, on August 19, 1994, Clinton announced that the Cuban rafters would no longer be transported to the United States; rather, they would be carried to the U.S. naval base at Guantánamo. He also asked Castro to deter the *balseros* from leaving the island. Subsequently, Clinton announced that Cuban Americans would no longer be allowed to send cash remittances to their relatives in Cuba; that visits to the island would be severely restricted, except for extreme humanitarian cases; and that a special Treasury Department license would be needed for journalists and academics going to the island. With the stroke of a pen, Clinton reversed U.S. policy on Cuban immigration. By late September, nearly 28,000 Cubans had been deposited in the "refugee camp" set up in Guantánamo. Despite efforts to make their accommodations comfortable, the frustrated Cuban detainees, who had no idea how long their stay would be while U.S. officials studied each case for the detainee's claim to refugee status, rioted several times.

Throughout the crisis, the Clinton administration conducted negotiations with the Cuban government at the United Nations. The talks resulted in an agreement announced May 2, 1995. Accordingly, the detainees would be gradually admitted to the United States until the camp was emptied by March 1996, but the agreement also stipulated that any rafter attempting to reach the United States illegally would be immediately repatriated. To avert a further immigration crisis, the United States set a 20,000 yearly limit on the number of visas available to Cubans wishing to immigrate to the United States, but on the same grounds as other nationalities. This meant that Cubans seeking asylum could enter the United States for political, not economic, reasons. On May 9, 1995, one week after the accords were signed, Clinton signaled that the new policy would be enforced when he ordered the U.S. Coast Guard to return thirteen *balseros* to Cuba. Generally, the Cuban American community expressed its disappointment at the end of the special treatment accorded them for thirty-five years, but Mas Canosa's CANF applauded the hard-line decisions as a means to increase the internal pressure on Castro. CANF ignored the contradiction of trying to strangle Castro's regime economically with the embargo at the same time the Cuban exiles funneled an estimated $2.2 billion to their relatives on the island since 1991.

In addition to its influence on cultural and immigration policies, the conservative Cuban American community, and particularly CANF, exerted great influence upon the passage of the Torricelli and Helms-Burton bills that tightened the economic embargo upon Cuba. But in the mid-1990s, after the passage of the Helms-Burton Bill, the chasm within the community widened further. Whereas CANF applauded the Helms-Burton Bill, other groups expressed greater interest in those sections of the legislation that promised assistance in establishing a democratic government in Cuba. In response to Clinton's January 1997 report entitled "Support for a Democratic Transition in Cuba," which offered $8 billion in economic aid for a post-Castro Cuba, six anti-Castro groups, minus the CANF, met in Washington to express their support for the proposal.

Two Cuban American groups at odds with CANF are *Cambio Cubano* (Cuban Change) and the Cuban Committee for Democracy. These groups represent Cuba's middle sector, those aspirants for a broader-based democracy on the island. The first, founded in 1992 by Eloy Gutiérrez-Menoyo, a former pro-Castro revolutionary who spent twenty-two years in a Cuban jail for deserting the revolutionary cause, advocates working within the Cuban system to expand continually economic and political opportunities. The second, founded a year later by University of Miami professor and exile Enrique Baloyra, supports the transition to a democratic Cuba from the outside. Both groups acknowledge that Castro betrayed the revolution but do not accept CANF's hard-line position or Mas Canosa's apparent desire to govern a post-Castro Cuba. They are equally critical of the U.S. embargo, asserting that it will only result in economic and political chaos on the island.

The division also was seen on a local level in Miami as revealed by three events in the fall of 1997. First, the Archdiocese of Miami proposed to sponsor a cruise to Havana in January 1998 so that Cuban Americans could partake in the proceedings of Pope John Paul II's visit to the island and meet briefly with relatives. According to the *Miami Herald*, many Cuban Americans expressed an interest in seeing the Pope, but feared personal reprisals from hard-line members of the local Cuban community. In addition, conservative Cuban business leaders and CANF pressured the Archbishop to cancel the planned trip. In late December he finally caved in. Instead, only a small charter flight was scheduled as a substitute.

For the few Cuban Americans from Miami who made the trip to Cuba for the papal visit, it was an emotional experience visiting with relatives and seeing long-ago neighborhoods. They returned to Miami with a greater sense of commitment to bring change to the island. David Cabarrocas, a Miami architect, spoke for many Cuban Americans when he observed: "Our historical error has been to allow one man to get rid of all his enemies—and to have them promise never to return until he dies. What a coup!"[2] Using Caritas, the charitable arm of the Cuban Catholic Church, a parish-to-parish program has taken root between Miami and Cuba. Although admittedly only a small step, it offers the possibility of establishing bridges and contacts.

Second, the future of the annual Latin America and Caribbean Music Market remained in doubt because a number of international record executives peddled the works of Cuban artists at the 1997 show. This violated a 1991 Miami-Dade County (Florida) resolution engineered by the Cuban American leaders that forbids vendors who work with the county from doing business with firms that have dealings with Cuba. The issue turned into one regarding free speech and the right of a minority to influence county-wide policy.

Finally, in March 1998, the *Miami Herald* uncovered a link between CANF leadership and Cuban exiles in San Salvador who plotted the rash of hotel bombings in Havana during the summer and early fall of 1997. The newspaper also reported on an alleged assassination attempt against Castro by Cuban exiles during the November 1997 meeting of Latin American leaders in Venezuela.

The conflicts that characterize the diversity of the Cuban American community and the continued hard-line position against an aging communist dictator have tarnished the community's national image. According to a national poll conducted in June 1997, Cubans are among the least favorably regarded group among recent immigrants. With the death of CANF founder and president Jorge Mas Canosa in November 1997, the future impact that the Cuban American community will have upon U.S. government policy towards Cuba is an open question.

NOTES

1. For a nearly a fifteen-year period, Mas Canosa and the CANF came to have significant influence over U.S. Cuban policy through conservative representatives in the U.S. Congress, including Senator Jesse Helms (R., N.C.) and Republican Representative Dan Burton (Ind.), and Democrats Robert Menendez and Robert Torricelli, both of New Jersey. Subsequently, others would join the group like south Florida Republican Representatives Ileana Ros-Lehtinen and Lincoln

Diaz-Balart. The group became known as the Cuban American lobby, with the popular assumption that it spoke for all Cuban Americans.

2. Fabiola Santiago, "Cuban Exiles Rethink Options after Papal Visit," *Miami Herald*, January 30, 1998, p. 1.

6

Conclusion: The Meaning of the Cuban Revolution

José Martí, Eduardo Chibás, and Fidel Castro shared many thoughts about Cuban society. Whereas Martí addressed the Spanish political tyranny and Chibás and Castro that of Cuba's *creole* elite, all three understood that the Cuban government did not exist for the masses of people. All three called for a social revolution whereby the benefits of economic development would be shared more equally among everyone. Each also understood the dangers of economic dependency brought about by the special relationship that Cuba had with the United States and the reliance on monoagriculture, particularly sugar production. Martí, Chibás, and Castro wanted to change that too. Whereas Martí and Chibás are most often described as nationalists, Castro would become a communist. Whatever the description, each advocated revolution.

The Cuban experience fits neatly into the definition of a Latin American revolution provided by political scientist Jan Knippers Black. According to Black, a society that has been controlled politically and economically by a small elite (both native and foreign) and propped up by the military is overturned by those who represent the middle and lower socioeconomic sectors. After the old regime is overthrown and the revolutionary leaders come to power, the promise of democratization and social justice goes unfulfilled. The revolutionary leaders come to control the nation's politics and economy. Castro's revolution in Cuba meets these prerequisites.[1]

When Cuba gained its independence from Spain in 1898, the Cuban *creoles* assumed the political mantle vacated by the Spanish *peninsulares*. From the presidency of Tomás Estrada Palma in 1902 through that of Gerardo Machado in 1933, the contest for control of the political arena remained a struggle among the leading families of Cuba's white elite. And once in power, government became a source of corrupt wealth, not to be lost. These *creoles* also had no intention of sharing political power with the lower socioeconomic groups, or of losing their social status. They welcomed U.S. businessmen who made extensive investments in the Cuban economy and who concluded that any change in Cuba's institutional order would adversely affect their business operations. In addition, an informal alliance developed between them and, with it, a cultural connection between the island and the mainland. Both the Cuban *creoles* and the North American businessmen looked to the U.S. government to protect their particular interests. The Platt Amendment provided the legal cover for the numerous U.S. interventions during this time period. Though policymakers in Washington may well have looked upon these interventions as a moral crusade to reform the corrupt Cuban political system, Cuban nationalists viewed the same as intrusions upon their nation's sovereignty to maintain elitist rule and protect U.S. economic investments.

At the same time that the elitists struggled among themselves in the political arena, the development of the Cuban economy in the early twentieth century and the availability of education to more people spawned a new and ever-growing middle class. Consisting of government workers, mid-level managers in private enterprise, small businessmen, professionals, technicians, journalists, and students, the middle sector understood the corruptness of the Cuban political system and the economic shortcomings caused by the U.S. domination of the Cuban economy. They wanted change. Toward that end, they organized into professional and student associations and labor unions to press their demands. But not until 1933 did they effect change, and then, only momentarily. "The Generation of 1930" found solace in the programs implemented during the brief presidency of Ramón Grau Martín in 1933, but the *creole* elite and the U.S. business community did not. Washington also encouraged a return to the traditional social order. For the moment, the United States looked with favor upon the coup d'etat engineered by Fulgencio Batista in January 1934.

For the next twenty-five years, until January 1959, Batista ruled with an iron fist, either directly as president or through puppets and shadow governments. Increasingly, politicians distanced themselves from public service and used the government for personal enrichment. At the same time, the middle sector became increasingly frustrated with their failed efforts to reform the political system. Groups within the middle sector often turned to violence, and the government reacted in kind. By the 1950s, the conflict within the political arena was exacerbated by worsening economic conditions.

Cuba's reliance on a monoagricultural society dated to Spanish times when the government at Madrid encouraged the development of sugar production for sale on the world market. Because of geographical proximity and favorable tariff policies, the United States quickly became Cuba's primary market. The connection did not change after 1898—in fact, it intensified. North Americans became the dominant players not only in the sugar industry, but also in mining, infrastructure projects, and tourism, and they were the source of most consumer goods for the Cuban public. The world demand and price it paid for sugar had its repercussions in Cuba, affecting the employment and consumption habits of everyone. But while the middle sector and urban laborers formed associations and unions in the 1920s, the unskilled workers—rural and urban—remained isolated. Over time, the gap in wages and the concomitant standard of living widened between the *creole* elite, the middle sector, and the urban and rural poor. These disparities became explosive issues in the 1950s.

As a university student, Castro came to understand the intensity of the conflict and, at first, thought that change could be effected through the existing political system. But that ideal vanished as a result of fraudulent 1952 elections in which he lost his bid for a place in the national congress. Thereafter, he argued that change could only come about through the destruction of the existing political and economic systems. He was committed to revolution.

Castro's insurgency was only one of many groups seeking to overthrow the Batista regime after 1952, and he benefited from their actions. He also offered something to each: for the middle sector, political participation and an improved standard of living; and for the poor, social justice. With such promises, he received their support, financial and otherwise. In this sense, Fidel Castro differed little from the Mexican revolutionaries from 1911 to 1917, Bolivian Victor Paz Estensarro from 1944 to 1954, and the Sandinista National Liberation Front in Nicaragua from 1972 to 1984.

Once in Havana in January 1959, Castro quickly abandoned his promise for democracy and pursued a deliberate path to consolidate his power. Although Batista escaped Castro's wrath by fleeing Havana before Castro's arrival, the dictator's compatriots were not so fortunate. Castro eliminated the former political and military *creole* elite through summary trials, lengthy jail sentences, and executions. Others escaped the country. Castro also confiscated their wealth, including landholdings. Through nationalized confiscation, Castro also moved against foreign-owned properties.

Within a year, the middle sector recognized that its aspiration to enter the Cuban political system would not be achieved. Castro not only postponed elections, but through law, intimidation, and a neighborhood spy system he also silenced the critics of his revolution. The criollo upper and middle sectors became the first to seek refuge in Miami.

Castro also maneuvered to isolate other political factions that contributed to Batista's downfall. Old-line communists, student activists, and other allies were removed from the decision-making process. Dissent would not be tolerated; political parties were outlawed, save the communist, which Castro reorganized until he was in firm control of it and could use it to serve his purposes. By 1965 the traditional social pyramid had collapsed and a new one resurfaced. At its apex stood Fidel Castro, with the support of Cuba's army, headed by his brother Raúl. Fidel was firmly in control. True to the theory about the politics of revolution, a new dictatorship had emerged.

Only the lower social sectors remained, and Castro implemented programs—health, housing, social security, and the like—to gain their support. Every sector of society was organized from athletics to women. The state provided every service either free or at minimal cost. To ensure that future generations were imbued with the proper ideological zeal, church schools were closed and the state directed education at all levels. Over time, loyalty to the revolution and membership in the communist party became the measuring stick for benefits to be received from the system.

With revolutionary zeal, Castro set out to remake the Cuban economy. In cooperation with his chief economic advisor at the time, Ernesto "Che" Guevara, Castro planned to make Cuba self-sufficient in foodstuffs and consumer goods. But the zeal was not matched with the resources nor the essential management skills. The revolution resulted in the loss of U.S. capital and prompted the out-migration of Cuba's managers and technicians. The effort to go it alone failed by 1970 when Cuba did not achieve its 10-million-ton sugar harvest. The economy was in disarray.

Whereas the Cuban economy was dependent upon the United States prior to 1959, it became increasingly dependent upon the Soviets and their eastern European bloc allies after 1970. Moscow determined that the geopolitical benefits of maintaining a communist nation in the U.S. backyard was worth an estimated $2 billion per year. The Soviets also supplied the necessary management techniques and subsequently trained the Cubans in the art of centralized planning. Into the mid-1980s, the program brought a degree of political tranquility and economic security to Cuba. Life may have been relatively comfortable for most Cubans, at least by comparisons to the turbulent 1960s, but the anticipation and possibility of achieving an increased standard of living was a far-fetched idea. Castro attempted to conceal the revolution's deficiencies by showcasing its accomplishments in medicine, health care delivery, education, and sports. But he could not hide a decaying infrastructure, inadequate housing, and the continued political tyranny. His 1986 call for a recommitment to the revolution failed to rekindle the national conscience.

In the international arena, Castro pursued an aggressive foreign policy in an effort to demonstrate Cuba's ability to stand tall against its historic nemesis, the United States, and act independent from its newfound benefactor, the Soviet Union. Even when he learned from the 1962 missile crisis that he was nothing more than a chess pawn in the Cold War confrontation between Moscow and Washington, Castro intended to fan the revolutionary flames in Latin America. His call for the violent overthrow of the hemispheric oligarchies in the 1960s and his support for Maurice Bishop in Grenada, the Sandinistas in Nicaragua, and Farabundo Martí in El Salvador in the 1970s and 1980s illustrated the consistency of his policy. Castro's military adventures in Africa and the Middle East and headship of the Nonaligned Movement were designed to make Castro a Third World leader deserving of equal treatment by the superpowers.

But the unfulfilled social revolution within Cuba and the world leadership role that Castro so badly wanted unraveled in 1989 as the Soviet Union began to disintegrate and finally collapsed two years later. Without its benefactor, the Cuban economy self-destructed, and the social programs it had instituted became empty promises. With an end to the Cold War, Castro no longer had a role to play. Despite all the adversity and with his charisma lacking its confident twinkle, still the seventy-one-year-old Fidel Castro promised to stay the course.

The calamity of the 1990s prompted Castro to bring many changes to Cuba, yet he continued many of his traditional policies. Cuba's dire economic circumstances in the 1990s forced Castro to abandon many of his socialist principles by permitting foreign capital to enter Cuba and repatriate profits; introducing market reforms that have enabled many Cubans to earn money for the acquisition of scarce consumer goods; and relying upon the charitable activities of the Roman Catholic Church to provide the social safety nets that the state can no longer supply. Still, he remains in firm control of the government apparatus, which refuses to tolerate political or social dissent. According to Amnesty International, the United Nations Human Rights Commission, and the United States Congress, Cuba's human rights record remains among the most horrific in the world. And Castro continues to blame the United States for all that has gone wrong in Cuba.

For two generations, Castro has been a nemesis to the United States. When Castro came to power at the height of the Cold War, policymakers in Washington sought his ouster through intrigue, armed invasion, and subsequently economic strangulation. When those efforts failed, Washington determined to isolate Castro from the international community, and with the exception of the 1962 missile crisis, gave him more attention than the realities of his power deserved. Washington justified these policies on the grounds that Castro's Cuba became one more link in Moscow's international communist conspiracy. Through it all, Castro proved most resilient.

The end of the Cold War and the collapse of the Soviet Union provided the opportunity for the United States to re-examine its Cuban policy. It did, briefly in 1992 and 1994. Rather than seek avenues towards accommodation, the U.S. government further tightened the economic noose, but this time its policy affected more than just Cuba. The Torricelli and Helms-Burton Bills have brought the United States into conflict with major trading partners and allies—Europe and Canada—and with its hemispheric neighbors. Not only do these countries question the international legalities of that legislation, they also question the wisdom and morality of U.S. policy toward a nation teetering on the brink of collapse. The criticisms intensified following the visit of Pope John Paul II to Cuba in January 1998.

Whatever the wisdom of Castro's determination to stay with socialism and the legality and morality of U.S. policy toward Cuba, change within Cuba cannot be far off. Though reports in early 1998 indicate that Fidel Castro is in reasonably good health, his charismatic hold over the Cuban people has dwindled. A collapsed economy and empty social programs have strained the national will. Identifying his successor is pure speculation. At the Fifth Communist Party Congress in October 1997, Fidel clearly indicated that he prefers his brother Raúl as next in line, and there is evidence to indicate that he is. In February Fidel was reelected President of the Council of State and Raúl First Vice President. During the last year, Raúl has been more visible within Cuba and has represented the country at many state functions abroad. His control over the army is unquestioned, and the military is needed to maintain order within the country. Considered more pragmatic than Fidel, Raúl was the one who pushed for the market reforms beginning in 1993.

One group of Cuban watchers believes that after Fidel Castro's departure the military will take over, filling a political vacuum created by the lack of a clear line of succession, despite Fidel's announced preference for his brother Raúl. They are labeled "the Poles" because this small group of officers admire General Wojciech Jaruzelski, whose 1980 coup in Warsaw supposedly prevented a Soviet invasion in the wake of popular demonstrations against the existing communist government. By parallel, the Cuban generals worry about a U.S. military intervention in Castro's wake and their ascension to political power would forestall such a move and provide time to stabilize the political arena before turning the reins of government over to civilians.

Other groups that might have leadership aspirations include the "Jurassics," orthodox communists grouped around communist party ideology chief José Ramón Machado and the party's school for cadres and administrators; the *Guervaristas*, spartan army and government officials who reject the privileges available to Cuba's ruling class, but also are politically flexible; and the *Aperturistas*, advocates of opening the economy to market forces, and who have been in virtual hibernation since Castro slowed the opening of the economy in 1995. Powerful individuals capable of assuming the leadership role include Manuel Pineiro, a top intelligence official; Eusebio Leal, head of the highly profitable organization responsible for the renovations in old Havana; Carlos Lage, vice president and economic czar; and Ricardo Alarcon, president of the national assembly. The number of political opportunists within Cuba is legion, but as one observer noted, "as long as Fidel is alive, they are all *fidelistas*."[2]

In Miami, however, some members of the Cuban American community have their own plans for a post-Castro Cuba. The aging *creole* elite, centered around the Cuban American National Foundation, want to plant democratic capitalism on the island. And until his death in November 1997, Jorge Mas Canosa had visions of his own Cuban presidency. Other Cuban Americans, like Eloy Gutierrez-Menoyo, leader of the Miami-based moderate Cambino Cubano exile organization, caution that such an imposition will be disastrous. Rather, he suggests that the outside world encourage the existing Cuban leadership to permit greater political and economic freedoms, otherwise confront a violent reception after Castro's departure.

The new Cuban political leadership will deal with a Cuba vastly different from what it was in 1959. The traditional elite and middle sector have disappeared, and a new society has developed under state control that, until the 1990s, provided a sense of social security not previously experienced. And in today's world of free-market economics, the Cuban people have been schooled in the perils of American capitalism and experienced the downside of Soviet dependency and a planned economy. The island faces its future as a paradox—at once an economic, political, and social uncertainty, and an opportunity.

So, too, U.S. government policy toward Cuba stands poised for change. A new generation of policymakers, unencumbered by Cold War experiences, is beginning to arrive in Washington. Many of them already question the wisdom of continuing the economic blockade and isolation of Cuba. At the same time, the death of Jorge Mas Canosa foreshadows a general change within the Cuban American community. The first generation of embittered Cuban emigrés is being replaced by their younger descendents who do not share the enmity towards Castro. Assimilated into the U.S. culture, they are more North American than Cuban in their concerns and interests.

Fidel Castro never realized the ideals of José Martí or Eduardo Chibás. Instead, he became ruler over a Cuba economically dependent upon the Soviet Union with a political system as closed as that which he challenged, and a society deprived of mobility as it had been before 1959. Yet he leaves a legacy of a triumphant revolution, representing for Latin America's downtrodden masses a victory over elitist and corrupt government and relief from social and economic injustices. Castro also held the United States at bay much to the admiration of many Latin Americans wary of "big brother" to the north, and by championing nonaligned nations' interests, he won respect for himself and Cuba in the international order. As such, the Cuban Revolution might survive even the death of its architect and only *jefe* (chief), Fidel Castro.

NOTES

1. Jan Knippers Black, "Participation and Political Process: The Collapsible Pyramid," in Jan Knippers Black, editor, *Latin America: Its Problems and Its Promise* (Boulder: Westview Press, 1984), 165–90.

2. "Cuba's Governing Party Looks Inward," *Miami Herald*, September 21, 1997, 15.

Biographies: The Personalities Behind the Cuban Revolution

Batista Y Zaldivar, Fulgencio (1901–1973)

Fulgencio Batista Y Zaldivar was the president of Cuba from 1940 to 1944 and again from 1952 until 1958. His political influence spanned from the the 1930s to the 1960s. He was born on January 16, 1901, the son of a railroad laborer in Banes, Oriente Province. Batista spent his early years in poverty and attended a Quaker missionary school. After leaving school, Batista worked at a variety of jobs—tailor apprentice, laborer in the cane fields, grocery clerk, barber—before joining the army at age twenty. The military afforded an opportunity for Batista's rapid upward mobility. An ambitious and energetic young man, he studied at night and graduated from the National School of Journalism. In 1928 Batista was promoted to sergeant and assigned as a stenographer at Camp Columbia in Havana.

In the late 1920s and early 1930s, President Gerardo Machado came under increasing attack for the political repression and corruption that characterized his regime and by the continually worsening economic conditions brought on by the Great Depression. This led to his ouster in August 1933 and the establishment of a provisional government headed by Carlos Manuel de Céspedes. These conditions afflicted the army where promotions became infrequent and pay restrictions possible. Frustrated and ambitious younger officers conspired with disenchanted students to seize control of the government on September 4, 1933. Batista led these officers in the overthrow of Céspedes's provisional government and its replacement by a short-lived five-man junta. Within a week, the junta was disbanded in favor of Provisional President Ramón Grau San Martín. Batista's reward was promotion to colonel and chief of the army. Grau's program displeased almost everyone and led Batista to force Grau's resignation in January 1934. For the next six years, Batista ruled through puppet presidents and shadow governments.

Elected president in 1940, Batista set out to win popular support with a wide-ranging program of welfare legislation in public administration, health, education, and public works. He established rural hospitals, pushed through minimum wage legislation, increased salaries for public and private employees, and started a program of rural schools under army control. Batista also legalized the Cuban Communist Party and in 1943 established diplomatic relations with the Soviet Union. The army received higher pay, pensions, better food, and modern medical care, thus ensuring its loyalty.

On December 9, 1941, Batista brought Cuba into World War II on the Allied side. Air and naval bases were made available to the United States, which purchased all of Cuba's sugar production and provided generous loans and grants. In 1944 Batista allowed the election of his old-time rival, Grau San Martín. After an extensive tour of Central and South America, Batista settled at Daytona Beach, Florida. There he wrote a book, *Sombras de América*, published in Mexico in 1946, in which he surveyed his life and policies. In 1948, while still in Florida, he was elected to the Cuban Senate from Santa Clara Province. He returned to Cuba that same year, organized his own party, and announced his presidential candidacy for the June 1952 elections. Batista, however, prevented the elections from ever taking place. Aware perhaps that he had little chance to win, he and a group of army officers on March 10, 1952, overthrew the constitutionally elected regime of President Carlos Prío Socarrás. Batista suspended the 1940 Constitution, as well as Congress, canceled the elections, and dissolved all political parties.

Opposition soon developed, led primarily by university students who rioted and demonstrated frequently. On July 26, 1953, young revolutionaries led by Fidel Castro unsuccessfully attacked the Moncada military barracks in Oriente Province. Some of the attackers were killed; others, including Castro, landed in jail. Batista seemed bent on remaining in power. In a rigged election in November 1954, he was "re-elected" for a four-year-term. Although Cuba was prosperous, Batista neglected social and economic problems. Corruption and graft in his administration reached unprecedented proportions. Political parties and groups called for new elections but with little success. As a political compromise became unlikely, the adherents to violence grew in number.

Students increased their activism. After his release, Castro went to Mexico to prepare an expedition, which landed in Cuba and began guerrilla operations. Other groups organized an urban underground. An attack on the Presidential Palace on March 13, 1957, by the students and followers of deposed President Prío nearly succeeded in killing Batista. The government met terrorism with counterterrorism. Political prisoners were tortured and assassinated. By 1958 national revulsion against Batista had developed. Finally, defections in the army precipitated the crumbling of the regime on December 31, 1958. Batista escaped to the Dominican Republic and later to the Portuguese Madeira Islands, where he wrote several books, among them *Cuba Betrayed* (1962) and *The Growth and Decline of the Cuban Republic* (1966), both of them apologies for his divisive role in Cuban politics. He moved to Madrid, Spain, where he died on August 6, 1973.

Blas Roca (Francisco Calderío) (1898–1987)

Blas Roca, a union organizer and politician, was born in 1898 as Francisco Calderío in Manzanillo, Oriente Province. He changed his name to Blas Roca when he became a member of the Communist Party. A shoemaker by trade, he became active in union activities before joining the party in 1929. In 1934 he was elected secretary general of the party, a post he held until 1961. From 1940 until 1952, he served in the Cuban House of Representatives. During Castro's regime, Blas Roca held several important government positions. From 1962 until 1965 he served on the national directorate and secretariat of the forerunners of the present Cuban Communist Party (PCC) and as editor of the communist newspaper *Hoy*. In 1965 he became a member of the PCC General Committee. Subsequent appointments included membership in the party's secretariat and politburo and to the council of state.

As president of the PCC's Constitutional Studies Commission, Blas Roca was instrumental in institutionalizing the Castro government and drafting the new constitution proclaimed in February 1976. In the October 1976 nationwide elections he was elected as the delegate from Matanzas municipality to the National Assembly and served as its elected president from 1976 until 1981. Also in December 1976 he was elected a vice president of the Cuban Council of State. Because of age and poor health, Blas Roca stepped down as president of the National Assembly in December 1981. Henceforth, his political activities slowed until his death in 1987.

Castro Ruz, Fidel (1926–   )

A lawyer by training, a revolutionary by vocation, Fidel Castro led the successful guerrilla movement that ousted dictator Fulgencio Batista in 1959 and launched the Cuban Revolution. Since then, he has led the Cuban Revolution as President, Chief of the Armed Forces, and First Secretary of the Communist Party of Cuba and has transformed Cuba into a socialist state aligned with the Soviet Union. The son of Angel Castro y Agiz and Lina Ruz González de Castro, he was born on August 13, 1926, on his family's sugar plantation near Birán, Oriente Province. Castro was educated in Jesuit schools in Oriente and later at the prestigious Belén High School in Havana. In 1945 Castro entered law school at the University of Havana at a time of intense student activism and violence. He joined the *Unión Insurreccional Revolucionaria*, and acquired a reputation for personal ambition, forcefulness, and fine oratory, yet he never became a prominent student leader.

In 1947 Castro left the university temporarily to enroll in an expedition against Dominican Republic dictator Rafael L. Trujillo, which did not materialize, and in 1948 he participated in one of the most controversial episodes of his life, the *Bogotazo*—series of riots in Bogotá following the assassination of Liberal party leader Jorge E. Gaitán. Caught up in the violence that rocked Colombian society, Castro joined the mobs and roamed the streets distributing anti-U.S. propaganda and inciting the populace to revolt. Pursued by Colombian police, he and the other students went to the Cuban embassy and were later flown back to Havana, where Castro resumed his studies.

At the university, Castro was exposed to different ideologies, but above all, the nationalistic program of Cuba's Orthodox Party—economic independence, political liberty, social justice, and an end to corruption—captured his imagination. The program, based upon the ideals of José Martí, found contemporary expression in the party's leader Eduardo Chibás, whom Castro admired and followed eagerly. In 1950 Castro graduated and began practicing law and engaged in politics in Havana. He became a congressional candidate on the Orthodox party slate for the June 1952 election. The election was never held because on March 10, 1952, Fulgencio Batista led a group in overthrowing President Carlos Prío Soccarás's regime. The incident convinced Castro that the only path to political change would be through the violent overthrow of Batista. Toward that end, he organized a group of followers and, on July 26, 1953, attacked the Moncada military barracks in Oriente Province. Castro was captured, tried, and sentenced to fifteen years in prison. Castro defended himself in the trial in a speech "History Will Absolve Me." In it, he attacked Batista's regime and outlined his political and economic ideas, most of them within the mainstream of Cuba's political tradition.

After being released by an amnesty in 1955, Castro traveled to Mexico, where he organized an expedition against Batista. On December 2, 1956,

Fidel, his brother Raúl, and eighty men landed in Oriente Province. Castro and twelve of his followers survived the landing and escaped to the Sierra Maestra Mountains, from which they conducted a guerrilla war against the Batista regime for the next three years. By 1958 a movement of national revulsion against Batista had developed. By the end of the year, the regime collapsed, and on January 1, 1959, Castro proclaimed a provisional government.

Although Manuel Urrutia and subsequently Osvaldo Dorticós served as presidents of the country, Fidel Castro wielded the real power. He successfully maneuvered both his opponents and supporters to consolidate his political pre-eminence. His reforms for Cuba's poorer classes gained him a wide base of support, but at the same time he angered the Cuban elite and foreign businessmen, mostly U.S. investors. His nationalization of agricultural lands commenced a diplomatic war of nerves with the Eisenhower administration in Washington that eventually led the United States to sever relations with Cuba on January 1, 1961. Following the failed CIA Bay of Pigs invasion in April 1961, Castro increasingly turned to the Soviet Union for economic support. He finally proclaimed to be a communist in December 1961. During the October 1962 missile crisis, Castro stood outside the dialogue between Soviet Premier Nikita Khrushchev and U.S. President John F. Kennedy that led to a resolution of the crisis, but the experience convinced Castro that he could never trust the Soviets. Until 1991 when the Soviet Union collapsed, relations between the two countries were often tense.

Castro accepted Che Guevara's advice in attempting to industrialize Cuba and create a "new socialist man" in the 1960s. When the efforts approached failure in the late 1960s, Castro increasingly criticized his colleague, took fuller control of the economy, and blamed the U.S. embargo for Cuba's economic plight. As the economy continued to stagnate in the 1970s, Castro led the government reorganization plans that resulted in the 1976 constitution, which gave the appearance of democratization. But Castro never lost control. Over the years, Castro increasingly relied upon individuals more noted for their loyalty and lack of imagination than on government and leadership skills, with the exception of Carlos Rafael Rodríguez. Otherwise, along with his brother Raúl, who is second in command, Castro tightened his grip on the nation. All labor, social, and professional organizations are directed by the state. The press is controlled. Academic research and literary and artistic expression must be within the bounds of the revolution. There is no room for opposition. Dissidence means arrest and prison sentences.

Little is known about Castro's private life. His marriage to Mirta Díaz-Balart produced one son, Fidelito, and ended in divorce. Fidelito is a trained physicist and for a time headed the Cuban Nuclear Commission. One sister, Juana, now a U.S. resident, is an outspoken critic of the regime. Some argue that Celia Sanchez Mundulay, an ally in the guerrilla war, served as Cuba's first lady, although they never married. She also became a close confidante and the only one capable of leveling criticisms at Fidel. The vacuum that followed her death in 1980 has not been filled.

With the collapse of the Soviet Union in 1991 and the concomitant adverse economic impact upon Cuba, critics argued that Castro's tenure would soon end. As recently as the Fifth Communist Party Congress in October 1997, Castro gave no hint of resigning except to indicate that his brother Raúl would be his most capable successor.

Castro Ruz, Raúl (1931–)

Raúl Castro was one of the original members of the 26th of July Movement that organized the successful overthrow of Fulgencio Batista in 1959. Raúl was born on June 3, 1931, on his father's plantation in Birán, in the northern portion of the Province of Oriente, the fifth of seven children of Angel Castro y Argiz and Lina Ruz González de Castro. He attended the Jesuit school Colegio Dolores in Santiago de Cuba and later the Belén High School in Havana. As a student at the University of Havana, Raúl's interests in politics became evident. Unlike his brother Fidel, Raúl was attracted to Marxism early and became a member of the *Juventud Socialista* (Socialist Youth), and affiliate of the Moscow-oriented *Partido Socialista Popular*, Cuba's communist party. In 1953, while still a student at the University of Havana, Raúl made his first trip behind the Iron Curtain when, after participating in the World Youth Congress in Vienna, he visited the Soviet bloc capitals of Bucharest, Budapest, and Prague.

Upon his return to Cuba, Raúl became involved in his brother's struggle against Batista's government. He shared Fidel's view that reform in Cuba could not be accomplished by constitutional means, but only by overthrowing the oppressive government. They also agreed that the pervasive influence of the United States in the nation's economy had to end. The younger Castro reportedly broke off from the communist organization to join his brother's fight.

On July 26, 1953, Raúl accompanied his brother and 160 followers in an attack on the Moncada Barracks in Santiago de Cuba. In the failed attack, Raúl and Fidel were captured. Subsequently, many of their followers were executed, but the Castro brothers received lengthy prison terms. Raúl was given a thirteen-year sentence but was released in a general amnesty in May 1955. After his release from prison, Raúl went to Mexico with Fidel to form and organize the 26th of July Movement. In December 1956 Raúl, Fidel, and eighty revolutionaries left Mexico in a yacht named *Granma* and landed in Oriente Province. Most of the rebels were killed by Batista's forces during and immediately after the landing, but the Castro brothers managed to escape to the Sierra Maestra Mountains along with sixteen others.

From the mountains, the Castro brothers conducted a guerrilla war against the Batista regime. With the rank of major, Raúl established a second front in the Sierra de Cristal mountains in northeastern Oriente. Named after underground leader Frank Páis (who was murdered in July 1957), Raúl's "Frank Páis Second Front" grew to a force of several hundred men. During his stay in the mountains, Raúl Castro gained a reputation for being the most hotheaded, impetuous, and violently anti-American among the rebels and for possessing a killer instinct. He reportedly matched the Cuban dictator Batista's acts of terror with equal ferociousness. In the summer of 1958, he kidnapped forty-seven Americans and three Canadians, ranging from engineers employed at the Moa Nickel Company to American servicemen stationed at Guantánamo Bay. Reportedly, Fidel disapproved of the kidnappings and ordered Raúl to release the hostages. Raúl did not comply. He kept the captives to negotiate with the Americans, and also because he knew that Batista would not plan any attacks while there were American citizens present in his camp. When the United States agreed to Raúl's demands, he released the prisoners on July 18, 1958. The kidnappings made world headlines and prompted new accusations about Raúl's link to communism. On January 26, 1959, following the success of the Revolution, Raúl decided to marry his fiancée, Vilma Espín, who had fought alongside him in the mountains (under the name of Deborah), and was reported to be his "political mentor." She was the daughter of an upper-class rum distiller, and held a chemical engineering degree from the Massachusetts Institute of Technology (MIT).

In the wake of the revolution, Raúl punished Batista's supporters. For example, he directed the execution of nearly one hundred officers and soldiers of the Batista army and ordered them buried in a mass grave near Santiago de Cuba. In 1959 Raúl was named Minister of the Revolutionary Armed Forces, which gave him ministerial rank and complete control in reorganizing the armed forces. He built the army into a highly professionalized modern military establishment closely modeled on the Soviet armed forces and equipped with the latest Soviet military hardware. He also made military service for Cuba's youths mandatory and sent thousands of young officers for training in the Soviet Union. He also completed advanced training there. He led the Cuban land forces against the exile forces in the Bay of Pigs invasion on April 17, 1961, and arranged for the deployment of Soviet long-range missiles in Cuba, which resulted in the Cuban Missile Crisis of 1962. He continually called for the elimination of the U.S. presence at Guantánamo Naval Base because it stood as a permanent focus of provocation. As commander of Cuba's two military intelligence organizations, Raúl directly thwarted numerous counterrevolutionary activities. In the 1970s and early 1980s, he visited the Soviet Union and eastern Europe and was invited as an observer to the Warsaw Pact maneuvers.

Over the years, Raúl significantly increased his political power. During the 1960s, he played a major role in transforming the framework of the Cuban government into a Soviet-like single political party structure. In the 1970s, while remaining commander-in-chief, Raúl became first vice president of the Council of State and the Council of Ministers. He also continued to serve as a member of the Politburo and as second secretary of the Communist party and since 1965 has been president of the Agrarian Reform Institute. He also is responsible for the Ministry of Interior, the Secretariat to the President, the Ministry of Public Health, and the Children's Institute. He was one of the principal figures in the move toward a more Sovietized bureaucratic order and long enjoyed Moscow's confidence as a politically reliable Cuban leader and as a competent administrator. Given the extent of power Fidel and Raúl have acquired, many critics describe Cuba as the Castro brothers' family business.

With the collapse of the Soviet Union in 1991 and the concomitant economic crisis at home, the Cuban military increased its prominence in various economic activities, including manufacturing and tourism. Once considered an ideologue, Raúl has shown greater flexibility since 1991 by endorsing limited capitalist foreign investment and market incentives. Although Raúl possesses considerable power, he lacks his brother's charisma, which leads many analysts to suggest that he could not successfully follow Fidel. Despite these observations, at the conclusion of the Fifth Communist Party Congress in October 1997, Fidel clearly suggested that Raúl should be his successor.

Céspedes, Carlos Manuel de (1819–1874)

Carlos Manuel de Céspedes was a nineteenth-century Cuban revolutionary. Born on April 19, 1819, the son of a sugar planter in Cuba's Oriente Province, Céspedes received his baccalaureate degree in Havana in 1840, after which he studied law in Spain. For participating in Cuban revolutionary activities, Céspedes was exiled to France. Already committed to opposing colonial repression when he returned to Cuba, Céspedes joined with other like-minded eastern planters and cattle ranchers in the isolated and less-developed corners of the Oriente Province, and together they used Masonic Lodges to organize and coordinate revolutionary activities.

On October 10, 1868, without consulting the other leaders, Céspedes held a public meeting at his plantation (La Demajagua) to issue the *Grito de Yara*, which proclaimed Cuba's independence from Spain, universal suffrage, and an end to slavery. He then encouraged his listeners to follow the path of such Latin American freedom fighters as Simón Bolívar and José de San Martín. Although he immediately freed his own thirty slaves, Céspedes later appealed to the slaveholders in western Cuba to join the revolt by calling for the gradual emancipation of their slaves, with compensation for the owners.

Although he acted alone, Céspedes was the acknowledged leader of the insurrection, and in April 1869 he was chosen president of the republic declared by the Constituent Assembly. Despite their commitment to independence, Céspedes and his coconspirators envisioned independence as a transitional step in the process of union with the United States. Only weeks after the independence proclamation, Céspedes led a delegation of Cuban revolutionaries to Washington, D.C., to petition the American secretary of state to consider Cuba's admission to the Union. A year later, the revolutionary Constituent Assembly of Guáimaro explicitly proclaimed annexation as the ultimate purpose of the Cuban rebellion.

The rebels enjoyed early successes, but the revolutionaries were divided by petty regionalism, class origins, and conflicts over military strategy. They lacked the unity and discipline essential for victory. Céspedes's authoritarian manner only intensified the centrifugal forces of the revolutionary movement. In 1873 Céspedes was deposed in absentia as president, and the following year, on March 22, he was killed in a skirmish with Spanish forces.

Chibás, Eduardo (1907–1951)

Eduardo Chibás was a political leader and founder of the Cuban Orthodox party. Born on August 26, 1907, in Oriente, Chibás became a student leader at the University of Havana in the 1920s, where he was among the original members of *Directorio Estudiantil* that protested against the administration of Gerardo Machado. After earning his law degree at Havana, Chibás lived in Miami, Florida, until 1933 because of his outspoken criticism of the Machado government. Chibás returned to Havana following the ouster of Machado in the summer of 1933 to support the presidency of Ramón Grau San Martín. He strongly criticized Fulgencio Batista's orchestrated overthrow of Grau in January 1934, and it led to his joining the Cuban Revolutionary party (*Auténticos*) and continued the criticism against Batista's handpicked puppet presidents. Chibás supported Grau's unsuccessful bid for the presidency in 1940 and his victorious campaign in 1944. But Chibás became disillusioned with Grau's nepotism and corruption and the violence conducted by political groups.

Chibás broke away from the *Auténtico* party in 1947 to establish the Orthodox party, which sought to end political corruption and rescue the principles of the 1933 revolution. Subsequently, Chibás was elected to the Senate and in 1948 finished third in the presidential elections won by Carlos Prío Socarrás. In 1952 he again ran for the presidency in a three-way campaign against Carlos Hevia and Batista. A few months prior to the election, on August 5, 1951, Chibás shot himself at the conclusion of an emotional radio broadcast in which he was drawing attention to government corruption. His death created a vacuum within the Orthodox party and facilitated Batista's March 1952 coup d'état. Thereafter many of the party members joined in opposition to the Batista regime and became involved in the revolutionary struggle that resulted in his overthrow in 1959.

Dorticós Torrado, Osvaldo (1919–1983)

Osvaldo Dorticós Torrado was a lawyer who served as president of Cuba from 1959 to 1976. Born on April 27, 1919, in Cienfuegos, he attended local private and public schools and was active in local politics. He earned his law degree from the University of Havana in 1941. Dorticós returned to Cienfuegos to practice law, subsequently serving as Dean of the Cienfuegos Bar Association and then vice-president of the National Bar Association.

An active opponent of the Batista regime from 1952 to 1959, Dorticós joined the Movement of Civic Resistance, a coalition of businessmen and professionals engaged in clandestine activities against the government. For these activities, he served a short jail sentence in 1957, after which he joined Fidel Castro's 26th of July Movement. As the Movement's coordinator for Cienfuegos, Dorticós supplied Che Guevara's troops in the nearby Escambray Mountains. He was again arrested and detained briefly by the Batista government in December 1958, after which he fled to Mexico.

Dorticós returned to Cuba after Fidel Castro's victory in January 1959 and served as Minister of Justice. He was responsible for a series of decrees that modified the 1940 constitution. Dorticós became president of Cuba in July 1959, following the resignation of Manuel Urrutia, and, at age forty, was the youngest to hold that position in Cuban history. Although real power lay in Castro's hands, Dorticós remained a loyal ally. Following the downfall of Anibal Escalante in 1962, Dorticós temporarily served as Secretary of the National Organization of the United Party of the Social Revolution (ORI). He received additional appointments as Minster of the Economy and Director of the Cuban Central Planing Board. In 1965 Dorticós became a member of the Cuban Communist party, serving on its politburo and central committee.

Dorticós's place in the regime was enhanced in the 1970s as Castro reorganized the government. He held positions in the National Assembly of the People's Power and the Council of State. He also served as vice president of the Council of Ministers and was a member of the Political Bureau of the Central Committee of the Cuban Communist party. Dorticós committed suicide on August 23, 1983.

Echeverría Bianchi, José Antonio (1932–1957)

José Antonio Echeverría Bianchi was a student leader and revolutionary who joined forces with Fidel Castro to oust Batista from political power by force. Born on July 16, 1932, in Matanzas Province, Echeverría attended the Marist Brothers School and the public high school in his hometown of Cárdenas. As a student in the University of Havana's School of Architecture, he became involved in student and national politics and was elected president of the University Students Association from 1954 to 1956. Opposed to the Batista dictatorship, Echeverría led numerous demonstrations against the regime. In 1955 he traveled to Costa Rica to support the José Figueres administration against attacks from the Nicaraguan dictator Anastasio Somoza. In 1956, along with Fauré Chomón, he founded the Revolutionary Directorate, an underground student organization committed to the violent overthrow of the Batista regime. That same year, Echeverría traveled to Chile where he participated in the Congress of Latin American Students and to Mexico where he signed a cooperative agreement with Fidel Castro. Upon his return to Cuba, the Directorate conducted sabotage and violent acts against members of the Cuban government and its supporters. On March 13, 1957, Echeverría and supporters of former President Carlos Prío Soccarás (1948–1952) led an unsuccessful attempt to assassinate Batista. While some of the group attacked the Presidential Palace, which failed, Echeverría led an assault on Havana's radio station, where they mistakenly announced that Batista had been killed. In an ensuing battle with the Havana police, Echeverría was shot and killed on March 13, 1957.

Escalante, Anibal (1909–1977)

Anibal Escalante served as secretary general of the Cuban Communist party and editor of its newspaper *Hoy*. Born in 1909 into an affluent family in Oriente, Escalante earned his law degree from the University of Havana in 1932. He joined the Communist party that same year and founded *Hoy*. He served as the paper's editor from 1938 until the early 1960s. When, in 1951, the paper's printing presses were destroyed and he was the target of an attempted assassination, Escalante charged the government-led Cuban Confederation of Workers with responsibility. In 1953 he was one of the five who directed the Communist party during Blas Roca's illness. During Batista's ban on communist activities from 1953 to 1959, Escalante remained in hiding.

After Fidel Castro's victory in 1959, Escalante resumed his editorship of *Hoy* and in June used the paper as a platform to assert that President Manuel Urrutia lost his revolutionary zeal. Whereas Urrutia wanted to keep the Cuban middle class and some sectors of the upper class within the Revolution, Escalante favored the more radical Communist party elements. Soon thereafter Escalante was charged with merging Castro's 26th of July Movement with the Revolutionary Student Directorate and the Cuban Communist party. The resultant Integrated Revolutionary Organizations, modeled after the Soviet Communist party, was perceived as a threat to Castro's power. As a result, in 1962 Escalante was forced from the National Directory. He went into exile, first in the Soviet Union, later transferring to Prague, Czechoslovakia.

Permitted to return to Cuba in 1964 as the administrator of a small state-run farm, Escalante remained out of the public eye until 1968, when he and his colleagues were accused of organizing a "microfaction" that conspired against the government. In an eight-hour speech before the Central Committee, Castro charged Escalante and his colleagues with supporting Moscow's side in the ideological argument with Cuba (peaceful coexistence versus armed struggle). Castro made Escalante an example of a "mistaken" revolutionary leader who clandestinely passed on information to Moscow and who attempted to destroy the unity of the Cuban Revolution. Escalante was sentenced to fifteen years in prison. He died in Havana on August 11, 1977. The Escalante trial was significant because it illustrated the conflict within Cuba between the "old" and "new" communists, with the latter coming out victorious.

Estrada Palma, Tomás (1835–1908)

Tomás Estrada Palma was the first president of Cuba (1902–1906). Born on July 9, 1835, near Bayamo, Oriente Province, Estrada Palma attended schools in Havana and the University of Seville in Spain, where he enrolled in the law school but failed to obtain a degree because family matters forced his return to Cuba.

With the outbreak of the Ten Years' War (1868–1878), Estrada Palma joined the rebels and in 1876 was selected president of the provisional government. Captured by Spanish forces in 1877, Estrada Palma was shipped to Spain, where he remained in jail until the end of the war. He then moved to Paris, France. There he began a discussion group for political exiles and took an interest in European intellectual life. In the early 1890s, he left Paris for New York and then Honduras, where he married Genoveva Guardiola, daughter of the Honduran president, and briefly served as Director of the Postal Services. At the insistence of José Martí, Estrada Palma and his family moved to New York in 1892 to form the Cuban Revolutionary Party. Following Martí's death on the Cuban battlefield in May 1895, Estrada Palma was named delegate-in-exile of the Cuban junta in New York City, carrying out diplomatic negotiations, primarily with the United States, raising funds, and promoting the Cuban cause. He accepted the title of provisional president of Cuba following Spain's defeat in 1898 and was elected president by an overwhelming majority in 1901.

Considered a decent, honest, and hardworking man, Estrada Palma expanded public education, directed the completion of the national railroad and repayment of debts, and oversaw reconstruction after a decade of war. But he had little faith in the ability of his compatriots to govern themselves and scolded them for their shortcomings. He consistently lectured the Cubans on political virtue and good government. He also preferred that Cuba remain a protectorate of the United States rather than a fully independent nation, until Cuba developed a sufficiently well-trained cadre of political, economic, and social leaders to make independence successful.

His image was further tarnished by the treaty linkages with the United States that provided it special privileges on the island. He negotiated the 1903 Permanent Treaty, which included the Platt Amendment that governed relations between the two countries and granted the United States the right to lease and establish naval bases at Guantánamo. That same year, he also signed a reciprocity treaty with the United States that gave Cuban products, particularly sugar, a preferential rate for import duties into the United States and gave selected American products preference in Cuban rates. Estrada Palma also openly encouraged U.S. investment on the island.

As the 1905 elections approached, political difficulties increased. Estrada Palma joined the Conservative Republican Party—or Moderate Party, as it then was called—and sought reelection. Estrada Palma regained the presidency unopposed because the Liberal party boycotted the elections. Tensions increased, however, as the Liberals charged a corrupt election and resorted to violence. In August 1906, an uprising took place in Pinar del Río Province that quickly spread throughout the island. Estrada Palma appealed for U.S. intervention. President Theodore Roosevelt sent Secretary of War William H. Taft to mediate between government and opposition, but Estrada Palma rejected Taft's proposed solution and resigned in September 1906. With Roosevelt's approval, Taft then ordered the landing of U.S. Marines. After dissuading the Liberals from fighting, Taft, again with Roosevelt's consent, proclaimed a provisional government led first by himself as acting governor and later by Charles E. Magoon. U.S. intervention lasted until January 1909. Estrada Palma retired quietly to his estate in Bayamo, where he resided until his death on November 4, 1908.

Gómez y Báez, Maximo (1836–1905)

Maximo Gómez y Báez was a major leader in Cuba's wars for independence. Born on November 18, 1836, in Baní, the Dominican Republic, Gómez attended a local seminary and a religious seminary. Gómez began his military career at age sixteen when he joined the Dominican army to fend off Haitian invaders. He accepted a Spanish commission as captain in 1861 and retained the post until the end of Spanish control of the colony in 1865. After the 1866 civil war in the Dominican Republic, in which Gómez lost his property, he fled to Cuba.

Settling in Bayamó, Gómez sympathized with Cuban revolutionaries over Spain's harsh treatment of the colony and with the exploitation of black slaves. In October 1868 he joined Carlos Manuel de Céspedes and other leaders in what became the Ten Years' War. His battlefield success soon earned him promotion to the rank of general and then commander-in-chief of the rebel army. He and fellow field commander, Antonio Maceo, were in constant conflict with the civilian leadership over extending the war into western Cuba where an attack upon the sugar plantations would wreak havoc on the island's economy and result in freedom for the slaves. Disillusioned and disappointed at the lack of military success, Gómez left Cuba just prior to the signing of the Treaty of Zanjón that ended the Ten Years' War. Subsequently, he supported the ill-fated Guerra Chiquita (the Little War, 1879–1880), an attempt by several Cuban rebels to continue the war against Spain.

Gómez next went to Honduras, where he remained until 1884, at which time he traveled to New York City. There, he momentarily joined forces with José Martí in organizing and collecting funds for a new rebellion in

Cuba. But Gómez and Martí soon clashed over the leadership role, and Goméz withdrew from the revolutionary ranks. Gómez then traveled to Cuba and back to the Dominican Republic. There he received a new call from Martí in 1892 for a final effort to liberate Cuba. Martí had organized a revolutionary party in exile and now offered Gómez the post of military chief.

Forgetting old differences, Gómez accepted and joined Martí and Maceo in their revolutionary endeavors. For the next few years, the three men worked tirelessly, organizing Cubans in and out of the island. On March 25, 1895, they issued the Manifesto of Monte Christi, renewing the Cuban revolution. When Martí died in a skirmish on May 19, 1895, Gómez assumed the leadership mantle by becoming commander-in-chief of the rebel army. Returning to the battlefield, Gómez finally implemented his plans for the invasion of the western Provinces. He decreed a moratorium on sugar production, promising death and destruction to property for anyone who ignored his order. The measure proved effective economically and contributed to his battlefield success. By 1897 his forces had moved into Matanzas and Havana.

The war stalemated, however, as the new Spanish leader, General Valerino Weyler, forced the rural populations into garrisoned towns and increased the number of Spanish troops on the island. In addition, the loss of Maceo in battle in 1896 meant that Gómez carried on the war himself. Gómez retreated to the eastern provinces and from there carried on successful guerrilla operations. Weyler was unable to defeat the Cuban rebels, much less engage them in a major battle. The determined Gómez refused any compromise with Spain, including an offer in January 1898 that would have made Cuba a self-governing province within the Spanish empire.

This was the existing condition in Cuba when the United States declared war on Spain on April 25, 1898. The Cuban forces collaborated with the U.S. army in the short campaign against Spain. By August, hostilities had ceased, and Spain agreed to relinquish sovereignty over the island. Gómez and his troops retired to the sugar mill Narcisa in Las Villas Province and there awaited the departure of Spanish troops. After the withdrawal, Gómez made a triumphant tour of the island and amid general joy entered Havana on February 24, 1899. But Gómez, the most popular hero of the war, soon clashed with the U.S. authorities and the Cuban legislative assembly. He requested that the Americans pay the Cuban army for the aid that American soldiers had received. The United States refused and, instead, offered $3 million or an estimated $75 for each soldier who turned in his weapons. Gómez refused this offer as well as a proposed U.S. loan for reconstruction, which the Assembly wanted. The Assembly also resented Gómez's secret conversations with representatives of the U.S. government to secure payment for the war veterans. The Assembly finally dismissed Gómez as commander-in-chief of the army. His dismissal only increased his popularity. As the end of the American occupation approached, Gómez emerged as the most popular figure for the presidency. Yet the old general refused to be considered and instead campaigned for and helped elect Tomás Estrada Palma, former rebel president and delegate-in-exile of the Cuban Republic in Arms. Gómez supported Estrada Palma's administration, but when the president announced his intention to re-elect himself, he met with Gómez's stiff opposition. Old and sick, General Gómez went on a speaking tour but could do little before his death on June 17, 1905.

Grau San Martín, Ramón (1887–1969)

Ramón Grau San Martín was a physician who twice served as Cuba's president (1933–1934 and 1944–1948). Born on September 13, 1887, the son of a wealthy tobacco farmer, in Pinar del Río Province, Grau earned a doctor of medicine degree from the University of Havana in 1908. He expanded his medical studies in France, Italy, and Spain before returning to Cuba and becoming a professor of physiology at the University of Havana in 1921. He wrote extensively on medical subjects, including a university textbook on physiology.

Grau achieved greater notoriety in politics. Beginning in 1927, Grau actively and consistently opposed the Gerardo Machado dictatorship. He was the only faculty member who refused to sign the edict authorizing Machado's honorary doctorate from the university. For his efforts, Grau was jailed in 1931, and following his release, exiled to the United States. In August 1933 following Machado's ouster, the provisional government, headed by Carlos Manuel de Céspedes, was itself quickly overthrown on September 4, 1933, by a military coup led by Sergeant Fulgencio Batista y Zaldívar. Grau was included in the short-lived five-man junta that replaced Céspedes.

When the pentarchy collapsed, Grau became provisional president. His four-month regime (September 10, 1933–January 14, 1934) became a high-water mark in the revolutionary process. The government was highly nationalistic and pro-labor. Backed by his faithful university students and propped by the military, Grau took several bold initiatives. He promptly abrogated the hated Platt Amendment, which had kept Cuba in a state of dependence on the United States. The revolutionary government effected other dramatic changes: an eight-hour work day, a requirement that at least 50 percent of a business's employees had to be native Cubans, compulsory trade unionization and the creation of professional associations, and an agrarian reform program designed to benefit peasants. In addition, the University of Havana became autonomous and its enrollment restrictions removed. Women received the right to vote. Not surprisingly, the government's activism spurred demonstrations for more-radical reforms but also earned it the enmity of the political elite and hostility from the United States, which encouraged the opposition to act. Batista led another military coup in January 1934, but the socioeconomic legacies of Grau's experiment lived on.

Grau went into temporary exile. He returned in time to be elected to the convention that drafted the 1940 constitution. That same year, he lost the presidential election to Fulgencio Batista. He ran again in 1944, this time successfully. He took office in the midst of post–World War II prosperity and used the increased government revenue to undertake a vast public works and school construction program and to expand social security benefits. He also encouraged economic development and agricultural diversification. Prosperity, however, brought increased nepotism and corruption, which, in turn, resulted in violence of tragic proportions. At the same time, the reformist zeal of the 1930s had greatly diminished and Grau faced increasingly stiff congressional opposition to his programs. Grau turned over the presidency to his protégé, Carlos Prío Soccarás in 1948 and then withdrew from public life until 1952 when he openly opposed Batista's coup d'etat. Grau ran for the presidency in Batista's controlled 1954 and 1958 elections, only to withdraw just prior to election day because of government fraud. After Castro came to power in 1959, Grau retired to his home in Havana until his death on July 28, 1969.

Guevara, Ernesto "Che" (1928–1967)

Ernesto "Che" Guevara was a Marxist revolutionary and guerrilla who became Fidel Castro's most trusted advisor. Born on June 14, 1928, in Rosario, Argentina, to parents of Spanish and Irish descent, Guevara spent his childhood in a nearby mountain town owing to his asthmatic condition. Influenced by the writings of the Chilean communist poet Pablo Neruda, Che (the Argentine equivalent of "pal") took a deep interest in history and sociology. After completing high school, Guevara entered the University of Buenos Aires to study medicine. Before earning his medical degree in 1953, Guevara took an extended transcontinental trip that included stops in Chile, Brazil's Amazonia, and Florida. In late 1953 Guevara left Argentina for good, settling first in Guatemala. There he supported the reformist regime of Jacobo Arbenz. When it was overthrown in 1954, he sought refuge in the Argentine embassy until he could travel to Mexico.

In 1955 a friend introduced Guevara to Fidel and Raúl Castro, who were then planning an expedition against the regime of Fulgencio Batista in Cuba. Guevara agreed to join the expedition, initially serving as its medical doctor. On December 2, 1956, the expeditionaries landed in eastern Cuba, becoming the nucleus of a guerrilla force that operated in the Sierra Maestra Mountains. The guerrillas, together with a loosely connected underground movement, undermined the government. When Castro created a second rebel column in 1957, he promoted Guevara to commander. Finally, a wave of popular discontent and desertions in the Cuban army precipitated the crumbling of the Batista regime on December 31, 1958. On January 1, 1959, Guevara was one of the first rebel commanders to enter Havana and take control of the capital.

Guevara shaped the Revolution's early economic policies in his capacities as director of the Industrial Department of the National Institute of Agrarian Reform (INRA), president of the National Bank of Cuba, and Minister of Industry. Guevara initiated central economic planning that required extensive state ownership of productive enterprises, but his plans for the rapid industrialization of Cuba failed. He sought to create a "new socialist man" dedicated to the Revolution and motivated by moral rather than material rewards. He hoped eventually to abolish the use of money. He also carried out several diplomatic missions, most notably to the Soviet Union and capitals in eastern Europe and Africa. By 1965, however, Guevara's influence began to wane, and in 1965 he resigned his position as Minister of Industry, the reasons for which have never been clear. Some scholars argue that Che and Fidel drifted apart; others argue that Guevara left in order to initiate a revolution in Latin America.

Guevara advocated insurrection as the only means to topple dictatorial governments and U.S. economic presence across Latin America. His *Guerrilla Warfare*, published in 1960, became a handbook for aspiring Latin American revolutionaries. Adhering to the *foco* theory, Guevara stressed that there was no need to await the presence of revolutionary conditions, but rather argued that insurrection itself would produce them. Inspired by Castro's success in Cuba and Guevara's call to arms, revolutionary movements erupted across Latin America in the 1960s, only to be crushed by military repression.

In this ambience, Guevara determined to apply his *foco* theory to Bolivia. He expected that the guerrilla operation in Bolivia would spread across the Andes, forcing U.S. intervention into another Vietnam. He began military actions there in March 1967, but it never gained support from local peasants. Guevara's forces also faced an inhospitable terrain, suffered from internal divisions, and quarreled with the Bolivian Communist party. Anxious to put an end to Guevara's movement, the United States provided the Bolivian army with supplies and advisors. On October 8, 1967, Guevara was captured and a day later executed. His body remained buried in an unmarked site until 1997, when it was recovered and returned to Cuba for a hero's internment.

Gutierrez-Menoyo, Eloy (1934–   )

Eloy Gutierrez-Menoyo was a Cuban revolutionary in the battle against Fulgencio Batista. In 1993 he founded *Cambio Cubano* (Cuban Change), a U.S.-based exile organization calling for peaceful change within Cuba. Born on December 8, 1934, in Madrid, Spain, Eloy was the youngest of six children. His father, Carlos Gutierrez-Zabaleta, was an ardent anti-Franco activist, who attained the rank of commander as a medical doctor in the Spanish Republican Army. In 1947 the family migrated to Cuba to escape the harshness of the Franco regime in Spain. Following Fulgencio Batista's coup in 1952, Eloy and his brother Carlos joined one of the many student movements opposing the dictator. Eloy was in charge of logistics for the 1957 assassination attempt upon Batista at the presidential palace, in which his brother Carlos lost his life.

In November 1957, eleven months after Castro raised his revolutionary banner on the island, Gutierrez-Menoyo became the leader of his own small guerrilla group operating in the mountains of central Cuba. By mid-1958 Gutierrez-Menoyo's Second Escambray Front army nearly equaled the size of Castro's forces. He arrived in Havana before Castro and in fact turned the city over to him. Gutierrez-Menoyo's men joined the united rebel army, and he was named major, the highest rank possible at the time. Expecting to play a prominent role in the post-Batista government, Castro quickly outmaneuvered Gutierrez-Menoyo, and as the regime became increasingly dictatorial and Marxist, Gutierrez-Menoyo became increasingly disillusioned. In January 1961, with twelve of his closest advisors, Gutierrez-Menoyo left Cuba for the United States.

Being a social democrat, Gutierrez-Menoyo was not well received by the ultra-right wing that dominated the Cuban exile group in Miami nor by the Central Intelligence Agency that was planning the Bay of Pigs invasion at the time. Gutierrez-Menoyo was detained by the U.S. Immigration Service until after the failed invasion. He then founded Alpha-66, a militant anti-Castro group that conducted sabotage attacks upon Cuba from Florida bases. Subsequently, he established a base of operations in Santo Domingo, from where he left for Cuba in December 1964 to plot Castro's overthrow.

Captured a month later by the Cuban army, Gutierrez-Menoyo was sentenced to thirty years in prison. As a prisoner in several Cuban jails over the next twenty-two years, he was subjected to severe beatings, torture, and other deprivations for refusing rehabilitation. His release in 1987 was negotiated by Spain's socialist prime minister Felipe González.

After a brief stay in Spain, Gutierrez-Menoyo returned to Miami, Florida, where he found himself out of step with the Cuban American National Foundation (CANF) on the best way to bring change to Cuba. In 1993 he founded *Cambio Cubano*, which advocates a dialogue with Castro and argues that peaceful change from within is the only vehicle for a peaceful post-Castro Cuba. He also calls for lifting the U.S. trade embargo placed upon Cuba. In June 1995 he further infuriated CANF by visiting Cuba and engaging in a four-hour discussion with Castro. Other moderate Cubans doubt that Gutierrez-Menoyo can effect any change in Cuba because of Castro's personal tight control over the island.

López, Narciso (1797–1851)

Narciso López, a Venezuelan by birth (October 17, 1797), became a general in the Spanish army and later led filibustering expeditions against Spanish power in Cuba in 1850–1851. In his mid-teens, he joined the Spanish army fighting against Simón Bolívar, rising rapidly in the ranks. When Spanish troops withdrew from Venezuela to Cuba in 1823, López accompanied them and settled in the island. He subsequently returned to Spain where he was promoted to the rank of general for his leadership against the Carlist rebels. López returned to Cuba in 1840 to serve briefly as governor general of Trinidad Province and to pursue private business interests.

After losing his patronage, López became disenchanted with Spanish rule and began to conspire against its authority over the island. In 1848 he joined with a group of Cubans who favored annexation to the United States and organized a plot named after his mining enclave "The Cuban Rose Mine." The scheme failed when Spanish authorities learned of the conspiracy and when the U.S. government, at the time considering the purchase of Cuba from Spain, moved against the expedition. López escaped capture by fleeing to the United States, where he organized an expedition with the support of southern leaders. In 1849 he sailed from New Orleans with a force of 600 men, mostly American veterans of the Mexican War, and landed in Cárdenas, Matanzas. The flag carried by López was to be later adopted as the Cuban national emblem. The expeditionaries overwhelmed the small Spanish force and captured the town but found little support among the local populace. López again escaped to the United States to organize another filibustering attack. In 1851, with 453 men, mostly Southerners and a few Cubans, López landed near Bahía Honda in a desolate area. With little local support, López was defeated and captured by the Spanish army and subsequently publicly garroted in Havana on September 1, 1851.

Scholars still disagree as to López's real objectives. Some point out that he wanted the island's independence; others insist that he desired Cuba's annexation to the United States. Perhaps he wanted a free Cuba but one where slavery could be preserved. Whatever his motivations, López's actions helped arouse anti-Spanish sentiment in the island and paved the way for later uprisings. To many Cubans, López was a precursor of Cuba's independence movement.

Maceo, Antonio (1845–1896)

Antonio Maceo served as second in command of the Cuban independence army. Born on June 14, 1845, in Santiago de Cuba, the son of a Venezuelan mulatto émigré and a free Cuban black, the young Maceo spent his early years on his father's small farm in Oriente, making occasional trips to Santiago de Cuba to sell agricultural products. Maceo received most of his education at home from private tutors.

Unhappy with Spanish domination and horrified by the exploitation of the black slaves, Maceo entered the Masonic Lodge of Santiago in 1864 and started to conspire with Cuban revolutionaries. When, on October 19, 1868, Carlos Manuel de Céspedes and other leaders began Cuba's Ten Years' War, Maceo joined the rebellion and five years later earned the rank of general. Maceo became a most effective guerrilla fighter as he outsmarted and outmaneuvered the Spanish generals and on successive occasions inflicted heavy losses on them. He kept tight discipline in his encampment, constantly planning and organizing future battles. Maceo won the respect and admiration from his men and fear and hatred from the Spanish troops. His incursions into the sugar zones not only helped to disrupt the sugar harvest but principally led to the freedom of the slaves, many of whom soon joined the ranks of the Cuban rebel army.

His prominent position among revolutionary leaders soon gave rise to intrigue and suspicion. Conservative elements who supported the war efforts began to fear the possibility of the establishment of a Negro republic with Maceo at its head. The example of Haiti still loomed in the minds of many, and was reinforced when the rebel commander General Maximo Gómez advocated an invasion of western Cuba in order to cripple sugar production and liberate the slaves. The invasion was postponed until 1875, and then it reached only to Las Villas Province in central Cuba. The destruction of the sugar estates increased the opposition from landed and sugar interests. As a result, the essential supplies, weapons, and money from exiles in the United States failed to arrive in Cuba. After a prolonged silence, Maceo finally answered those who accused him of attempting to establish a black republic. On May 16, 1876, Maceo asserted that he neither advocated nor would support a black republic. He also cautioned against accepting any U.S. assistance in the Cuban struggle for independence. He reasoned that such assistance would only hinder a free Cuba's development.

With neither side able to win a decisive victory, the Spanish and Cuban rebel leadership agreed to the Treaty of Zanjón on February 11, 1878. Though most of the Cuban rebel generals accepted the pact, Maceo refused to capitulate and continued the fight with his depleted army. Subsequently, he held a historic meeting, known as the "Protest of Baragúa," with the head of the Spanish forces, Marshal Arsenio Martínez Campos, requesting independence for Cuba and complete abolition of slavery. When these two conditions were rejected, he again resumed fighting briefly, but, without financial support and with his forces exhausted, Maceo realized that the situation was hopeless.

Maceo left for Jamaica and then New York, where he joined with Major General Calixto García, then organizing a new rebellion. This uprising, know as *La Guerra Chiquita* (the Little War, 1879–1880), ended in disaster, after which the disillusioned Maceo traveled to the Dominican Republic and finally settled in Honduras. In the mid-1880s, he again joined yet another military adventure headed by General Maximo Gómez, only to witness its self-destruction due to mistrust among the leadership. Never losing sight of a free Cuba, Maceo spent the remainder of the decade wandering throughout the Caribbean and Central America before settling in Costa Rica, where he engaged successfully in tobacco and sugar production. There he received a call from Martí, in 1893, for a final effort to liberate Cuba. Maceo joined Martí and Gómez in organizing the Cubans in and out of the island, until finally, on February 24, 1895, the War of Independence began.

One month later, Maceo and a group of expeditionaries landed in Oriente Province to join the rebellion. Now Gómez and Maceo were able to implement their plan to invade the western provinces and carry the war to the other extreme of the island. The two generals and Martí met on Cuban soil to map the war strategy. Maceo advocated a strong military junta rather than civilian control to direct the effort. He argued that dissension and incompetence of the civilian government during the Ten Years' War had led to the failure of the rebellion. Although the question of civilian versus military control was not resolved, Gómez was made commander-in-chief of the army, Maceo military commander of Oriente, and Martí head of the revolution abroad and in nonmilitary matters. Martí's death only days after the meeting, on May 19, 1895, dealt a strong blow to the morale of the Cuban forces, but Maceo and Gómez continued the fight. Maceo waged a bitter but successful campaign against larger Spanish forces in the Provinces of Pinar del Río and Havana. On December 7, 1896, while preparing the next campaign in the small town of San Pedro del Cacahual, Spanish forces attacked and in the skirmish Maceo was killed.

Although he did not live to see his country freed from Spain, Maceo's military genius and warnings to avoid any connection with the United States earned him a place in the pantheon of Cuban heroes.

Machado y Morales, Gerardo (1871–1939)

Gerardo Machado y Morales was the fifth president of Cuba (1924–1933), whose administration was marred by excessive corruption and repression of the political opposition. Born on September 28, 1871, in Santa Clara, Las Villas Province, Machado spent his childhood at his family's cattle estate, attended private schools, and in his early twenties engaged in growing and selling tobacco. He followed his father's footsteps when he joined the Cuban rebel army in 1895, rising to the rank of brigadier general. After the war ended, Machado turned to politics and business. He became mayor of Santa Clara and during the presidential administration of José Miguel Gómez (1909–1913) was appointed Inspector of the Armed Forces and later Secretary of the Interior. For seven years after his service in the Gómez administration, Machado engaged in farming and joined with American capitalists investing in public utilities. Machado's business ventures made him independently wealthy.

Returning to politics in the early 1920s, Machado won control of the Liberal party and, with his slogan "water, roads, and schools," was elected Cuba's fifth president in 1924. Machado's first administration coincided with a period of prosperity. Sugar production expanded, and the United States provided a close and ready market. Machado embarked on an ambitious public works program, which included the completion of the Central Highway, the construction of the National Capitol, the enlargement of the University of Havana, and the expansion of health facilities. He also sponsored a tariff reform bill in 1927 providing protection to fledgling Cuban industries. Despite these accomplishments, Cuba's dependence on sugar continued and U.S. influence and investments increased. For example, Cuba financed the public works programs with U.S. loans. Machado also resorted to force in the suppression of student and labor demonstrations and strikes.

Before his first administration ended, Machado sought re-election. Claiming that his economic program could not be completed within his four-year term and that only he could carry it out, Machado announced his decision to have himself re-elected and to extend the presidential term to six years. He cleared the political path through bribes and intimidation that brought the opposition parties, the congress, and the judiciary under his control. Under these conditions, Machado won re-election in 1928 with virtually no opposition.

Machado's second term was wrought with problems. Affected by the political and economic shock waves caused by the world depression, he became an increasingly ruthless dictator. Many Cubans, led primarily by university students, organized resistance to the regime. Student demonstrations became so severe in 1930, that Machado ordered the closing of all schools in the country. In 1931 former President Mario G. Menocal led a short-lived uprising in Pinar de Río Province, and an anti-Machado expedition landed in Oriente Province, only to be crushed by the army. Two of the most prominent of these opposition groups, the ABC (a clandestine organization composed of intellectuals and the middle sectors of society) and the university's Student Directorate, undermined Machado's position through sabotage and terrorism. As urban violence increased, so did repression. Machado's police raided secret meeting places, arresting students and ABC leaders, whom they tortured or killed.

In an effort to find a peaceful solution to Cuba's political situation, in 1933 U.S. President Franklin D. Roosevelt dispatched Special Envoy Sumner Welles to mediate between government and opposition. The mediation was supported by most political factions and leaders. Confronted with a political deadlock, the opposition orchestrated a general strike that paralyzed the nation and prompted Machado to seek the assistance of communist labor leaders to use their influence to end the strike. Fearing U.S. intervention, the Cuban armed forces staged a coup d'état on August 12, 1933, which forced Machado to leave the country. Machado eventually settled in the United States, where he died in Miami Beach on March 29, 1939.

Martí y Pérez, José Julián (1853–1895)

José Julián Martí y Pérez was a revolutionist, poet, journalist, and the principal organizer of Cuba's war against Spain. Indeed, Martí became Cuba's greatest hero and most influential writer. Born on January 28, 1853, in Havana of poor Spanish immigrants, Martí spent his early years as an eager student and a prolific poet. Martí was still in school at the outbreak of the Ten Years' War (1868–1878), Cuba's first war for independence. At age sixteen and while enrolled at Havana's *Instituto de Segunda Enseñanza de L Habana*, he published a newsletter, *La Patria Libre* (Free Fatherland). Soon afterwards he was arrested as a political dissident and sentenced to six years at hard labor. After serving several months, his sentence was commuted to banishment in Spain. Shortly after his arrival in Madrid in January 1871, Martí published a political essay, *El Presidio Político en Cuba*, an indictment of Spanish oppression and conditions in Cuban jails. In Spain, Martí resumed his studies and in 1874 received a degree in philosophy and law from the University of Saragossa.

From Spain, Martí traveled through Europe and in 1875 went to Mexico, where he worked as a journalist. After a short visit to Cuba in 1877, he settled in Guatemala, where he taught literature and philosophy. That same year, he married Carmen Zayas Bazán, daughter of a Cuban exile. Unhappy with Guatemala's political conditions, Martí returned to Cuba for two months in 1877 and again from August 1878 to September 1879. With the termination of the Ten Years' War, Martí assumed that conditions on the island would be improved, but they were not. Spanish authorities soon discovered his revolutionary activities and again deported him to Spain. He escaped to France and from there moved to the United States and Venezuela.

Finally, in 1881, he made New York the center of his activities, although he continued to travel and write about the many problems of Latin American nations. He wrote a regular column for *La Opinión Nacional* of Caracas, *La Nación* of Buenos Aires, and twenty other newspapers throughout Latin America. Not only his journalistic articles but also his poetry and prose became popular. Martí became a precursor of the Modernist movement in literature. In 1882 his most significant poems, composed for his son, were published in a book called *Ismaelillo*. Martí's best-known poems are his *Versos sencillos* (1891), which emphasize such themes as friendship, sincerity, love, justice, and freedom. Martí also won the hearts of many Latin American youngsters with his *Edad de oro* (1889), a magazine especially devoted to children. Martí's greatest contributions to Spanish-American letters were his essays. Written in a highly personal style, the Modernist renovation of language characterized his writing and marked the beginning of the new Latin American prose. By the early 1890s, he stood prominently as a major Latin American literary figure.

During the same time period, Martí concluded that Cuba's destiny could only be realized by achieving independence from Spain via open conflict. He also believed that the war had to be quick in order to prevent U.S. intervention. The task of uniting Cuba's diverse factions proved monumental. On one side were those who favored autonomy under Spain, and on the other were those who favored annexation to the United States. He also had to deal with the threat of U.S. expansionism and the authoritarian inclination of the veteran generals of the Ten Years' War. Martí's fear of a military dictatorship after independence led, in 1884, to a break with Máximo Gómez and Antonio Maceo, two generals engaged in conspiratorial activities. Martí's withdrawal proved to be temporary. By 1887 the three men were working together, with Martí assuming political leadership.

In 1892 Martí formed the Cuban Revolutionary party in the United States. For the next three years, he directed his efforts toward organizing the war against Spain. His oratory inspired his listeners, his honesty and sincerity inspired faith, and his conviction in the ideas he was pursuing inspired respect and loyalty for him and his cause. His writings were not merely rhetorical exercises; rather they were moral teachings aimed at making a better person. Martí's importance transcended Cuba. Like Bolívar, he thought in terms of a continent and advocated the unity of Latin America. His writings and ideas had a powerful impact not only in his homeland but throughout Latin America. When in 1895 he gave the order for the resumption of hostilities against Spain, Martí landed in Cuba to lead the war only to lose his life in an unimportant skirmish with Spanish troops at Dos Rios, Oriente, on May 19, 1895.

Although Cuba achieved its independence in 1898, Martí's political doctrines had little impact upon subsequent events, and only a few thought that his statue should be erected in Havana's Central Park. Only when the island was swept by a nationalist fervor in the 1920s and 1930s did Martí re-emerge as the political and moral mentor of the new generation of Cuban leaders. He remained so through the Castro revolution. Because his writings were contradictory, Martí may have sympathized with Karl Marx's concern for the worker, but he was not a Marxist. And though he distrusted U.S. expansionist attitude and some of the sordid consequences of its late-nineteenth-century industrial revolution, he still admired the country for its dynamism and the determination of its people.

Mas Canosa, Jorge L. (1939–1997)

Jorge L. Mas Canosa was the founder and chairman of the Cuban American National Foundation (CANF). Born on September 29, 1939, in Santiago, Cuba, to a major in Fulgencio Batista's army, Mas was educated in local elementary and secondary schools and the Presbyterian Junior College in North Carolina. A week after Castro's victory in 1959, Mas returned to Cuba, where he entered law school at Oriente University. There he joined fellow students in anti-Castro activism. His anti-Castro stance forced him to flee to Miami in 1960 to escape punishment. There he joined fellow Cuban exiles in the Bay of Pigs invasion in 1961, although his ship circled offshore while the main landing force met its doomed fate. Subsequently, he briefly served in the U.S. Army. Upon his return to Miami, Mas worked as a dishwasher, milkman, and shoe salesman to support his wife and three sons. He also was associated with the Cuban exile groups *Representacion Cubana en el Exilio* (RECE) and Commando of United Revolutionary Organizations (CORU). Both groups were linked to the CIA-sponsored covert attacks upon Cuba's economic infrastructure in the mid-1960s and 1970s. During the same time period, he moved into the construction business, eventually becoming the owner of Church & Tower, a multimillion dollar operation that gained its initial prominence laying underground telephone cable. Over the years, Mas came to play a prominent role in several Miami community organizations.

By 1980 he determined that the hit-and-run tactics conducted by commando groups against Castro would not topple the Cuban dictator. Along with other Miami-based Cuban businessmen, he founded the Cuban American National Foundation (CANF) as a nonprofit educational organization to enlighten public opinion about Castro's policies and the need to impose harsh measures upon the regime in order to force its demise. Mas found a sympathetic ear in the Ronald Reagan and George Bush administrations and had significant influence upon their foreign policies. He supported the *contras* in their effort to oust the Sandinista regime in Nicaragua, believing that success on the isthmus would bring about a tougher U.S. policy toward Cuba. He supported the foundation of and received funds from the National Endowment for Democracy. He was instrumental in the establishment of Radio Martí in 1982 and soon became director of its operations. Subsequently, he supported TV Martí, which began operating in 1990 with a $16 million annual budget. CANF's influence led to the congressional passage of the 1992 Cuban Democracy Act and the 1996 Helms-Burton Bill, which tightened the economic embargo on Cuba.

Mas was not without controversy, however. Despite his denials, critics and many of his former supporters claimed that he envisioned himself as president of a post-Castro Cuba. Toward that end, he assembled a team of economists, engineers, and other specialists to plan a $15 billion infusion into a free-market economy on the island to be directed by the Cuban exile community in the United States. These plans have caused controversy within the Cuban community and led to the formation of more moderate

Cuban exile groups. Mas's critics, in turn, have come under attack from CANF, as have the *Miami Herald* and national legislators for expressing opinions about Castro and U.S. policy contrary to those of Mas and CANF. America's Watch, which usually reserves its criticisms for foreign dictators, has accused CANF of creating a repressive climate for freedom of expression against and within the Cuban-exile community. A vacuum in the leadership of the Cuban-American community resulted from his death on November 23, 1997.

Miró Cardona, José (1907–1974)

José Miró Cardona was the first prime minister of revolutionary Cuba in 1959. Born in Havana July 28, 1907, Miró attended local schools. Following his graduation from the University of Havana Law School in 1938, Miró became a successful and respected member of the Cuban bar. He held several important positions, including professor of penal law and Dean of the University of Havana's Law School and president of the Cuban Bar Association. Miró supported the call for Batista to step down in 1956 and became an influential member of the Civic Dialogue intended to seek a peaceful solution to Cuba's political crisis. He gained political notoriety in 1958 when he gained asylum in the Uruguayan embassy in 1958 for reportedly being the author of a public document that called for Batista's resignation. He went into exile to become secretary-general of the Civic-Democratic Revolutionary Front, an organization that coordinated the activities of several anti-Batista groups.

Following Castro's 1959 victory, Miró returned to Havana as prime minister of the revolutionary government. Subsequently, he was appointed as ambassador to Spain, only to be recalled in a policy dispute with Castro. His opposition to Castro's reforms for the University of Havana led Miró into exile in June 1960. Selected president of the Cuban Revolutionary Council in March 1961, Miró would have become President of Cuba had the Bay of Pigs invasion been successful in April 1961. Thereafter, Miró resided in Puerto Rico where he continued his anti-Castro activities and worked as a professor of penal law at the University of Puerto Rico until his death on August 10, 1974.

Prío Socarrás, Carlos (1903–1977)

Carlos Prío Socarrás was a lawyer and politician who served as president of Cuba from 1948 to 1952. Born in 1903 to a middle-class family in Bahía Honda, Pinar del Rio Province, Prío Socarrás went to local schools and then moved to study law at the University of Havana. He joined in student protests against Gerardo Machado when Machado decided to seek a second presidential term in 1928. Before Machado closed the university because of the demonstrations, Prío Socarrás formed a close relationship with law professor Ramón Grau San Martín. As a member of the "Generation of 1930," Prío Socarrás served as the leader of the *Directorio Estudiantil* in 1930 that called for Machado's ouster. These students claimed to be the heirs of José Martí and the legitimate representatives of the Cuban national will. As young, middle-class idealists, they naively believed that Cuba's ills could be solved solely with the removal of Machado from the presidency. When that happened in 1933 and the installation of the Grau provisional presidency followed, that belief disappeared. When Grau was ousted in early 1935, Prío Socarrás became a founding member of the *Auténtico* party, which called for economic and political nationalism, social justice, civil liberties, and greater Cuban control of its natural resources. He was a delegate to the 1940 constitutional convention and won recognition for university autonomy.

Prío Socarrás held many government positions in the 1940s: senator from 1940 to 1948; prime minister from 1945 to 1947; and labor minister in 1947 and 1948. He easily won the 1952 presidential election as the candidate for the *Auténtico* party. Prío Socarrás adhered to the 1940 constitution, at least initially, and his government pushed many reforms and improvements such as social security for agricultural workers, stabilizing rents, public works and highway construction, establishment of the national bank, and building the national library. But his administration also was plagued with nepotism and corruption and the sponsorship of gang violence, all of which contributed to the public's growing loss of confidence in Prío Socarrás. On March 10, 1952, three months before the scheduled presidential elections, Fulgencio Batista engineered a coup d'état. Prío Socarrás gained asylum in the Mexican embassy and shortly departed for that country. In 1953 he moved to Florida where he engaged in anti-Batista activities in violation of a 1939 U.S. neutrality law, for which he was briefly interned.

Prío Socarrás returned to Cuba under Batista's 1955 political amnesty but returned to Miami a year later when Batista charged him with conspiring to overthrow the government. Again, he conspired to bring down Batista, and again he served a short jail term in the United States. In July 1958, he joined Castro in Caracas, Venezuela, to form the "Junta of Unity" against the Batista regime. With Castro's triumph in 1959, Prío Socarrás returned to Cuba and vocalized his support for the new government. Eventually disillusioned with the direction of Castro's regime, Prío Socarrás returned to Miami where he remained until his suicide in 1977.

Rodríguez, Carlos Rafael (1913–1997)

Carlos Rafael Rodríguez was a Communist party leader, lawyer, and economist who became an important political figure in the Castro regime. Born on May 23, 1913, in Cienfuegos, Rodríguez earned his law degree from the University of Havana and thereafter served intermittently on the university faculty. As a student, he joined the active opposition against the Gerardo Machado administration and met with a small nucleus of communists. Following Machado's ouster in 1933, Rodríguez became mayor of Cienfuegos and until 1939 served as editor of two publications *Mediodía* and *Universidad*. In 1938 he joined the Cuban Socialist party, Cuba's pro-Soviet Communist party, and was elected to its central committee. In 1943 and 1944 he served as the Court Attorney for the city of Havana.

As Minister without Portfolio and a member of the National Committee for Post-War Studies during Fulgencio Batista's administration (1940–1944), he became interested in economics and wrote many articles on Marxist theory. He opposed Batista's subsequent brutal dictatorship (1952–1959) and in 1958 traveled to the Sierra Maestra Mountains to form an alliance between the old-line communists and Castro's 26th of July Movement. Rodríguez remained with the guerrillas for the rest of the war and formed a close alliance with Castro and his associates.

Immediately following Castro's victory in 1959, Rodríguez served as publisher of *Hoy*, helped to draw up government decrees, and became involved with university reforms. He subsequently supported Castro in the power struggle with the old-line communists. In 1962 he was appointed President of the National Institute of Agrarian Reform (INRA), and he became Minister a year later when INRA was upgraded to the ministry level. His policies of land confiscation and the establishment of state farms resulted in food shortages and prompted Castro to assume INRA's leadership in 1965, at which time Rodríguez was transferred to the Communist party's secretariat.

Beginning in 1970, Rodríguez's government role became more prominent. That year, he became President of the National Commission on Economic, Scientific and Technical Collaboration of the Council of Ministers. In 1971 he became vice president of the Council of Ministers. He later became a member of the political bureau of the secretariat of the Communist party, a member of the National Assembly of the People's government, and a vice president of both the Council of State and the Council of Ministers. He has served as Castro's principal liaison with the former Soviet Union and Eastern Bloc countries, negotiating Cuba's entry into the East European Common Market (COMECON). Even after his removal from his position in the Politiburo in a government reorganization in October 1997, Ro-dríguez continued to be considered one of the most important figures in the Cuban government until his death on December 8, 1997.

Urrutia Lleó, Manuel (1901–1981)

A lawyer and judge, Manuel Urrutia Lleó was appointed President of Cuba in January 1959. Born in 1901 in Yaguajay, Las Villas Province, Urru-tia graduated from the University of Havana Law School in 1923. In 1928 he was appointed municipal judge of Oriente Province and later magistrate for Santiago. He first gained national recognition in May 1957 when he pre-sided over the trial of one hundred of Castro's followers for their role in the 1953 attack on the military barracks at Moncada. Urrutia determined that the *Fidelistas* should be acquitted, a decision that brought him strong criti-cism and a judicial reprimand from the Batista government.

In December 1957 Urrutia went into exile in Miami as Fidel Castro's fa-vored candidate for the presidency once the civil war was over. Urrutia flew to Castro's stronghold in the Sierra Maestra in November 1958 to consult with the revolutionaries. In January 1959, following the triumph of the Revolution, Urrutia took over the presidency. Castro's decision to appoint him president was apparently based upon the assumption that he was ac-ceptable to both the moderate and radical factions of the revolutionary movement. Once in office, Urrutia appointed a civilian cabinet composed mainly of anti-Batista political figures who came from the middle and up-per sectors of society. He then proceeded to tear down Batista's governmen-tal structure. Through a series of decrees, he dissolved congress; removed from office all congressmen, provincial governors, mayors, and municipal councilmen; abolished all of Batista's censorship and martial law restric-tions; and initiated a widespread purge of Batista supporters in the bureauc-racy. Still, Urrutia showed little ability in the art of politics during this volatile period as he criticized openly the increasing communist influence in government. It soon became clear that real power resided in the person of Fidel Castro and his band of young rebel army officers. Castro publicly an-nounced major policy changes without consulting Urrutia's cabinet and complained about the slowness of reforms. In his speech of July 17, 1959, Fidel Castro accused Urrutia of posing an obstacle to the revolution and of fabricating the legend of a communist danger to Cuba. Urrutia resigned and was placed under house arrest before taking refuge in the Venezuelan em-bassy and subsequently going into exile. Castro replaced Urrutia with Os-valdo Dorticós as President of Cuba.

Eventually, Urrutia settled in the United States where he became a university professor and organizer of an anti-Castro movement. In 1964 he authored his own account of the Revolution in *Fidel Castro and Co., Inc.: Communist Tyranny in Cuba*. He died in New York City on July 5, 1981.

Primary Documents
of the Cuban Revolution

Considered the father of Cuban independence, José Martí's name was invoked by every twentieth-century Cuban *independentista*, including Fidel Castro. Among his many thoughts was the conviction that Spanish America differed sharply from the United States and that the United States never cared to understand the difference between the two. Martí remained cautious of the U.S. intentions in Latin America and feared that it would use its power to dominate any relationship. In the excerpt below, written after the 1888–1889 Pan American Conference in Washington, DC, Martí cautions his readers not to be awestruck by the advances found in the United States and advises the Latin Americans to steer clear of any alliance with it. The implication is clear to the Cubans, who are already dependent upon the U.S. economy.

Document 1
JOSÉ MARTÍ CAUTIONS AGAINST CLOSE TIES
TO THE UNITED STATES

A nation grows and influences other nations according to the elements composing it. The action of one country in alliance of countries will conform to its salient elements, and not differ from them. If a lush and fragrant pasture is made available to a hungry horse, the horse will rush in, bury itself in the grass up to the withers [ridge between the shoulders of a horse], and angrily nip at anyone who bothers it. . . .

To see ahead is one essential quality in the building and governing of nations. Governing is nothing more than foreseeing. Before joining another nation, it must be seen what harm or what benefit can accrue naturally out of the elements composing that nation.

It is not necessary merely to ascertain whether the nations are as great as they appear, and whether the same accumulation of power that dazzles the impatient and incapable has not come about at the cost of higher qualities, and by virtue of qualities which threaten those who admire that power. But rather, even when the greatness is genuine and profound, durable, just, useful, and cordial, it is quite possibly of another kind and the result of other methods that the greatness that can be aspired to unaided, and reached of its own accord through proper methods—the only viable ones—by a nation with a different concept of life and living in a different atmosphere and in a different way. When life is shared, ideas and customs must be shared. For those who must live together, it is not enough for their objectives in life to be the same, but their way of living as well. Either they fight or scorn each other, or they hate each other for their differences in manner as they did for those of their objectives. Countries without communal methods, even when their goals are identical, cannot unite to achieve their common purposes with identical means.

And he who knows and sees cannot honestly say—for this can be said only by the one who does not know or see or who because of his own interests is unwilling to know or see—that even in the United States of today there may be a prevalence of this most human and virile (although always egotistical and victorious) element of the rebellious colonists, who are sometimes the younger sons of the nobility and sometimes of the Puritan bourgeoisie. But this element—which consumed the native race, fomented and lived from the slavery of another race, and reduced or robbed the neighboring countries—has been sharpened instead of softened by the continuous grafting of the European hordes, a tyrannical breeding of political and religious despotism whose only common quality is the appetite accumulated by exercising over the rest the authority that was exercised over themselves. They believe in need, in the barbarous right as the only right: "This will be ours because we need it." They believe that the Spanish American nations are formed principally of Indians and Negroes. As long as the United States knows no more about Spanish America, and respects it no more, although with the numerous incessant, urgent, and wise explanations of our people and resources it could come to respect us—can this country invite Spanish America to an alliance that would be honest and useful to our Spanish American nations?

Whoever says economic union says political union. The nation that buys, commands. The nation that sells, serves. Commerce must be balanced to assure freedom. The nation eager to die sells to a single nation, and the one eager to save itself sells to more than one. A country's excessive influence over the commerce of another becomes political influence. Politics is the work of men who surrender their feelings to an interest. When a strong nation supplies another with food, the strong nation becomes useful to it. When a strong nation wants to engage another in battle, it demands allegiance and service from those nations dependent upon it. The first thing a nation does to gain dominion over another is to separate it from other nations. Let the country desiring freedom be free in business affairs. Let it distribute its commerce among countries as strong as itself. If it must prefer one, let it prefer the one that needs it least and scorns it least. Let there be no alliances against Europe, nor with Europe against an American nation. The geographical fact of living together in America does not oblige political union, except in the mind of some candidate or some college graduate. Business interests follow the slopes of land and water, and stay close on the heels of whoever can offer something in exchange, be it monarchy or republic. Union with the world, and not with a part of it; not with one part against another. If the family of American republics has one mission in life, it is not that of having one of them ride roughshod over future republics.

Source: José Martí, "The Monetary Congress of the American Republics," in Philip S. Foner, ed., *Inside the Monster* (New York: Monthly Review Press, 1975), 371–73.

> The Platt Amendment was an annex to the 1902 Cuban constitution that granted the United States extensive influence in the country, essentially establishing it as a U.S. protectorate. At the end of the Spanish-American War in 1898, the U.S. Army administered Cuba until the adoption of a self-governing constitution. U.S. authorities, however, were not pleased with the failure of the Cuban elite to win local elections prior to independence, prompting a fear that U.S. national interests would be threatened if the non-elites directed an independent Cuba. Furthermore, within the policy parameters that dated to the Monroe Doctrine in 1823, the United States wanted to maintain its influence on the island and secure it from European advances. Toward that end, Secretary of War Elihu Root persuaded Senator Orville Platt to attach an amendment to the 1901 Army appropriations bill. The Cubans reluctantly added the Platt Amendment to their 1902 constitution and incorporated it into a 1903 treaty with the United States. Significantly, until its abrogation in 1934, the amendment limited Cuba's economic and political foreign policies and granted the United States the right to intervene in times of political turmoil. The Platt Amendment became a major target of Cuban nationalists, who viewed U.S. intervention in Cuba's political affairs as imperialist actions de-

signed not only to protect U.S. interests but also continually to secure the position of the Cuban upper class.

Document 2
THE PLATT AMENDMENT

I.

That the government of Cuba shall never enter into any treaty or other compact with any foreign power or powers which will impair or tend to impair the independence of Cuba, nor in any manner authorize or permit any foreign power or powers to obtain by colonization or for military or naval purposes or otherwise, lodgment in or control over any portion of said island.

II.

That said government shall not assume or contract any public debt, to pay the interest upon which, and to make reasonable sinking fund provision for the ultimate discharge of which, the ordinary revenues of the island, after defraying the current expenses of government shall be inadequate.

III.

That the government of Cuba consents that the United States may exercise the right to intervene for the preservation of Cuban independence, the maintenance of a government adequate for the protection of life, property, and individual liberty, and for discharging the obligations with respect to Cuba imposed by the treaty of Paris on the United States, now to be assumed and undertaken by the government of Cuba.

IV.

That all Acts of the United States in Cuba during its military occupancy thereof are ratified and validated, and all lawful rights acquired thereunder shall be maintained and protected.

V.

That the government of Cuba will execute, and as far as necessary extend, the plans already devised or other plans to be mutually agreed upon, for the sanitation of the cities of the island, to the end that a recurrence of epidemic and infectious diseases may be prevented, thereby assuring protection to the people and commerce of Cuba, as well as to the commerce of the southern ports of the United States and the people residing therein.

VI.

That the Isle of Pines shall be omitted from the proposed constitutional boundaries of Cuba, the title thereto being left to future adjustment by treaty.

VII.

That to enable the United States to maintain the independence of Cuba, and to protect the people thereof, as well as for its own defense, the government of Cuba will sell or lease to the United States lands necessary for coaling or naval stations at certain specified points, to be agreed upon with the President of the United States.

VIII.

That by way of further assurance the government of Cuba will embody the foregoing provisions in a permanent treaty with the United States.

Source: The Platt Amendment, U.S., 56th Congress, Second Session, Chapter 3, 1901, 31 United States Statutes at Large, 897–98.

The protests that followed Fulgencio Batista's carefully orchestrated coup d'etat on March 10,1952, had little impact on the course of Cuban history, except one: the July 26, 1953, attack, led by Fidel Castro, upon the Cuban army barracks at Moncada in Santiago. The attack was a resounding failure and resulted in the death of all but a few of Castro's 165 followers. The remainder were jailed. Castro survived the attack, only to be tried separate from his comrades and in secret. Castro conducted his own defense and his closing statement provided a lengthy criticism of Cuba's corrupt political and legal systems, and a discourse on the wretched socio-economic conditions of the island's poor. A portion of Castro's speech called for revolutionary social change, and it serves as a guideline for his future programs.

Document 3
HISTORY WILL ABSOLVE ME

A revolutionary government with the support of the people and the respect of the nation, once it cleans out all venal and corrupt officeholders, would proceed immediately to industrialize the country, mobilizing all inactive capital (currently over 1,500 million dollars) through the National Bank and the Bank for Industrial and Agricultural Development, submitting that giant task to the study, organization, planning, and final realization by technicians and men of absolute capability, free from political meddling.

A revolutionary government, after making the 100,000 small farmers owners of the land for which they now pay rent, would proceed to end the land problem once and for all. This would be done first by establishing, as the Constitution orders, a limit to the amount of land a person may own for each type of agricultural undertaking, acquiring any excess by expropriation; by recovering the lands usurped from the state; by improving the swamplands; by setting aside zones for tree nurseries and reforestation. Second, it would be done by distributing the rest of the land available among rural families, preferably to those large in number; by promoting cooperatives of farmers for the common use of costly farm equipment, cold storage, and technical-professional guidance in the cultivation of crops and the breeding of livestock. Finally, it would be done by making available all resources, equipment, protection, and know-how to the farmers.

A revolutionary government would solve the problem of housing by lowering rent 50 percent, by giving tax exemption to houses inhabited by their owners; by tripling the taxes on houses built to rent; by substituting the ghastly one-room flats with modern multistory buildings; and by financing housing projects all over the island on a scale never before seen, which would be based on the criterion that if in the rural area the ideal is for each family to own its parcel of land, then in the city the ideal is for each family to own its house or apartment. There are enough bricks and more than enough manpower to build a decent house for each Cuban family. But if we continue waiting for the miracle of the golden calf, a thousand years will pass and the problem will still be the same. On the other hand, the possibility of extending electrical power to the farthest corner of the Republic is today better than ever before because today nuclear energy applied to that branch of industry, lowering production costs, is already a reality.

With these three initiatives and reforms, the problem of unemployment would disappear dramatically, and sanitation service and the struggle against disease and sickness would be a much easier task.

Finally, a revolutionary government would proceed to undertake the complete reform of the educational system, placing it at the same level as the foregoing projects, in order to prepare adequately the future generations who will live in a happier fatherland.

Source: Fidel Castro, *History Will Absolve Me* (New York: Fair Play for Cuba Committee, 1961), 41–42.

The debate over the responsibility for the failed Bay of Pigs invasion of Cuba in April 1961 has not abated since the event. In February 1998 the Washington, D.C.-based National Security Archive, a privately funded agency that seeks the release of important government documents through the Freedom of Information Act, secured the release of the lone remaining copy of the *Inspector General's Survey of the Cuban Operation and Associated Documents* (the Inspector General responsible for the report was Lyman Kirkpatrick). Although its existence—and the fact that it was critical of the CIA—had been long known, the document was not available until recently. Only twenty copies were made; nineteen were recalled and destroyed. The only remaining one was said to have been kept locked in a safe of the CIA director. Presented here is a summary of the report's conclusions.

Document 4
CENTRAL INTELLIGENCE AGENCY ANALYZES THE FAILURE OF THE BAY OF PIGS INVASION, APRIL 1961

1. The Central Intelligence Agency, after starting to build up the resistance and guerilla forces inside Cuba, drastically converted the project into what rapidly became an overt military operation. The Agency failed to recognize that when the project advanced beyond the stage of plausible denial it was going beyond the area of Agency responsibility as well as Agency capability.

2. The Agency became so wrapped up in the military operation that it failed to appraise the chances of success realistically. Furthermore, it failed to keep the national policy-makers adequately and realistically informed of the conditions and considered essential for success, and it did not press sufficiently for prompt policy decisions in a fast moving situation.

3. As the project grew, the Agency reduced the exiled leaders to the status of puppets, thereby losing the advantages of their active participation.

4. The Agency failed to build up and supply a resistance organization under rather favorable conditions. Air and boat operations showed up poorly.

5. The Agency failed to collect adequate information on the strengths of the Castro regime and the extent of the opposition to it; and it failed to evaluate the available information correctly.

6. The project was badly organized. Command lines and management controls were ineffective and unclear. Senior Staffs of the Agency were not utilized; air support stayed independent of the project; the role of the large forward base was not clear.

7. The project was not staffed throughout with top-quality people, and a number of people were not used to the best advantage.

8. The Agency entered the project without adequate assets in the way of boats, bases, training facilities, agent nets, Spanish-speakers, and similar

essential ingredients of a successful operation. Had these already been in being, much time and effort would have been saved.

9. Agency policies and operational plans were never clearly delineated, with the exception of the plan for the brigade landing; but even this provided no disaster plan, no unconventional war annex, and only extremely vague plans for action following a successful landing. In general, Agency plans and policies did not precede the various operations in the project but were drawn up in response to operation needs as they arose. Consequently, the scope of the operation itself and of the support required was constantly shifting.

Source: National Security Archive, The Gelman Library, George Washington University, Washington, D.C. *Inspector General's Survey of the CUBAN OPERATION, October, 1961* (Copy 1 of 20), 143–45.

> Speaking before an estimated 1 million people in Havana's Revolutionary Plaza on February 4, 1962, Fidel Castro called for Latin American revolutionaries to rise up against the hemisphere's oligarchical governments, all of which, Castro insisted, were supported by the United States. It signaled his fundamental foreign policy goal for the early 1960s: to turn the Andes into Latin America's own Sierra Maestra. Significantly, the declaration came one day after the United States imposed its economic embargo on Cuba and one month after the United States had engineered Cuba's expulsion from the Organization of American States.

Document 5
SECOND DECLARATION OF HAVANA

In 1895 Martí had already pointed out the danger hovering over the Americans and called imperialism by its name: imperialism. He pointed out to the people of Latin America that more than anyone, they had a stake in seeing to it that Cuba did not succumb to the greed of the Yankees. . . . But Cuba rose up. Cuba was able to redeem itself from the bastard tutelage. Cuba broke the chains that tied its fortunes to those of the imperial oppressor, redeemed its riches, reclaimed its culture. . . . The history of Cuba is but the history of Latin America.

To the accusation that Cuba wants to export its revolution, we reply: Revolutions are not exported, they are made by the people. . . . What Cuba can give to the peoples, and has already given, is its example. . . . And what does the Cuban revolution teach? That revolution is possible, that the people can make it, that in the contemporary world there are no forces capable of halting the liberation movement of the peoples. . . . Our triumph would never had been feasible if the revolution itself had not been inexorably destined to arise out of existing conditions in our socioeconomic reality, a reality that exists to an even greater degree in a good number of Latin American countries. . . .

It inevitably occurs that in the nations where the control of the Yankee monopolies is strongest, the exploitation of the oligarchy cruelest, and the situation of the laboring and peasant masses almost unbearable, the political power appears most solid. The state of siege becomes habitual, every manifestation of discontent by the masses is repressed by force. The democratic path is closed completely. The brutal character of dictatorship, the form of rule adopted by the ruling classes, reveals itself more clearly than ever. It is then that the revolutionary explosion of the peoples becomes inevitable. . . .

The duty of every revolutionist is to make the revolution. It is known that the revolution will triumph in the Americas and throughout the world, but it is not for revolutionists to sit in the doorways of their houses waiting for the corpse of imperialism to pass by. The role of Job does not suit a revolutionist. Each year that the liberation of Latin America is speeded up will mean the lives of millions of children saved, millions of intellects saved for culture, an infinite quantity of pain spared the people. Even if the Yankee imperialists prepare a bloody drama for Latin America, they will not succeed in crushing the people's struggles; they will only arouse universal hatred against themselves. And such a drama will also mark the death of their greedy and carnivorous system. . . .

No nation in Latin American is weak—because each forms part of a family of 200 million brothers, who suffer the same miseries, who harbor the same sentiments, who have the same enemy, who dream about the same better future and who count upon the solidarity of all honest men and women throughout the world. . . .

Great as was the epic of Latin American independence, heroic as was that struggle, today's generation of Latin Americans is called upon to engage in an epic that is even greater and more decisive for humanity. For that struggle was for liberation from Spanish colonial power, from a decadent Spain invaded by the armies of Napoleon. Today the call for struggle is for liberation from the most powerful world imperialist center, from the strongest force of world imperialism and to render humanity a greater service than that rendered by our predecessors. . . .

But this struggle, to a greater extent than the earlier one, will be waged by the masses, will be carried out by the people: the people are going to play a much more important role now than they did then, the leaders are less important and will be less important in this struggle than in the one before. . . .

This epic before us is going to be written by the hungry Indian masses, the peasants without land, the exploited workers. It is going to be written by the progressive masses, the honest and brilliant intellectuals, who so greatly abound in our suffering Latin American lands. A struggle of masses and of ideas. An epic that will be carried forward by our peoples, mistreated and scorned by imperialism; our people, unreckoned with until today, who are now beginning to shake off their slumber. Imperialism considered us a weak and submissive flock; and now it begins to be terrified of that flock; a gigantic flock of 200 million Latin Americans in whom Yankee monopoly capitalism now sees its gravediggers.

Source: Fidel Castro, *Declaracion de la Habana* (Havana: n.p., n.d.), 1, 28–29, 31–32 (translation by Thomas M. Leonard).

> At the beginning of the Revolution, Fidel Castro sought to end Cuba's economic dependence upon sugar and to develop an economy completely self-sufficient in food production and essential consumer goods. His vision prompted the Cuban Central Planning Board optimistically to anticipate economic growth at 10–15 percent annually from 1962 to 1965. The plan failed. In explaining the failure, Che Guevara placed responsibility upon the U.S. embargo, an assertion that remained a constant factor in Cuban foreign policy and domestic political thought ever since. To correct the economic backsliding, Guevara suggested the resurrection of an export-based economy, predicated upon the traditional products of sugar, nickel, and cattle in order to obtain the hard currencies needed to purchase heavy machinery in the world marketplace.

Document 6
CHE GUEVARA ON THE CUBAN ECONOMY, 1964

So far the industrial development achieved can be described as satisfactory, if we take into account the problems caused by the North American blockade and the radical changes which have occurred in only three years as regards our foreign sources of supply. Last year our sugar production fell from 4.8 million metric tons to 3.8 million, but this was offset by an increase, in general terms, of 6 percent in the rest of industry. This year, 1964, given the greater strength of our internal productive organization and our greater experience in commercial relations with our new sources of supply, the industrial advance should be still greater.

The transformations so far made in the Cuban economy have produced great changes in the structure of our foreign trade. As regards exports the changes have been limited chiefly to the opening up of new markets, with sugar continuing to be the main export article. On the other hand, the composition of our imports has changed completely during these five years. Imports of consumer goods, particularly durables, have decreased substantially in favor of capital equipment, while a small decrease can be noted in the imports of intermediate goods. The policy of substitution of imports is showing slow but tangible results.

The economic policy of the Revolution having attained a certain integral strength, it is clear that imports of durable consumer goods will once more increase, to satisfy the growing needs of modern life. The plans being made for the future provide for both an absolute and a relative increase in the importation of these articles, taking into account the social changes which have occurred. It will be unnecessary, for example, to import Cadillacs and other luxury cars, which in former years were paid for to a great extent with the profits derived from the labor of the Cuban sugar worker.

This is only one aspect of the problems which are at present being studied. The policy we shall follow in years to come will largely depend on the flexibility of our foreign trade, and on the extent to which it will permit us to take full advantage of opportunities which may present themselves. We expect the Cuban economy to develop along three principle [*sic*] lines between now and 1970.

Sugar will continue to be our main earner of foreign exchange. Future development implies an increase of 50 percent in present productive capacity. Simultaneously a qualitative advance will take place in the sugar sector, consisting of a substantial increase in the yield per unit of land under cultivation, and an improvement in technology and equipment. That improvement will tend to make up for the ground lost through inefficiency during the last ten to fifteen years. During that period the complete lack of expansion of our market led to technological stagnation. With the new possibilities which have opened up in the socialist countries, the panorama is changing rapidly.

One of the main bases for the development of our sugar industry, as well as for the development of the country as a whole, is the agreement recently signed between the U.S.S.R. and Cuba. This guarantees to us future sales of enormous quantities of sugar at prices much above the average of those paid in the North American and world markets during the last twenty years. Apart from this and other favorable economic implications, the agreement signed with the U.S.S.R. is of political importance inasmuch as it provides an example of the relationship that can exist between an underdeveloped and a developed country when both belong to the socialist camp, in contrast to the commercial relations between the underdeveloped countries exporting raw materials and the industrialized capitalist countries—in which the permanent tendency is to make the balance of trade unfavorable to the poor nations.

The second line of industrial development will be nickel. The deposits in northeastern Cuba offer great possibilities for making this part of the island the future center of the metallurgical industry. The capacity of the nickel-smelting works will be increased, making Cuba the second or third largest producer in the world of this strategic metal.

The third line of this future development will be the cattle industry. The large number of cattle, great indeed in proportion to the size of the population, offers rich possibilities for the future. We estimate that within about ten years our cattle industry will be equalled in importance only by the sugar industry.

As I have indicated, the role played by foreign trade in the Cuban economy will continue to be of basic importance, but there will be a qualitative change in its future development. None of the three principal lines of development will imply any effort to substitute imports, with the exception of the cattle industry, during the first years. After these first years the character of our new economic development will be fully reflected in our exports, and although the policy of substitution of imports will not be abandoned, it will be balanced by exports. For the decade following 1970 we are planning a more accelerated process of substitution of imports. This can only be achieved on the basis of an industrialization program of great scope. We shall create the necessary conditions for such a program, making full use of the opportunities offered to an underdeveloped economy by our external trade.

Has the indisputable political importance in the world achieved by Cuba an economic counterpart? If so, should that importance lead to the contemplation of more serious economic relations with other countries, materializing in trade? In such an event, how would we build up this trade which has been greatly reduced due to the North American blockade.

In considering these questions I leave aside reasons of a utilitarian nature which might lead me to make an apology for international trade, for it is evident that Cuba is interested in an active, regular, and sustained interchange of trade with all countries of the world. What I am trying to do is to present an exact picture of the present situation. The North American government is obsessed by Cuba, and not only because of its abnormal colonialist mentality. There is something more. Cuba represents, in the first place, a clear example of the failure of the North American policy of aggression on the very doorstep of the continent. Further, Cuba provides an example for future socialist countries of Latin America and so an unmistakable warning of the inevitable reduction of the field of action of U.S. finance capital.

North American imperialism is weaker than it seems; it is a giant with feet of clay. Although its present potentialities are not seriously affected by violent internal class struggles leading to the destruction of the capitalist system, as foreseen by Marx, those potentialities are fundamentally based on a monopolistic, extraterritorial power exercised by means of an unequal interchange of goods and by the political subjection of extensive territories. On these fall the full weight of the contradictions.

As the dependent countries of America and other regions of the world cast off the monopolistic chains, and establish more equitable systems and more just relations with all the countries of the world, the heavy contributions made by them to the living standard of the imperialist powers will cease, and of all the capitalistic countries the United States will then be the most seriously affected. This will not be the only outcome of an historical process; displaced finance capital will be forced to seek new horizons to make good its losses and, in this struggle, the most wounded, the most powerful, and the most aggressive of all the capitalist powers, the United States, will employ her full strength in a ruthless competition with the others, adopting, perhaps, unexpected methods of violence in her dealings with her "allies" of today.

Thus the existence of Cuba represents not only the hope of a better future for the peoples of America but also the prospect of a dangerous future for the seemingly unshakable monopolistic structure of the United States. The North American attempt to strangle Cuba implies a desire to stop history; but if, in spite of all kinds of aggression, the Cuba state remains safe, its economy becoming increasingly strong and its foreign trade more important, then the failure of this policy will be complete and the move toward peaceful coexistence will become more rapid.

Source: Ernesto Guevara, "The Cuban Economy," in Rolando E. Bonachea and Nelson P. Valdes, eds., *Che* (Cambridge: The MIT Press, 1969), 144–47.

In the years after 1965, Fidel Castro and his economic advisors recognized the need to export increasing amounts of sugar in order to earn the foreign capital necessary to pay its trade debt with the Soviet Union and to import the machinery necessary for industrial development. This need turned into a national crusade for the harvesting of a ten-million ton sugar crop in 1970. In so doing, all other aspects of the economy were ignored. Still, the ten-million ton harvest was not realized. In his annual message commemorating the Revolution, on July 26, 1970, Castro admitted the government's failure to incorporate the input from the people. His speech to the Federation of Cuban Women (FMC) on August 23, 1970, excerpted here, is indicative of appeals made to trade unions, professional associations, and other organizations for their recommitment to and participation in the revolutionary process.

Document 7
FIDEL CASTRO'S SELF CRITICISM, 1970: SPEECH TO THE FEDERATION OF CUBA WOMEN

At the beginning, the vanguard was minority; the conscious revolutionaries were minority. However, as a result of the revolution, as a result of that flame that caught hold in the hearts and minds of our people, as a result of the struggle, the vanguard is no longer a minority. We now have a people in which the revolutionary feelings and ideas have taken deep root. We no longer have to look at things from the standpoint that it is a minority that will do the job of developing awareness. No! We must also see it from the standpoint that a minority, charged with specific tasks and functions, must get its awareness from the people. [*Applause*] It is no longer a question of our developing other people ideologically, but of our own ideological development, as well. It is no longer a question of helping the people develop their awareness, but of having the people help us develop ours.

It is an unquestionable fact that our people have made great strides forward in revolutionary awareness, in their sense of equality; and it is also an unquestionable fact that we are living in a period of arduous work—one which, objectively, we must make sacrifices. And under such circumstances, there is no room for theoretical disquisitions. We must be realists, realists. And the moral principle we should embrace—above all, the revolutionary vanguard, those in posts of responsibility, should be to make even more sacrifices than those we ask of the people. . . . And nobody should be surprised if any manifestation of privilege taking should arouse the most profound indignation among the masses. This is only logical.

These are matters that have to do with the tasks and duties of revolutionaries and of all those in posts of responsibility. These are essential, fundamental matters. . . . And, to the extent that we assimilate this thoroughly and correctly, we will be establishing the best, the optimal conditions for winning the battles that lie ahead of us, for overcoming the obstacles that lie ahead. . . .

This revolution is able to count on a magnificent people of which we should be more than proud, more than satisfied. Now we must know how to be worthy of this people. We must also know how to develop and carry our mass organizations forward to the utmost limits of their infinite possibilities.

This will be one of the duties and one of the basic tasks facing our party, as well as to give the people ever greater participation in the solution of their own problems. The time has come to take qualitative strides forward in the functioning of the process.

Source: Granma, August 24, 1970, pp. 3–4 (translation by Thomas M. Leonard).

Beginning in the early 1970s, Fidel Castro embarked on a foreign policy that relied less on aiding armed struggles in Latin America and more on diplomacy in international organizations. Within the Nonaligned Movement he found ample opportunity to identify with its members' anticolonial crusade. Throughout the decade, Castro relied upon a combination of military civilian assistance programs and diplomacy to enhance his image among his newly found colleagues. The high-water mark came in 1979 when Havana hosted the Movement's sixth summit conference and Castro was selected to lead the organization for the next four years. The ascendancy was short-lived. In December 1979, the Soviet Union invaded Afghanistan, a member state of the Non-aligned Movement. In the months that followed, Cuba unsuccessfully tried to balance its commitment to both the Soviets and the Move-ment, but in the end lost its standing among its Third World colleagues. In the excerpt presented here, taken from his 1979 Havana keynote address, Castro proudly points to Cuba's international status at the time.

Document 8
KEYNOTE ADDRESS
NONALIGNED MOVEMENT SUMMIT CONFERENCE
HAVANA SEPTEMBER 1979

Ninety-four states and liberation movements are represented here as full members of this Sixth Summit Conference. This summit conference is, therefore, the one aligned with the largest attendance and with the greatest number of Nonaligned and national liberation movement leaders ever held. This is not something for which our modest country should take credit; rather it is an unmistakable sign of the vigor, strength, and prestige of the Movement of Nonaligned Countries.

In our international relations, we express solidarity with deeds, not fine words. Cuban technicians are now working in twenty-three countries that be-long to our movement. In the vast majority of these countries, because of their economic limitations, this cooperation is provided without charge, in spite of our own difficulties. Right now, Cuba has twice as many doctors serving abroad as does the UN World Health Organization. . . .

Noble, self-sacrificing Cubans have died thousands of miles from home while supporting liberation movements, defending other people's just causes, and fighting against the expansion of North American racists as well as other forms of imperialistic attack on human dignity and the integrity and independence of other nations. They express the purity, selflessness, solidarity, and internationalist consciousness that the revolution has forged among our people. . . .

That we maintain fraternal relations with the Soviet Union and the rest of the socialist community? Yes, we are friends of the Soviet Union. We are very thankful to the Soviet people, because their generous cooperation helped us to survive and overcome the very difficult and decisive periods in our people's life, when we were even in danger of being wiped out. We are grateful to the glorious October revolution because it ushered in a new era in human history, made it possible to defeat fascism, and created a world situation in which the peoples' self-sacrificing struggle led to the downfall of the hateful colonial system. To ignore that is to ignore history itself.

Not only Cuba but also Vietnam; the Arab countries under attack; the peoples in the former Portuguese colonies; the revolutionary processes in many other counties throughout the world; and the liberation movements that fight against oppression, racism, Zionism, and fascism in South Africa, Namibia, Zimbabwe, Palestine, and elsewhere owe a great debt of gratitude to socialist solidarity. I wonder whether the United States or any other NATO country has ever helped a single liberation movement anywhere in the world.

We are firmly anti-imperialist, anticolonial, antineocolonial, antiracist, anti-Zionist, and antifascist because these principles are part of our thinking, they constitute the essence and origin of the Movement of Nonaligned Countries and have formed its life and history ever since its founding. These principles are also very fresh in the life of the peoples we represent here.

Was any country that now belongs to our movement really independent more than thirty-five years ago? Is there any member that hasn't known colonialism, neocolonialism, fascism, racial discrimination, or imperialist aggression; economic dependence; poverty squalor; illiteracy; and the most brutal exploitation of its natural and human resources? What country doesn't bear the burden of the technological gap a lower standard of living than the former metropolises, unequal terms of trade, the economic crisis, inflation, and underdevelopment imposed on our peoples by centuries of colonial exploitation and imperialistic domination?

Cuba will be in the front line defending these principles, independence, and the unique, prestigious, fraternal, and ever more constructive and influential role of the Nonaligned movement in international life, so that the energetic and rightful voice of our peoples may be heard.

Source: Granma Weekly Review, September 9, 1979, p. 1.

> Beginning in 1986, the Communist Party of Cuba initiated a program to incorporate new and younger persons into the party's decision-making process. The hope was to create a more working-class leadership that closely resembled Cuban society and one more capable of leading the revolutionary process into the future. Within two years, however, the winds of political change that began to sweep across the Soviet Union and eastern Europe in 1988 and 1989 brought much concern to Fidel Castro. In late 1988 and into early 1989, Castro exhorted his people not to be persuaded by those changes. He clearly indicated that Cuba would remain committed to the socialist path and criticized those countries for not doing the same. In the excerpt from a speech on January 8, 1989, Castro proudly pointed to revolutionary Cuba's accomplishments of the preceding thirty years. The date is significant because three months hence, in April 1989, Soviet Premier Mikhail Gorbachev visited Havana and indicated that changes would be forthcoming in Soviet-Cuban relations.

Document 9
THIRTY YEARS OF THE CUBAN REVOLUTION

I'm not going to make a long and tedious recounting here of the revolution's deeds, works, and successes. . . . Perhaps a few things ought to be mentioned here in general terms for our foreign guests concerning the colossal efforts made by our country and some of the results achieved.

I'll begin by mentioning what our enemies mention first, namely, education and public health, because our enemies say that we have had colossal successes in education and in health. . . .

Today, illiteracy has technically—I say technically—been cut to 1.5 percent, that is, it involves people who because of old age or some other problems could not be taught to read and write in any way. Therefore, we can say that illiteracy has been reduced to zero.

Today the opportunity to study extends to 100 percent of the country's children—nationwide—both in the cities and the countryside. . . .

There are hundreds of technical schools turning out skilled workers in the country. There are around 100,000 regular university students and more than 200,000 if we consider those who study by alternate means such as workers' guided studies, nurses getting their degrees, primary school teachers getting their primary education degrees, and so on, making a total of 200,000 university students, although many of these are already working. In other words, they will not be future university graduates looking for jobs, but instead they are studying something relating to the jobs they already have. . . .

In the field of health I can say, for instance, that the infant mortality rate, which in 1987 had been lowered to 13.3 per 1,000 live births in the first year of life, this year, when we hoped to bring it below 13, we managed to take it to less than 12, so that our infant mortality rate for 1988 came to 11.9. This places us—and this rate has been sustained—among the twenty countries with the lowest infant mortality rates in the world, and even below the rates of many industrially developed countries. I think this has truly been an extraordinary accomplishment. . . .

One interesting statistic concerns tuberculosis. The 1988 rate was 5.9 per 100,000 people, which places Cuba below Canada and the United States. This is saying a lot—Cuba's tuberculosis rate is below those of Canada and the United States.

Plenty could be said about all this, but it would take too long—what is being done, for instance, with German measles, tetanus, and other diseases that have practically disappeared. So our society is getting rid of a series of diseases, which can be done only through a truly sound medical network.

A novel institution, that of the family doctor, was introduced here. We already have more than 6,000 doctors engaged in this type of practice, and in a few years we'll have 20,000 family doctors. The doctors are now starting to be placed in factories, schools, and day-care centers, so we'll have a truly extraordinary medical network. . . .

We're developing new fields in medicine. Our country is already doing heart transplants and for a long time it has been doing kidney transplants. We are also beginning to do nerve transplants; we now have a center engaged in developing that activity with rather good prospects. We're also doing ocular microsurgery and are advancing considerably in a series of fields that are part of what we might call sophisticated medicine.

In the social sphere, there's practically no unemployment in our country. Statistically speaking, we do have some unemployed people, which is not because of lack of jobs, because we still have a shortage of labor power in many places—in agriculture, in the mountains, in reforestation, in construction. Rather it has to do with the preference of some young people for certain kinds of work. But that doesn't mean that there are no jobs available for every young man or woman, independent of the fact that it can't always be the type of job that perhaps they prefer.

Social security covers all the workers in the country, 100 percent. And, of course, one of the most sacred obligations of the state relates to pensions, retirement, and all the other social security benefits extended to families in need of them. . . .

How could the social accomplishments achieved by our country have come about without economic development? And this in spite of the fact that we must develop our country under very difficult conditions, because for the past thirty years we have had to contend with the imperialist blockade of our country. What other countries are subject to that type of blockade? Very few. With a zealous hatred, the empire forbids even the export of medical equipment to Cuba, not even medicines. Not even an aspirin can be brought to Cuba from the United States. It's a merciless blockade to which very few socialist countries are subject. I believe it's only the People's Republic of Korea, Vietnam, and Cuba. And with Cuba it's a fierce blockade, for the imperialists exert pressure on their allies everywhere not to trade with Cuba, not to deal grant loans to Cuba, not to transfer technology to Cuba.

Nevertheless, our country's economy has grown during these thirty years at a rate higher than 4 percent a year under the conditions of the blockade. I can give you some figures.

To give you one example, our electrical generating capacity has grown more than eightfold during these thirty years, eightfold! Steel production, which was very low in our country, has grown more than sixteenfold. Cement production has grown fivefold; we used to produce 700,000 tons whereas today we produce more than 3.5 million tons. Our production capacity is even greater, but in certain years the industry didn't get the right kind of maintenance. We're now trying to increase cement production until we reach not less than 4.6 million tons, in line with our economic and social development plans.

Production of fertilizers has grown fivefold. Citrus fruit production has grown seventeenfold. Egg production has grown eightfold, and so on with many other products. Nickel production has doubled and keeps growing. The machine industry is young in our country and is now developing rapidly. More than 6,000 cane harvesters have been manufactured, just to give one example of machine industry production output. To a greater or lesser extent, all our agricultural and industrial production has increased. Our textile industry is another example. Growth has been sustained in all the branches of our economy, in some more and in others less.

The fishing industry, an important source of food, has grown tenfold over these years of the revolution. And it would have grown much more if it hadn't been for an international measure that we supported because it was just, although it didn't benefit us. I'm referring to the 200–mile economic zone. If it hadn't been for this measure that we, as a Third World country, supported, we would have increased our fishing production twenty-five or thirty times over, because we already had a relatively large fishing fleet and the trained personnel for ocean fishing.

Source: Granma, January 11, 1989, pp. 3–5 (translation by Thomas M. Leonard).

> With the collapse of the Soviet Union and Eastern Europe, Cuba lost its primary trading partners. Its economy slumped badly and resulted in a "Special Period," one of further deprivation and sacrifice by the Cuban people. In the passage presented here, Fidel Castro reflects upon the thirty years of his Revolution, its general accomplishments, and the crisis at hand. He repeats the oft stated concept that the U.S. trade embargo is responsible for Cuba's economic plight, and clearly indicates that Cuba will remain committed to the socialist cause.

Document 10
REVOLUTIONARY IDEAS ARE NOT OBSOLETE

We have worked for 30 years at the task of defending a revolution which will soon be 32 years old. We have come through difficult times: those of the first few years, of the struggles against bandits in the Escambray Mountains and the Bay of Pigs invasion. Then later came the Missile Crisis, which will also have its anniversary in a few days and of which there has been a lot of talk lately. For two or three days I have been reading international wire dispatches reporting the excerpts of a supposed autobiography or notes by Khrushchev being published in the United States. It is claimed that I had advised Khrushchev to make a preemptive nuclear attack on the United States.

Perhaps Khrushchev interpreted, or could have interpreted, some of my messages in that way, but it really wasn't like that. I'm not going to explain now, but fortunately I still have the messages I exchanged with Khrushchev during the most difficult hours of the crisis and on subsequent days. I still have them because I thought that one day they wuld be interesting as historical documents. But since lately so many indiscretions have been committed and so many papers have been published on this matter, perhaps I'll find it necessary to publish those messages now, so that people will know what was said and to make clear what my viewpoints were on this matter at the heart of the Missile Crisis. I want today's generation to understand what Cuba's position was at that moment.

This may disturb the US government, which is always looking for ways to create hatred and animosity towards Cuba among the US public. I repeat, things are not as they say. The positions which I held then are those that I hold now, and what I said then I would say now in just the same way. I do not regret one word of what I said or one bit of what I did. Nevertheless, in the midst of all this gossip and scandalmongering, it's a good idea to make public some of these documents. Look how the Missile Crisis is still in the news, that period our people lived through, an extremely difficult period which we confronted calmly and level-headed.

Since then we have lived through all kinds of threats in these years. We have carried out extraordinary internationalist missions which will remain eternally in the history of our people's spirit of revolutionary solidarity. . . .

At certain moments some have called us a satellite, some have even believed that we take orders from outside the country—many times they wanted to humiliate us with such offensive assertions. But solidarity is a principle, to be brothers and sisters in revolution is a principle; it has been, it is, and it always will be. As for those who think that we were once satellites, I hope that they realize beyond the remotest shadow of a doubt that we never were, nor are we now, nor will we ever be, anybody's satellite.

We have to say that we made this revolution on our own—nobody made it for us, nobody defended it for us, nobody saved it for us. We made it ourselves, we defended it ourselves, we saved it ourselves, and we will continue to defend and save it as many times as necessary.

However, as we have said many times, it was a privilege, a stroke of good fortune, and extraordinary fact for our country, for our revolution, that the October Revolution took place. The thousand times glorious October Revolution!

In these days when some people want to smash statues of Lenin into pieces, we feel the figure of Lenin growing in our hearts and our thoughts.

Lenin and his ideas have meant so much to us and still mean a lot to us, we who have interpreted his ideas and those of Marx as they should be interpreted: in an original manner, unique to each country, to each revolutionary process. These ideas retain their validity in our revolutionary process, at a time when some are frightened to call themselves communists.

Lenin's work has endured throughout history and has helped to change the world. Lenin's work meant the emergence of the first socialist state in human history, and this state saved humanity from fascism. Without the blood shed by the Soviet people, fascism would have been imposed on the world, at least for a period of time, and all humanity would have known intimately the horrors of fascism. The first socialist state meant an advance for the peoples' liberation movements and the end of colonialism, and it meant so much to us when they imperialists wanted to destroy our revolution, when they blockaded us and tried to starve us out. . . .

It's shameful to see the extremes to which the imperialists have gone, asking the Soviet Union to please help them destroy the Cuban revolution. They ask the Soviet Union to join their blockade against Cuba. The blockade—which determined in part the close relations between the socialist camp and Cuba and the Soviet Union and Cuba—still exists against our country and is more rigorous and merciless than ever. And now the United States which has not been able to defeat us is asking the Soviet Union to join the US blockade against Cuba. . . .

What are we trying to do and what are we actually doing given the situation? We say that if we confront a special period in peacetime, a tough special period, our task must not only be one of survival but also of development. First, it would be a period of adapting ourselves to the situation, maintaining the country's basic development programs, the essential things such as the food program. . . .

The second program is biotechnology, the pharmaceutical industry and research centers, because these offer a world of resources to our country—a whole world! If we only had enough cement and steel cables for that and only enough resources for that, we would use them, because except for the food program this program is the most important. . . .

The third most important branch is that of tourism, which can also bring in large revenues for our country, because this is a country which has clean air and pure seas. This sun which cracks the stones is the same sun that Europeans and Scandinavians love in the winter, because it is very good for relaxing. It's not great for growing sweet potatoes, but it's excellent for recreation. . . .

However, comrades, there is one thing I want you to keep in mind: only a socialist system could confront these problems. In a capitalist system, what they would do with electricity is double or triple the price and that's that. The poor and people with low incomes would be without electricity and that would be it. Only a socialist model can confront the problem differently and is capable of rationing electricity instead of solving the problem by raising prices.

What do the capitalists do? What are they doing in a lot of Latin American countries? Every day we read the news and they haven't yet begun to feel the effects of the approaching fuel crisis. Thousands of people are being thrown out on the street, prices are multiplying, the people are harassed and only a minority of the very privileged can solve their problems.

No, we will not abandon a single person. This is characteristic of our socialism, our system. We challenge the capitalists to solve their problems and confront their difficulties in this way.

If we have to reduce the days worked, we will reduce them. If we can't work five days a week, we'll work four. And if we don't have enough raw materials and fuel in the industry to work four, we'll work three and there will be plenty of free time left which can be invaluable when put to good use.

We are now asking the country to carry out an extraordinary internationalist mission: saving the revolution in Cuba. Saving socialism in Cuba. And that will be the greatest internationalist service that our people can render humanity.

Revolutionary ideas haven't become obsolete or anything like that—they're going through difficult times but they will return with added strength. And they will return sooner if there is more injustice in the world, more exploitation, more hunder, greater chaos in the world. Revolutionary ideas will return and it's up to us, the standard-bearers of those ideas, to raise them up high, for that's the mission history has assigned to us. And as I said, we have the intelligence, the moral virtue, the courage and the heroism to fulfill this mission.

Source: Fidel Castro, "Revolutionary Ideas Are Not Obsolete," in Gianni Mina, *An Encounter with Fidel Castro* (Sydney, Australia: Ocean Press, 1991), 263–67.

The United States 1961 Foreign Assistance Act required that the State Department provide Congress with annual reports on the human rights practices of all nations receiving foreign aid from the United States and all member states of the United Nations. Congress went further with the 1974 Trade Act, which provided the president with the authority to cut foreign aid to those countries guilty of gross human rights violations, a rationale sometimes used to justify the continuance of the U.S. trade embargo against Cuba. The excerpts presented here are from the State Department's 1992 report and are indicative of those that preceded with regards to Cuba. The report places responsibility for the government's control over society and its violations of civil and human rights at Fidel Castro's doorstep.

Document 11
HUMAN RIGHTS IN CUBA

Cuba is a totalitarian state dominated by Fidel Castro, who is Chief of State, Head of Government, First Secretary of the Communist Party, and

Commander-in-Chief of the armed forces. President Castro seeks to control all aspects of Cuban life through a broad network of directorates ultimately answerable to him through the Communist party, as well as through the bureaucracy and the state security apparatus. The party is the only legal political entity and is headed by an elite group whose membership is ultimately determined by Fidel Castro. All government positions, including judicial offices, are controlled by the party. Though not a formal requirement, party membership is a de facto prerequisite for high-level official positions and professional advancement. . . .

[During 1992] government agents were responsible for several extrajudicial killings. . . . [In violation of Cuban law] beatings, neglect, isolation, and other abuse by police and prison officials were often directed at detainees and prisoners convicted of political crimes or who persist in expressing their views. . . .

The Constitution says that all legally recognized civil liberties can be denied anyone actively opposing the "decision of the Cuban people to build socialism." Authorities invoke this open-ended article to justify lengthy detentions of activists on the grounds that they constitute "counterrevolutionary elements" . . . [who] are often imprisoned for "enemy propaganda," "illicit association," "contempt for authority" (usually for criticizing Fidel Castro), "clandestine printing," or the broad charge of "rebellion." Rebellion has been used against those people advocating peaceful democratic change. . . . One index of the extent of repression is the high number of arrests for political crimes in recent years. According to reliable sources, from 1986 to 1990, 4,568 people were arrested and imprisoned at the Department of State Security (DSE) headquarters. . . .

Cuban law and trial practices do not meet international standards for fair and impartial trial. Almost all cases are tried in less than 1 day. . . . The judiciary's independence is compromised by the subordination of the courts to the Communist Party. . . . There is no known case in which a court has ruled against the Government on any political or security matter. . . . Often the sole evidence provided, particularly in cases with political significance, is the defendant's confession. The confession is usually obtained under duress and without legal advice or the knowledge of the defense lawyer. . . .

[The Ministry of the Interior] employs an intricate system of informants and block committees (CDR's) to monitor and control public opinion. Guardians of social conformity, CDR's are neighborhood security committees tasked with closely monitoring the daily lives of individual residents. . . . CDR's report suspicious activity, such as reception of foreign radio or television broadcasts in the home, conspicuous consumption, unauthorized meetings or attitudes toward the Government or the revolution. . . . Cubans do not have the right to receive publications from abroad and expect that their international correspondence will be read by state security. Overseas telephone calls are hard to make and are monitored; conversations with foreigners are reported. . . . Authorities regularly search people's homes without probable cause for the purposes of intimidation and harassment. . . .

The Government does not allow direct criticism of the revolution or its leaders. Laws are enforced against antigovernment propaganda, graffiti, and insults against officials. The penalty is 3 months to 1 year in prison. If Fidel Castro or members of the National Assembly or Council of State are the object , the sentence is 1 to 3 years. . . . Any assembly of more than three persons, even in a private home, is punishable by up to 3 months in prison and a fine. Though not universally enforced, it is often used as a legal pretext to harass and imprison human rights activists. . . . Another measure used to harass activists are acts of repudiation, officially sponsored mob gatherings outside the homes of suspected "counterrevolutionaries.". . .

The Constitution states that electronic and print media are state property and "cannot become, in any case, private property." The media are controlled by the Communist Party and operate under party guidelines. They faithfully reflect government views and are used to indoctrinate the public. No other public forum exists for airing views. Artistic, literary and academic freedoms are also circumscribed by the Government. Education is the exclusive prerogative of the State. The school system follows Marxist-Leninist precepts as interpreted by the Government. . . .

Cuban citizens have no legal right to change their government or to advocate a change. The Constitution's Article 5 states that the only political organization allowed is the Communist party. A small group of leaders select members of its highest governing bodies—the Politburo and the Central Committee.

Source: United States Department of State, *Country Reports on Human Rights Practices for 1992* (Washington, D.C.: United States Government Printing Office, 1993), 371–78.

The following two documents illustrate the conflict within the Cuban-American community. The first, the "Declaration of the 19th," is by Eloy Gutiérrez-Menoyo, a former rebel commander who fought against the Batista dictatorship. Subsequent to Batista's ouster, Gutiérrez-Menoyo split with Castro and went into exile in Florida, where he founded "Alpha 66," a group of dissidents who sought to wreak havoc on Cuba. In December 1964 Gutiérrez-Menoyo was captured during one of the group's incursions into Cuba and served twenty-two years in prison for his acts of treason against the Cuban government. Following his release, Gutiérrez-Menoyo founded *Cambio Cubano* in 1992 to demand peaceful change within Cuba. Gutiérrez-Menoyo envisions himself as remaining true to the causes of the Revolution and in direct contrast to the goals of the Cuban American National Foundation (CANF).

Led by Jorge Mas Canosas, a group of wealthy Cuban businessmen residing in Miami founded CANF in 1981. A nonprofit organization, it relies upon contributions from the Cuban community and seeks the ouster of Fidel Castro by any means, including an ever-tightening trade embargo. Its hard-line policies had great influence upon the Reagan and Bush administrations. Its late chairman, Jorge Mas Canosa, admitted to having presidential ambitions in Cuba. As the excerpt presented here indicates, CANF advocates a major role for the Cuban-American leadership in any post-Castro Cuba.

Document 12
CAMBIO CUBANO: DECLARATION, AUGUST 19, 1996

Economically speaking the depenalization of the dollar while positive is quite pallied unless it means more ample economic measures to improve [the] Cuban economy, making it more efficient, and that this improvement will benefit the *less-powerful majorities* [by] allowing them to become participants and users of that growing wealth. . . . It is dangerous for the Cuban government and interesting for any observer of the Cuban situation, the act that in allowing access to the dollar they are creating a new superior socioeconomic group that for the first time will obtain advantages that they have not earned by virtue of their physical or intellectual effort or by their degree of adhesion to the Cuban government. . . .

The right to enter or leave a country is a universal right. . . . It is time that the manipulation of the Cuban people to enter or leave the country be ended. . . .

The Cuban government should carefully design plans that, while attractive to foreign capital, will not be in detriment of the Cuban people. It is also necessary to develop creative mechanisms that will allow the participation of the working classes in the shares that the Cuban State will have in those new enterprises. In fact, it is opportune to point out that the Cuban government should move in the direction of no-State participation in the enterprises where popular sectors are interested. This could be achieved through new formulas stimulating self-incentive, co-ownership and the method of ownership of shares of stock. It is possible to avoid repetition [of] . . . the usual situations of racism and social injustices that occurred at the time of the establishment of the first republic. . . .

It is possible now . . . to support farmers by allowing them to become proprietors of the farms. It is possible to adopt a policy of flexibility with regard to cooperatives, so that these cease to be subjected to [a] centralized plan of control, so that unproductive lands be given to families, groups or individuals which make them productive again. . . .

The present situation of isolating tourist resorts and locations is a measure that has caused great damage. The Cuban government should recognize this defect in that project and should look for ways to correct this situation which is humiliating for the Cuban people. . . .

We are urging the Cuban government to continue with changes, honestly and with absolute transparency and with the certain goal that such economic changes be the carriers of political liberties and civil guarantees for the Cuban people who have the right to live free of any kind of fear.

Source: Declaration of the 19th (Miami, Fla.: Cambio Cubano, 1996), 2–3 (a flyer).

Document 13
CUBAN AMERICAN NATIONAL FOUNDATION: ON CUBA'S FUTURE

In Eastern Europe, freedom came as a surprise. Not even the West Germans were prepared; therefore, many errors ensued. That should not happen in Cuba. We know that Cuba will be free. Castro, reeling from the end of subsidies from his former Soviet benefactors, faces a growing democratic opposition movement and a moribund command economy which will shrink by roughly 20 percent in 1992 alone. It would be foolish for the Cuban exile community, Western policymakers, or international businesses to ignore the prospect of change and fail to consider the challenges and opportunities which a post-Castro Cuba will present.

Cuba citizens are not free to assemble and openly discuss options for a transition towards democracy and a market economy. Given this reality, Castro's successors would face the complex challenges of transition without the basic tools of comprehensive research and market-oriented experience which can hasten economic progress.

Those of us who live in freedom have a responsibility to fill that vacuum, learn from the experiences of reformers in the former Soviet bloc and prepare data and policy recommendations to help a new Cuban government rebuild Cuba's shattered economy.

We, the Cuban people, have what no post-Communist transition regime currently has. We have 20 percent of our population living in the United

States. Cuban exiles can provide a tremendous base of entrepreneurial skill, professional, and economic support, and participation. Cuban-American investment in the first year of a post-Castro Cuba could provide more than $3 billion in capital inflows to rebuild the island.

All that is needed is the vision and the will to seize this opportunity and eliminate, once and for all, the last vestiges of the most cruel political experiment of the 20th century.

Source: The Cuban American National Foundation, *For a Free and Democratic Cuba* (Miami, Fla.: Colonial Press, n.d.), 15, 16.

Following the failed Bay of Pigs invasion in April 1961, the United States pursued policies that imposed economic hardships upon Cuba in hopes of toppling Fidel Castro's regime. Subsequently, U.S. policymakers also came to view Castro as a puppet for Soviet ambitions in Latin America. Still obsessed with Castro's dictatorship following the collapse of the Soviet Union, the United States tightened its embargo in hopes of bringing the regime to its knees. The consistency in U.S. policy from 1962 until 1996 is the focus of the following exerpts from presidential statements about Cuba.

Document 14
JOHN F. KENNEDY, FEBRUARY 3, 1962
(WHITE HOUSE STATEMENT)

The President announced today an embargo upon trade between the United States and Cuba. He said that on humanitarian grounds exports of certain foodstuffs and medicines and medical supplies from the United States to Cuba would be excepted from this embargo. . . . The President pointed out that the embargo will deprive the Government of Cuba of the dollar exchange it has been deriving from sales of its products in the United States. The loss of this income will reduce the capacity of the Castro regime, intimately linked with the Sino-Soviet bloc, to engage in acts of aggression, subversion, or other activities endangering the security of the United States and other nations of the hemisphere.

Source: Public Papers of the Presidents, John F. Kennedy, 1962 (Washington, D.C.: Government Printing Office, 1963), 106.

Document 15
JIMMY CARTER, OCTOBER 1, 1979
(ADDRESS TO THE NATION)

Recently, we obtained evidence that a Soviet combat brigade has been in Cuba for several years. The presence of Soviet combat troops in Cuba is of serious concern to us. . . . This unit appears to be a brigade of two or three thousand men. It is armed with about 40 tanks and other modern military equipment. It's been organized as a combat unit. Its training exercises have been those of a combat unit. . . . It presents no direct threat to us. . . . [but] it contributes to tension in the Caribbean and the Central American region. The delivery of modern arms to Cuba and the presence of Soviet naval forces in Cuban waters have strengthened the Soviet-Cuban military relationship. They've added to the fears of some countries that they may come under Soviet or Cuban pressure. . . . During the last few years, the Soviets have been increasing the delivery of military supplies to Cuba. The result is that Cuba now has one of the largest, best equipped armed forces in this region. These military forces are used to intrude into other countries in Africa and the Middle East. . . .

[W]e will monitor the status of the Soviet forces by increased surveillance of Cuba. . . . We will assure that no Soviet unit in Cuba can be used as a combat force to threaten the security of the United States or any other nation in this hemisphere. Those nations can be confident that the United States will act in response to a request for assisstance to meet any such threat from Soviet or Cuban forces.

This policy is consistent with our responsibilities as a member of the Organization of American States and a party to the Rio Treaty. It's a reaffirmation of John F. Kennedy's declaration in 1963 "that we will not permit any troops from Cuba to move off the island of Cuba in an offensive action against any neighboring countries."

Source: Public Papers of the Presidents, Jimmy Carter, 1979 (Washington, D.C.: Government Printing Office, 1980), II, 102–4.

Document 16
RONALD REAGAN, FEBRUARY 19, 1986
(RESPONDING TO A PRESS CONFERENCE QUESTION)

We are very much aware of recent Soviet-Cuban and Libyan attempts to penetrate this hemisphere. In Nicaragua, we see the attempt by the Sandinistas, with help from Cuba and its Soviet patron, to consolidate repressive communist rule. And right here in the Caribbean exists one of the most repressive regimes on Earth the government of Fidel Castro in Cuba. . . . Castro has created an island prison in the middle of the Caribbean as a grim reminder of what can happen if we are not prepared to defend our freedom. In Grenada, a handful of tyrants almost succeeded with help from Cuba and the Soviet Union, in creating a repressive, militarized state which would have been a threat to the other nations of the Caribbean Basin and the United States. The United States rejects the idea that the Soviets should be able to spread their influence through subversion in this region. We believe that free people everywhere should support those who fight for freedom and against repression. That is what we are doing in Nicaragua and that is why we responded to requests to rescue Grenada in 1983. . . . We believe the democracies of the Caribbean should be allowed to develop without threats of subversion from the Soviet Union or Cuba. And Mr. Gorbachev knows that we will oppose any attempts by the Soviet Union and its allies to threaten the security of this hemisphere.

Source: Public Papers of the Presidents, Ronald Reagan, 1986 (Washington, D.C.: Government Printing Office, 1987), I, 223.

Document 17
GEORGE BUSH, OCTOBER 23, 1992 (REMARKS IN MIAMI ON THE SIGNING OF THE CUBAN DEMOCRACY ACT KNOWN AS THE TORICELLI BILL)

People are choosing liberty all over the world by their votes. The Cuban people deserve no less. That's why this Cuban Democracy Act strengthens our embargo. It will speed the inevitable demise of the Cuban Castro dictatorship. The legislation that I sign today reflects our determination, mine and yours, that the Cuban Government will not benefit from U.S. trade or aid until the Cuban people are free. And it reflects another belief: I'm not going to let others prop up Castro with aid or some sweetheart trade deal.

All of this is not designed to hurt the Cuban people. . . . Cuba suffers because Castro refuses to change. . . . Our policy is the only way to put, plain and simple: Democracy, Mr. Castro, not sometime, not someday, but now. Put it this way: We will not provide life support to a dictatorship that is dying. There will never be normal relations with Cuba as long as Castro sustains this illegitimate regime, as long as he intimidates and does violence to a brave and courageous people.

Source: Public Papers of the Presidents, George Bush, 1992–1993 (Washington, D.C.: Government Printing Office, 1993), II, 1939.

Document 18
WILLIAM J. CLINTON, MARCH 12, 1996 (REMARKS ON SIGNING THE CUBAN LIBERTY AND DEMOCRATIC SOLIDARITY [LIBERTAD] ACT KNOWN AS THE HELMS-BURTON BILL)

I sign it (LIBERTAD) with a certainty that it will send a powerful, unified message from the United States to Havana, that the yearning of the Cuban people for freedom must not be denied. This bill continues our bipartisan effort to pursue an activist Cuba policy, an effort that began some four years ago with the Cuban Democracy Act.

Under the provisions of that legislation, our administration has encouraged Cuba's peaceful transition to democracy. We have promoted the free flow of ideas to Cuba through greater support for Cuba's brave human rights activists, a dramatic increase in nongovernmental humanitarian aide to the Cuban people, long distance telephone service. And the more the Cuban people are free to express the freedoms and rights their neighbors enjoy the more they will insist on change. We have also kept the pressure on Cuba by maintaining a tough embargo policy. The legislation I sign today further tightens that embargo. . . .

The Cuban people must receive the blessings of freedom they have been so long denied. And I hope and believe that this day is another important step toward that ultimate goal that so many of you in this audience have worked so hard for, for so very, very long.

Source: Weekly Compilation of Presidential Documents (Washington, D.C.: Government Printing Office, 1996), 32:2, 478.

> Critics of U.S. policy toward Cuba date to John F. Kennedy's embargo in 1962. They have argued that the embargo forced Fidel Castro to turn to the Soviet Union for economic assistance, which in turn caused Castro to become the point man for Soviet interests in Latin America. Over time, the critics argued that the embargo failed to dislodge Castro and, in fact, played into his hands. He could blame the United States for his own failed policies. David R. Henderson's essay illustrates the critics' position.

Document 19
WHY OUR CUBA POLICY IS WRONG

Proponents of the American embargo against Cuba argue as follows: By squeezing the Cuban economy enough, the U.S. government can make Cubans even poorer than Fidel Castro has managed to over 37 years through his imposition of Stalin-style socialism. Ultimately, the theory goes, some desperate Cubans will rise up and overthrow Castro.

There are at least three problems with this strategy. The first, and most overarching, is that it's immoral. It could succeed only by making average Cubans—already living in grinding poverty—even poorer. Most of them are completely innocent and, indeed, already want to get rid of Castro. And consider the irony: The defining feature of socialism is the prohibition of voluntary exchange between people. Pro-embargo Americans typically want to get rid of socialism in Cuba. Yet their solution—prohibiting trade with Americans—is the very essence of socialism.

The second problem with the embargo strategy is more practical: It hasn't worked. To be effective, an embargo must prevent people in the target country from getting goods, or at least substantially increase the cost of getting goods. But competition is a hardy weed that shrugs off governmental attempts to suppress it. Companies in many countries, especially Canada, produce and sell goods that are close substitutes for the U.S. goods that can't be sold in Cuba. Wander around Cuba, and you're likely to see beach umbrellas advertising Labatt's beer, McCain's French fries, and President's Choice cola. Moreover, even U.S. goods for which there are no close substitutes are often sold to buyers in other countries who then resell to Cuba. A layer of otherwise unnecessary middlemen is added, pushing up prices somewhat, but the price increase is probably small for most goods.

Some observers have argued that the very fact that the embargo does little harm means that it should be kept because it's a cheap way for U.S. politicians to express moral outrage against Castro. But arguing for a policy on the grounds that it's ineffective is simply bizarre.

The third problem is political. The embargo surely makes Cubans somewhat more anti-American than they would be otherwise, and it makes them somewhat more in favor of—or at least against—Castro. He still publicizes the "blockade," his word for the embargo, as the cause of Cuba's awful economic plight and reminds his subjects ceaselessly that the U.S. government is the instigator. Some Cubans probably believe him.

Far from ending the embargo, the U.S. has gone in the other direction with the Helms-Burton law, named for Sen. Jesse Helms (R-North Carolina) and Rep. Dan Burton (R-Indiana). Its most controversial provision permits U.S. lawsuits against foreign companies if they use any property in Cuba that was confiscated from U.S. citizens. Starting on Aug. 1, 1998, even U.S. citizens who were Cubans at the time their property was stolen can sue. While this may sound reasonable to anyone who believes in property rights, the idea, applied consistently without regard for time or context, would lead down a path where few want to go. Native Americans, for instance, can, and do, make similar claims.

To enforce this provision of the Helms-Burton law, the U.S. government will make America off-limits to corporate officers, principals, or shareholders with a controlling interest in firms that profit from confiscated U.S. property in Cuba. The government has already used the law against a handful of Canadian and Mexican executives. Not just the violators, but also their spouses, minor children, and agents will be kept out of the U.S. Again, note the irony. One of the most important achievements of free societies—one that distinguishes them most from totalitarian regimes—is that when one family member breaks the law, that person, not the other family members, pays the penalty. Totalitarian governments violate this principle of individual responsibility all the time, and Castro is the main such violator left in the world. Now the U.S. has joined him. Helms and Burton say they want to beat Castro. Castro has already beaten them—and us.

The more open trade is between Cuba and the rest of the world, the more experience Cubans will have with foreigners and foreign goods. They will learn that they don't have to be poor, that meat once a day doesn't have to be a luxury, and that they don't have to die from socialized medicine. The "dollarization" of the Cuban economy, under which Castro allows people to exchange dollars for goods, has already started this process. The flow of dollars from relatives in southern Florida has promoted dollarization further, making recipients of these dollars less dependent on the Cuban government for their daily bread. When President Clinton reduced the amount Cuban exiles in the U.S. could legally send to their relatives, he made Cuba more dependent.

One piece of evidence that advocates of the embargo must confront is Castro's own action just before Congress voted on the Helms-Burton act. Here was a law that President Clinton had opposed and that, therefore, faced an uphill battle. Yet on February 24, 1996, just days before the vote, Castro had his air force shoot down two unarmed civilian jet planes piloted by members of the Miami-based exile group Brothers to the Rescue. No one on either side of the embargo debate has claimed that Castro is stupid. With his awesome intelligence machine, Castro certainly knew this action would make passage of the Helms-Burton law more likely. He presumably wanted to use it as new ammo in his propaganda. The embargo advocates point out that if full trade relations are resumed with the U.S. and Cuba, then Cuba's government will qualify for U.S. government aid. Such aid would definitely prop up Castro's regime, as similar aid has done for tyrants in Africa and elsewhere. So let's end the embargo, not give foreign aid to Cuba, and watch as Fidel fades forever into much deserved oblivion.

Source: David R. Henderson, "Why Our Cuba Policy Is Wrong," *Fortune* (October 13, 1997): p. 48.

From January 21 to January 25, 1998, Pope John Paul II made an historic visit to communist Cuba, a nation that had been self-declared officially atheistic for thirty years (1962–1992). Following his welcome in Havana, Pope John Paul II traveled to the cities of Santa Clara, Camaguey, and Santiago de Cuba before returning to Havana's Revolutionary Plaza to preside over public masses. He met privately with Fidel Castro and with the Cuban Conference of Bishops and other clerics and lay workers before returning to Rome. During the homily of each service,

Pope John Paul II criticized some aspect of Cuban life and the United States embargo. Presented here are excerpts from those addresses in which he criticized the Castro government for many of the ills confronting the Cuban society and the United States for contributing to the suffering of the Cuban people through its embargo.

Document 20
POPE JOHN PAUL II AT SANTA CLARA, JANUARY 22, 1998

The family, the fundamental cell of society and the guarantee of its stability, nonetheless experiences the crises which are affecting society itself. This happens when married couples live in economic or cultural systems which, under the guise of freedom and progress, promote or even defend an anti-birth mentality and thus induce couples to have recourse to methods of regulating fertility which are incompatible with human dignity. There is even an acceptance of abortion, which is always, in addition to being an abominable crime, a senseless impoverishment of the person and of society itself. . . .

The social situation experienced in this beloved country has created not a few difficulties for family stability: for example, material scarcities—as when wages are not sufficient or have very limited buying power—dissatisfaction for ideological reasons, the attraction of the consumer society. These and other measures involving labor and other matters have helped to intensify a problem which has existed in Cuba for years; people being obliged to be away from the family within the country, and emigration, which has torn apart whole families and caused suffering for a large part of the population. . . .

The family, the school and the church must form an educational community in which the children of Cuba can "grow in humanity." Do not be afraid; open your families and schools to the values of the gospel of Jesus Christ, which are never a threat to any social project. . . .

It is true that in the area of education, public authority has certain rights and duties, since it must serve the common good. Nonetheless, this does not give public authority the right to take the place of parents, without expecting others to replace them in a matter which is their own responsibility, should be able to choose for their children the pedagogical method, the ethical and civic content and the religious inspiration which will enable them to receive an integral education. They must not expect everything to be given to them.

Source: The Vatican's World Wide Web Site: http//www.vatican.va/holy_father/john_paul_ii/travels/hf_jp-ii_spe_.

Document 21
POPE JOHN PAUL II AT CAMAGUEY, JANUARY 23, 1998

What can I say to you, the young people of Cuba, who live under material conditions which are sometimes difficult, who are sometimes frustrated in your legitimate aspirations and are even sometimes deprived of hope itself? Guided by the spirit and in the power of the risen Christ, resist every kind of temptation to flee from the world and from society. Do not succumb to the lack of vision which leads to destroying one's personality through alcoholism, drugs and sexual irresponsibility and prostitution, the constant pursuit of new experiences. Do not take refuge in sects, alienating spiritual cults or groups which are completely foreign to the culture and tradition of your country. . . .

Cuba's future depends on you, on how you build your character and on how you translate into action your commitment to transform the world. And so, I say to you: With fortitude and temperance, with justice and prudence, face the great challenges of the present moment; return to your Cuban and Christian roots, and do all that you can to build a future of ever greater dignity and freedom.

Source: The Vatican's World Wide Web Site: http//www.vatican.va/holy_father/john_ paul_ii/travels/hf_jp-ii_spe_. (January 23, 1998).

Document 22
POPE JOHN PAUL II AT SANTIAGO DE CUBA,
JANUARY 24, 1998

Lay Catholics . . . have the duty and the right to participate in public debate on the basis of equality and in an attitude of dialogue and reconciliation. Likewise, the good of a nation must be promoted and achieved by its citizens themselves through peaceful and gradual means. In this way each person enjoying freedom of expression, being free to undertake initiatives and make proposals within civil society, and enjoying appropriate freedom of association, will be able to cooperate effectively in the pursuit of the common good. . . .

The church, immersed in civil society, does not seek any type of political power in order to carry out her mission; she wishes only to be the fruitful seed of everyone's good by her presence in the structures of society. . . . Christ charged her to bring this message to all peoples, and for this she needs sufficient freedom and adequate means. . . .

The church is called to bear witness to Christ by taking courageous and prophetic stands in the face of the corruption of political or economic power. . . .

I wish to send my greeting also to all of Cuba's children, who, in whatever part of the world, venerate our Lady of Charity . . . asking her, Loving Mother of all, to unite her children once more through reconciliation and brotherhood.

Source: The Vatican's World Wide Web Site: http//www.vatican.va/holy_father/john_ paul_ii/travels/hf_jp-ii_spe_. (January 24, 1988).

Document 23
POPE JOHN PAUL II AT HAVANA, JANUARY 25, 1998

I am confident that they [the people of Cuba] will continue to preserve and promote the most genuine values of the Cuban heart. Faithful to the heritage received from your forbearers and despite difficulties, the Cuban spirit must ever show its trust in God, its Christian faith, its ties to the Church, its love for the culture and traditions of the homeland, its vocation to justice and freedom. In the process of doing precisely this, all Cubans are called to contribute to the common good in a climate of mutual respect and with a profound sense of solidarity.

In our day, no nation can live in isolation. The Cuban people, therefore, cannot be denied the contacts with other peoples necessary for economic, social and cultural development, especially when the imposed isolation strikes the population indiscriminately, making it ever more difficult for the weakest to enjoy the bare essentials of a decent living, things such as food, health and education. All can and should take practical steps to bring about changes in this regard. May nations, and especially those which share the same Christian heritage and the same language, work effectively to extend the benefits of unity and harmony, to join efforts and overcome obstacles so that the Cuban people, as the active agents of their own history, may maintain international relations which promote the common good. In this way they will overcome the suffering caused by material and moral poverty, the roots of which may be found, among other things, in unjust inequalities, in limitations to fundamental freedoms, in depersonalization and discouragement of individuals, and in oppressive economic measures—unjust and ethically unacceptable—imposed from outside this country.

Source: The Vatican's World Wide Web Site: http//www.vatican.va/holy_father/john_ paul_ii/travels/hf_jp-ii_spe_. (January 25, 1998).

Glossary of Selected Terms

Agrarian Reform Laws: The first major agricultural law was implemented in May 1959. It set a 1,000 acre limit as the maximum amount of land that could be owned by individuals or corporations, although a few productive farms of up to 3,000 acres were permitted. Under this law 8.6 millon acres of land were placed under state control. The 1963 Agrarian Reform Law provided for the state expropriation of all private holdings over 165 acres. About 11,000 farms were taken over. For those farmers totally dispossessed by the act, the government compensated them at 250 pesos per month for ten years.

Auténtico Party: The popular name given to the *Partido Revolucionario Cubano*, which was founded in 1934 by student supporters of Ramón Grau Martín. *Following the precepts of José Martí, the Autenticos* called for economic and political nationalism, social justice, and civil liberties. Through the 1930s and early 1940s, the party opposed Fulgencio Batista and his puppet presidents, but when its own Grau Martín was elected president in 1944, the *Autentico* leadership became as equally corrupt.

Balseros: Or "rafters," this term refers to the estimated 30,000 Cubans who escaped the island between 1990 and 1994 virtually in anything that floated, including tubes, styrofoam, and wooden planks.

Batistianos: A descriptive term applied to those persons who supported Cuban dictator/president Fulgencio Batista in the late 1950s.

Brigade 2506: This Cuban exile force of 1,297 men was trained by the U.S. Central Intelligence Agency in Guatemala for the overthrow of Fidel Castro. It landed at the Bay of Pigs in the early morning of April 17, 1961 without adequate air cover and was quickly forced to surrender to Castro's Revolutionary Army. After a public trial in Havana, the 1,180 survivors were imprisoned for a year and a half before they were ransomed for U.S. medical supplies and several million dollars. The designation 2506 came from the serial number of one of the members who accidentally died during training.

Caracas Pact: Signed in the Venezuelan capital on July 28, 1958, between Fidel Castro's 26th of July Movement and the student-led Revolutionary Directorate in Cuba, but excluded the Communist party. The pact called for a common strategy to oust Batista from power, the installation of a provisional government headed by Manuel Urrutia, to be followed by elections, and for economic and social reforms and the implementation of human rights for all Cuban people.

Committees for the Defense of the Revolution (CDRs): Created in September 1960, these block-to-block organizations acted as vigilante committees to ensure internal security and public control. The committees identified counterrevolutionaries at the local level and informed the proper government authorities. By the early 1980s the CDRs reached a membership of nearly 5 million divided into some 30,000 bases. Virtually every neighborhood, school, factory, and farm had a CDR. Their functions expanded to include normal police activities and the holding of indoctrination seminars.

Communist Party of Cuba (PCC): In 1961 a merger of Fidel Castro's 26th of July Movement with the Popular Socialist Party and the Revolutionary Directorate into the Integrated Revolutionary Organizations (ORI) was the first step toward the creation of the United Party of the Socialist Revolution (PURS), which in 1965 was transformed into the Communist Party of Cuba, the only legal party on the island. Throughout the 1960s, the party was disorganized and exercised little influence in government, giving way to the personal leadership of Fidel Castro and his closest advisors. During the 1970s the party consolidated its power base and came to dominate the government's bureaucracy and leadership positions in the workplace cadres. Though membership reached nearly one-half million members in the mid-1980s, women remained underrepresented in the party's hierarchy. Without opposition, the party continued its hold on government positions and dominated the national assembly into the 1990s despite the economic hardships confronting the nation.

Creole: A popular term used throughout Spanish America to refer to those people of pure Spanish blood who were born in the New World. During colonial times this group of people lacked political rights, despite their economic wealth and high social status. With independence, they replaced the Spanish-born administrators and had little desire to incorporate the masses into the political process. In Cuba, the *creoles* became members of the Conservative and Liberal political parties in the decades immediately after independence.

Cuba Libre: An expression used by Cuban exiles in the United States during the 1890s to mean a free and independent Cuba—free from Spanish rule and independent from any world power, an inference to the United States.

Cuban American National Foundation (CANF): Founded in 1981 by Jorge Mas Canosa and other members of the Cuban elite exile community residing in Miami, it sought the ouster of Fidel Castro from power in Cuba by any means possible. CANF exerted great influence on U.S. policy toward Cuba until Canosa's death in 1997.

Cuban Confederation of Labor (CTC): Established in 1939 under communist leadership, the CTC received official status in 1942. In the early Cold War years (1945–1950), the CTC was shunted by all political leaders, and the break was so complete under President Carlos Prío Socarrás (1948–1952) that the union leadership fled into exile. After Batista seized power in 1952, the CTC came to his support and denounced the general strikes directed at the government by Fidel Castro and other antigovernment groups. Under Castro's regime the CTC continually lost importance until its 1973 charter made it a voluntary organization.

Cuban Democracy Act of 1992: A U.S. law, popularly known as the Torricelli Bill, that tightened the U.S. embargo on Cuba by prohibiting U.S. companies, operating in third countries, from doing business in Cuba and prohibiting ships trading with Cuba from visiting U.S. ports six months after stopping at the island.

Cuban Liberty and Democratic Solidarity Act of 1994: Popularly known as the Helms-Burton Bill after its sponsors (Senator Jesse Helms, R., N.C. and Representative Dan Burton R., Ind.), it further tightened the U.S. embargo on Cuba by promising to punish foreign businesses that use properties in Cuba formerly owned by U.S. citizens, including corporations. The international controversy surrounding the bill prompted U.S. President William J. Clinton to continually postpone its full implementation.

Cuban Revolutionary Party (PRC): Founded by José Martí in 1892 in Key West, Florida, for the purpose of unifying all sectors of Cuban society to achieve the island's independence from Spain. The party lasted until shortly after Martí's death in 1895.

Federation of Cuban Women (FMC): Founded in 1960, the FMC became an instrument of the Cuban government to mobilize, socialize, and integrate women into the Revolution. Headed by Raúl Castro's wife, Vilma Espín, the FMC came to enroll about 80 percent of the Cuban women and direct a variety of female orientated activities.

Fidelistas: A popular Spanish language term applied to those who profess support of Fidel Castro.

Freedom Flights: Between 1965 and 1973 an estimated 260,000 Cubans left the island in this controlled exodus program paid for by the United States government. Technically opened to all who wanted to leave Cuba, those of military age or with critical job skills were denied permission to depart the island.

Independent Colored Party (AIC): The *Agrupcion Independiente de Color* was organized by a group of radical blacks in the early 1900s to combat political discrimination based on racial lines. After the party fared poorly in the 1908 elections, it became increasingly frustrated to the point where it went into open rebellion in 1912, only to be swiftly defeated by government forces. The party's failure left the Afro-Cuban community outside national politics until Castro's Revolution in the United States.

Junta Central de Planificacion **(JUCEPLAN):** The Cuban Central Planning Board was set by the Castro regime in 1960 to plan and direct Cuban economic development. JUCEPLAN swiftly transformed Cuba's private enterprise into a centralized state-controlled economy, which resulted in an immediate jump in inflation, disorganization, bureaucratic chaos, and inefficiency. Over time, as the Cuban Central Planning Board came increasingly under the military's control, a sense of order and direction was implemented.

Marielitos: Refers to the estimated 125,000 Cubans who left the island from the port of Mariel in 1980 for South Florida via a flotilla of private boats sponsored by the Cuban American community.

National Institute of Agrarian Reform (INRA): Established under the 1959 law, INRA's director became a cabinet minister under the 1963 agrarian law. It was responsible for all matters related to agricultural production, land reform, credit, trade, and management of the collectivized farms. It disappeared altogether in 1974 when the Ministry of Agriculture absorbed its functions.

Operation Mongoose: The name given to an unsuccessful Central Intelligence Agency's operation in the early 1960s designed to disrupt the Cuban economy and politically discredit Fidel Castro.

Orthodox Party: Properly known as the *Partido del Pueblo Cubano*. Led by Eduardo Chibás, the party was founded in 1946 in response to the corruption of the Ramón Grau San Martín administration. Using a broom as its symbol to clean up government, the party also promised to fulfill the social promises of the 1933 revolution. Following Fulgencio Batista's coup in 1952 and subsequent repression of his political opposition, many members of the Orthodox party, including Fidel Castro, committed themselves to the forceful ouster of the dictator.

Personalismo: A Spanish language term used throughout Latin America to signify that people followed the political leadership of an individual, rather than the ideology or program he advocated.

Período Especial: A term introduced by Fidel Castro in 1991 to describe the economic hardship endured by Cuba following the end of its special economic relationship with the former Soviet Union and Eastern Europe.

Platt Amendment: A U.S. Congressional Resolution that was thrust upon the 1902 Cuban constitution. Until its abrogation in 1934, it limited Cuba's foreign policy and international financial transactions, and granted the United States the right to intervene to maintain political order. By special treaty arrangement in 1934, only the proviso that grants the United States rights to the Guantánamo Bay naval base remain in effect.

Popular Socialist Party (PPS): The original name given to the Cuban Communist Party when it was founded in 1925. At first, a small and disorganized group, the party focused on the organization of labor in the 1930s, which culminated in the formation of the Cuban Confederation of Labor in 1939. The party supported Fulgencio Batista and initially criticized Fidel Castro's violent opposition to the regime. Not until Castro's victory was in sight did the PPS join in the fight against Batista. In 1965 the PPS was absorbed into Fidel Castro's Communist Party of Cuba. Two of its leaders, Carlos Rafael Rodríguez and Blas Roca, played prominent roles in the Castro regime.

Revolutionary Directorate: A revolutionary student group organized by José A. Echeverría in December 1955 to promote an insurrectionary response to the repression of the Batista regime. After Echeverría's death in 1957, the Directorate turned to guerrilla warfare and split into two factions, one joining with Fidel Castro's guerrilla army with the 1958 Caracas Pact, and the other, led by Eloy Gutíerrez-Menoyo, formed the "Second Front of the Escambray" to fight independently. After Castro took control of Cuba, the entire Directorate joined the Integrated Revolutionary Organizations (ORI) in 1961, the first step toward the establishment of the Cuban Communist Party and the demise of the Directorate.

Sergeants' Revolt: On September 5, 1933, disenchanted lower ranking army officers led by Fulgencio Batista joined militant civilian opposition groups to overthrow President Carlos Manuel Céspedes. The event marks the emergence of Batista as the most powerful person in Cuban politics until his ouster by Fidel Castro in 1959.

Treaty of Paris: Concluded on December 10, 1898, and proclaimed on April 11, 1899, the treaty brought an end to the Spanish-American War and required Spain to relinquish its control of Cuba, Puerto Rico, and the Philippine Islands. The treaty provided for the United States to occupy the island until the establishment of a civilian government.

26th of July Movement: Name given to Fidel Castro's revolutionary cause adopted from the date of his ill-fated attack on the Moncada army barracks in Santiago de Cuba in 1953. Its forces "invaded" Cuba from the yacht *Granma* in December 1956 and thereafter conducted a guerrilla war against Fulgencio Batista until his ouster in 1959. Subsequently, the movement merged with other revolutionary groups to form the Communist Party of Cuba.

Young Communist League (UJC): Established in 1961, it replaced the Union of Young Rebels and merged the country's youth groups into one mass organization. Its objective was to raise the revolutionary consciousness and self-discipline of young Cubans. The 1975 constitution placed the UJC under the direction of the Cuban Communist Party. Membership can begin at age fourteen and is competitive, and can be a stepping stone into the PCC at age twenty-seven.

Annotated Bibliography

GENERAL WORKS, REFERENCE GUIDE AND HISTORIOGRAPHY

Bethell, Leslie, ed. *Cuba: A Short History*. Cambridge: Cambridge University Press, 1993. A one-volume reprint of the four Cuba essays that appeared originally in the multivolume *Cambridge History of Latin America* and span the years 1750 to the 1980s.

Black, Jan Knippers, et al. *Area Handbook for Cuba*. 2nd ed. Washington, D.C.: Government Printing Office, 1976. Although dated, the volume covers a wide range of topics including history, politics, economics, government, and foreign relations.

Carley, Rachel. *Cuba: 400 Years of Architectural Heritage*. New York: Whitney Library of Design, 1997. An important photograph collection from colonial times to the present.

Chilcote, Ronald, ed. *Cuba, 1953–1978: A Bibliographical Guide to the Literature*. White Plains: Kraus International Publishers, 1986. The most comprehensive guide for the time period.

Cuban Studies/Estudios Cubanos. Pittsburgh: Center for Latin American Studies at the University of Pittsburgh, 1975–present. An annual publication that provides the most-current information regarding publications about Cuba.

Curriculum Resource Center, Roger Thayer Latin American Studies Center, Tulane University, New Orleans, Louisiana 70118. The Center operates a free lending service for teachers. A guide to its collection of print and non-print materials is available for purchase. Materials on Cuba are available.

Díaz, José Alvarez, et al. *A Study of Cuba*. Coral Gables: University of Miami, 1965. Provides useful economic, political, administrative, and geographic data spanning the time since colonization through the early years of the revolution.

Fort, Gilbert V., ed. *The Cuban Revolution of Fidel Castro Viewed from Abroad*. Lawrence: University Press of Kansas, 1969. An important guide to the literature from abroad.

Hispanic Division of the Library of Congress. *Handbook for Latin American Studies*. Washington, D.C., 1936– . An annual publication since 1936. It contains annotated references for the key works published in English and Spanish for each of the Latin American countries.

MacGaffey, Wyatt, and Clifford R. Barnett. *Cuba*. Wesport: Greenwood Press, 1974. A reprint of a seminal work originally published in 1962. Follows a similar format to Black's *Area Handbook*.

Oberg, Larry R. *Contemporary Cuban Education: An Annotated Bibliography*. Stanford: Stanford University Press, 1980. A useful bibliographical guide to revolutionary Cuban education.

Pérez, Louis A., Jr. *Cuba: Between Reform and Revolution*. 2nd ed. New York: Oxford University Press, 1995. Provides a most detailed analysis of the Cuban historical experience from the time of Spanish conquest.

———. "In Service of the Revolution: Two Decades of Cuban Historiography, 1959–1979," *Hispanic American Historical Review* 60 (February 1980), 79–89. Provides a survey the literature of the revolution's first twenty years.

———. *The Cuban Revolutionary War, 1953–1958*. Metuchen, N.J.: Scarecrow Press, 1976. An early guide to the vast amount of literature dealing with the Cuban revolution.

———, comp. *Cuba: An Annotated Bibliography*. Westport: Greenwood Press, 1988. A valuable recent addition to the research tools on Cuban historiography.

———, ed., *Essays on Cuban History*. Gainesville: University Press of Florida, 1995. Brings together a wide range of topical essays, including history, historiography, and archival materials available in Cuba.

Smith, Robert Freeman. *Background to Revolution*. New York: R. E. Krieger, 1966. Contains twenty-six essays on historiography, history, U.S.-Cuban relations, economic development, race and slavery, labor, agriculture, and class structure.

———. "Twentieth-Century Cuba Historiography." *Hispanic American Historical Review* 44 (February 1964), 44–73. Provides a thorough analysis of the principal historical works and trends on Cuban historiography from colonial times.

Suárez, Andrés. "The Cuban Revolution: The Road to Power." *Latin American Research Review* 7 (Fall 1972): 5–29. Provides an analysis of the varieties of interpretations concerning the triumph of the 26th of July Movement.

Suchlicki, Jaimie. *Cuba: From Columbus to Castro*, 4th ed. Washington, D.C.: Brassey's, 1997. Provides a brief but most useful interpretative history of Cuba with an emphasis on the twentieth century.

―――. *Historical Dictionary of Cuba*. Metuchen, N.J.: The Scarecrow Press, 1988. Slightly dated, but still a valuable reference book that provides essential historical facts and describes events and prominent leaders in Cuban history.

Thomas, Hugh. *Cuba: The Pursuit of Freedom*. New York: Harper and Row, 1971. An encyclopedic volume that serves as a valuable English-language work on Cuba for the years from 1762 through the early 1960s.

Timmerman, Jacobo. *A Cuban Journey*. New York: Knopf, 1990. A critical analysis of the Cuban Revolution by a Chilean journalist.

DOCUMENTS

Economic Commission for Latin America and the Caribbean. *Annual Statistics for Latin America and the Caribbean*. Santiago and New York: United Nations, 1968– . An annual compilation of economic data on all of Latin America, including Cuba.

―――. *Economic Survey of Latin America and the Caribbean*. Santiago and New York: United Nations, 1949– . An annual publication that includes a descriptive narrative of the state of each Latin American nation's economy.

General Secretariat, Organization of American States. *The Situation of Human Rights in Cuba*. Washington, D.C.: Organization of American States, 1983. A most critical report on the lack of human rights and on prison conditions in Cuba.

International Commission of Jurists, *Cuba and the Rule of Law*. Geneva: International Commission of Jurists, 1962. An early account of human rights issues in revolutionary Cuba.

United States Department of State. *Country Reports on Human Rights Practices for (Year)*. Washington, D.C.: Government Printing Office, 1974– . This annual report to the U.S. Congress incudes a section on the abuse of human rights in Cuba.

Wilkie, James W., ed. *Statistical Abstract for Latin America*. Los Angeles: University of California at Los Angeles, Latin American Center, 1995. A most important reference for obtaining data regarding social conditions in Cuba. The volume is periodically revised.

BIOGRAPHIES, PERSONAL ACCOUNTS, DIARIES, ETC.

Anderson, Jon Lee. *Che Guevara: A Revolutionary Life*. New York: Grove Press, 1996. A reporter who interviewed several of Guevara's colleagues and examined not previously seen Cuban documents, Anderson concludes that Guevara was an idealistic revolutionary.

Batista, Fulgencio. *Cuba Betrayed*. New York: Random House, 1962. A defense of his own regime, which includes criticisms of the United States for letting Cuba fall to Castro.

Bourne, Peter G. *Fidel: A Biography of Fidel Castro*. New York: Dodd, Mead, 1986. Emphasizes the psychological characteristics that motivated Castro.

Castañeda, Jorge. *Compañero: The Life and Death of Che Guevara*. New York: Alfred A. Knopf, 1997. A thoughtful and scholarly reassessment of Guevara as one who was taken in by the ideals of Marxism-Leninism.

Castro, Fidel. *In Defense of Socialism, 1988–1989*. New York: Pathfinder Press, 1989. This collection deals with the crucial years in which Castro attempts to reignite a revolutionary zeal among the Cuban people while facing the loss of Soviet support.

———. *Building Socialism in Cuba, 1960–1962*. New York: Pathfinder Press, 1985. A vast collection of speeches that trace Cuba's transition to a socialist state.

———. *Cuba's International and Foreign Policy, 1975-1980*. 3rd. ed. New York: Pathfinder Press, 1981. Castro speaks out on events in Grenada, Nicaragua, and Africa and on relations with the United States.

Dubois, Jules. *Fidel Castro: Rebel-Liberator or Dictator*. Indianapolis: Bobbs-Merrill, 1959. An unequivocal defense of Castro by a French socialist.

Foner, Philip S., ed., translated by Elinor Randal. *Our America by José Martí: Writings on Latin America and the Struggle for Cuban Independence*. New York and London: Monthly Review Press, 1977. A collection of Martí's writings that focuses on his views of Latin America and particularly Cuba and its first war of independence, The Ten Years' War (1868–1878).

———. *Inside the Monster: Writings on the United States and American Imperialism*. New York and London: Monthly Review Press, 1975. A selection of Martí's writings that offers his perspectives on U.S. society, politicians, and businessmen. Though he admires American individualism, Martí distrusts the businessmen.

Geyer, Georgie Anne. *Guerrilla Prince: The Untold Story of Fidel Castro*. Boston: Little, Brown, 1991. Focuses on the personal aspects of Castro's life.

Gray, Richard B. *José Martí, Cuban Patriot*. Gainesville: University of Florida Press, 1962. Considered one of the more critical studies of Martí and his role in the Cuban independence movement.

Guevara, Ernesto Che. *Guerrilla Warfare*, 3rd ed. Wilmington: Scholarly Resources, 1997. In addition to Guevara's explanation of guerrilla warfare, two introductory essays place Guevara within the entire Latin American experience.

———. *Motorcycle Diaries: A Journey through South America*. London: Verso Press, 1995. Guevara's observations and personal experiences on his 1953 motorcycle trip through Chile, Peru, Brazil, and Venezuela.

———. *Reminiscences of the Cuban Revolutionary War*. New York: Pathfinder, 1969. Castro's chief lieutenant provides insight into the leadership and strategies of the revolutionary movement.

Halperin, Maurice. *The Rise and Decline of Fidel Castro*. Berkeley: University of California Press, 1972. One of the earlier critical analyses of Castro and his political intentions for Cuba.

Kenner, Martin, and James Petras, eds. *Fidel Castro Speaks*. New York: Grove Press, 1969. A collection of speeches that focuses on the pitfalls of capitalism in Latin America and Cuba's effort to correct them through communism.

Kirk, John M. *José Martí: Mentor of the Cuban Nation*. Gainesville: University Press of Florida, 1983. A detailed and valuable study of Martí's principles and visions for Cuba. Kirk concludes that Martí was not a socialist.

Lavan, George, ed. *Che Guevara Speaks: Selected Speeches and Writings*. New York: Merit Publishers, 1967. A collection of Che Guevara's essays, speeches, and interviews from 1959 until 1967 that illustrate his intellectual growth from a petty bourgeois to a committed communist.

Lewis, Oscar, Ruth M. Lewis, and Susan M. Rigdon. *Four Men Living a Revolution: An Oral History of Contemporary Cuba*. Urbana: University of Illinois Press, 1978. Presents oral histories of men and women, old and young, black and white, all living in a Havana apartment.

Liss, Sheldon B. *Fidel!: Castro's Political and Social Thought*. Boulder: Westview Press, 1994. An intellectual biography of Castro.

Llerena, Mario. *The Unsuspected Revolution: The Birth and Rise of Castroism*. Ithaca: Cornell University Press, 1978. A memoir of the anti-Batista struggle by an early supporter and later opponent of Fidel Castro.

Macaulay, Neill. *A Rebel in Cuba: An American's Memoir*. Chicago: Quadrangle Books, 1970. Account of a young idealist at the time who fought with Castro, only to leave the island as the revolution radicalized.

Mathews, Herbert. *Fidel Castro*. New York: Random House, 1969. Provides a sympathetic political biography.

Pando, Magdalen M. *Cuba's Freedom Fighter: Antonio Maceo, 1845–1896*. Gainesville: University Press of Florida, 1980. A sympathetic account of Maceo's life.

Phillips, R. Hart. *Cuba, Island of Paradox*. New York: McDowell, Obolensky, 1959. This *New York Times* reporter provides a perceptive first-person account of Cuba from the early 1930s to Castro's triumph in 1959.

Provenzo, Eugene, Jr., and Conceción García. "Exiled Teachers and the Cuban Revolution." *Cuban Studies/Estudios Cubanos* 8 (Winter 1983): 1–15. A study of Cuban teachers in exile and their attitudes toward the revolutionary educational system.

Quirk, Robert. *Fidel Castro.* New York: W. W. Norton, 1993. A particularly rich treatment of the early years of the revolution through 1968.

Szulc, Tad. *Fidel: A Critical Portrait.* New York: William Morrow and Co., 1986. Completed with the collaboration of Cuban officials, including Castro, this is one of the most detailed studies about Castro.

Urrutia Lleo, Manuel. *Fidel Castro and Company, Inc.* New York: Praeger, 1984. Cuba's first post-Batista president finds Castro and his cohorts deliberately putting Cuba on the path to communism.

HISTORIC CUBA

Aguilar, Luis E. *Cuba 1933: Prologue to Revolution.* Ithaca: Cornell University Press, 1972. A comprehensive account of this time period written by a Cuban exile.

Beals, Carlton. *The Crime of Cuba.* Philadelphia: J. B. Lippincott, 1933. A most critical study of Cuban politics and U.S. policies in Cuba under the Platt Amendment.

Fitzgibbon, Russell H. *Cuba and the United States, 1900–1935.* Menasha, Wis.: George Banta Publishing Company, 1935. Although dated, this volume remains the standard political account of the U.S. intervention in Cuba from 1902 to 1934 under the terms of the Platt Amendment.

Foner, Philip. *The Spanish-Cuban-American War and the Birth of American Imperialism.* 2 vols. New York: Monthly Review Press, 1972. One of the more comprehensive accounts of the war for independence, written from a Marxist perspective.

Healy, David. *The United States in Cuba, 1898–1902.* Madison: University of Wisconsin Press, 1983. One of the better accounts of the first U.S. occupation, this volume focuses upon the reasons for U.S. policy and the interactions between U.S. officials and Cuban authorities.

Helg, Aline. *Our Rightful Share: The Afro-Cuban Struggle for Equality, 1886–1912.* Chapel Hill: University of North Carolina Press, 1995. An examination of the events leading to the black revolt of 1912.

Matiello, Francine. "Rethinking Neocolonial Esthetics: Literature, Politics and the Intellectual Community in Cuba's *Revista de Avance,*" *Latin American Research Review* 38 (Fall 1993): 3–31. A valuable account of the artistic and literary works during the 1920s that illustrates the extent of discontent with corrupt politics and U.S. presence in Cuba.

Nelson, Lowry. *Rural Cuba*. Minneapolis: University of Minnesota Press, 1950. One of the better studies dealing with the Cuban peasantry that focuses largely on the twentieth century.

Offner, John L. *The Unwanted War: The Diplomacy of the United States and Spain over Cuba, 1895–1898*. Chapel Hill: University of North Carolina Press, 1992. This study is more sympathetic to the U.S. intervention in the Cuban war for independence.

Pérez, Louis A., Jr. *Army Politics in Cuba, 1898–1958*. Pittsburgh: University of Pittsburgh Press, 1976. An examination of the political role of the Cuban military in pre-revolutionary Cuba.

———. *Cuba and the Platt Amendment, 1902–1934*. Pittsburgh: University of Pittsburgh Press, 1986. Examines the impact of the Platt Amendment on Cuba's class formations, state structures, and political culture.

———. *Cuba between Empires, 1878–1902*. Pittsburgh: University of Pittsburgh Press, 1986. Examines the dynamics within Cuba that led to the war of independence and the U.S. intervention.

Rubens, Haratio S. *Liberty, The Story of Cuba*. New York: Harper, 1932. A first person account of the Cuban war for independence, 1895–1898, by the Cuban legal counsel assigned to New York City.

Stoner, Lynn. *From the House to the Streets: The Cuban Woman's Movement for Legal Reform, 1898–1940*. Durham, N.C.: Duke University Press, 1991. Provides an overview of middle- and upper-class female activism.

Suchlicki, Jaimie. *University Students and Revolution in Cuba, 1920–1968*. Coral Gables, Fla.: University of Miami, 1969. Provides an excellent understanding of student politics over a two-generation time span.

REVOLUTIONARY CUBA

"A Promise Kept," *Cuba Review* 8 (March 1978). A special issue devoted to all aspects of the Cuban health system from dental and medical clinics to government health policies.

del Aguila, Juan M. *Cuba: Dilemmas of a Revolution*. Boulder: Westview Press, 1984. A brief examination of the economic, social, and political changes brought to Cuba during the first twenty-five years of the revolution.

Alroy, Gil C. "The Peasantry in the Cuban Revolution." *Review of Politics* 29 (January 1967): 87–99. An analysis of the revolutionary effort to incorporate the peasantry into the new government system.

Ameringer, Charles D. "The Auténtico Party and the Political Opposition in Cuba, 1952–1957." *Hispanic American Historical Review* 65 (May 1985): 327–51. Provides an account of the mainstream opposition to the Batista regime.

Azicri, Max. *Cuba: Politics, Economics and Society.* London: Pinter Publishers, 1988. An examination of the role that education, cinema, poetry, music, and theater had during the revolutionary years.

Bonachea, Rolando E., and Nelson P. Valdés, eds. *Cuba in Revolution.* Garden City, N.Y.: Doubleday & Company, 1972. A collection of essays by Cubanologists who analyze the first decade of Castro's revolution from economic, political, and social perspectives.

Bunck, Julie Marie. *Fidel Castro and the Quest for a Revolutionary Culture in Cuba.* University Park: Pennsylvania State University Press, 1994. Buck examines Castro's effort to incorporate children, women, labor, and sports into the revolutionary process.

Butterworth, Douglas. *The People of Buena Ventura: Relocation of Slum Dwellers in Post-Revolutionary Cuba.* Urbana: University of Illinois Press, 1980. An ethnographic study of a working-class community in Havana.

Carbonell, Néstor. *And the Russians Stayed: The Sovietization of Cuba.* New York: William Morrow, 1989. An exile family's account of the first years of the revolution.

Cole, Johnetta B. "Women in Cuba: The Revolution within the Revolution." In Beverly Lindsay, ed., *Comparative Perspectives of Third World Women.* New York: Praeger, 1980, pp. 162–78. A good starting point for the study of women in the revolutionary period, this essay examines the status before and after 1959 in such areas as health, education, employment, housing, and culture.

Domínguez, Jorge I. *Cuba: Order and Revolution.* Cambridge, Mass.: Belknap Press of Harvard University Press, 1979. A valuable survey of the twentieth century that focuses upon the events since 1959.

Draper, Theodore. *Castroism: Theory and Practice.* New York: Praeger, 1965. An early monograph that frames the passionate debate in defense of Castro's revolution.

Edwards, J. David. "The Consolidation of the Cuban Political System." *World Affairs* 129 (Summer 1976): 10–16. Focuses on the 1976 constitution, people's power, and the expanding role of the Communist party and armed forces in the early 1970s.

Fabrico, Roberto. *The Winds of December.* East Rutherford, N.J.: Fairleigh Dickinson University Press, 1980. The most complete and most comprehensive account of the final months of the armed struggle against Batista.

Fagen, Richard R. *The Transformation of Political Culture in Cuba.* Stanford: Hoover Institution Press, 1969. An important study that focuses on the 1961 literacy campaign, schools of revolutionary instruction, and the establishment of the Committees for the Defense of the Revolution.

Farber, Samuel. *Revolution and Reaction in Cuba, 1933–1960.* Middletown, Conn.: Wesleyan University Press, 1976. A comprehensive account of the evolution of political and social groupings that emerged from the 1930s and their role in the events of the 1950s.

Feinsilver, Julie M. *Healing the Masses: Cuban Health Politics at Home and Abroad*. Berkeley: University of California Press, 1993. A thorough examination of medical policies and health care systems in Cuba after the revolution.

Figueroa, Max, Abel Prieto, and Raül Gutiérrez. *The Basic Secondary School in the Country: An Education Innovation in Cuba*. Paris: UNESCO Press, 1974. An examination of the secondary rural school programs.

González, Edward. *Cuba under Castro: The Limits of Charisma*. New York: Houghton, Mifflin, 1974. Concentrates on the origins of the Cuban revolution dating to the nineteenth century.

Handleman, Howard. "Cuban Food Policy and Popular Nutritional Levels." *Cuban Studies/Estudios Cubano* 11–13 (July 1981–January 1982): 127–46. A discussion of government nutrition policies and food distribution programs after the revolution.

Huberman, Leo, and Paul M. Sweezy. *Socialism in Cuba*. New York: Monthly Review Press, 1969. A sympathetic account of the revolution's health, education, and economic strategies.

Karol, K. S. *Guerrillas in Power: The Course of the Cuban Revolution*. New York: Hill and Wang, 1970. A detailed discussion the antecedents of the revolution through Castro's failed economic policies of 1970.

Kirk, John M. *Between God and the Party: Religion and Politics in Revolutionary Cuba*. Gainesville: University Press of Florida, 1989. This volume is considered the seminal work on relations between the Catholic Church and the revolutionary government.

Kozol, Jonathan. "A New Look at the Literacy Campaign in Cuba." *Harvard Educational Review* 2 (August 1978): 341–77. An examination of the historical development of the literacy campaign of the early 1960s.

Lewis, Oscar, Ruth M. Lewis, and Susan M. Rigdon. *Four Women: Living the Revolution: An Oral History of Contemporary Cuba*. Urbana: University of Illinois Press, 1977. Lengthy interviews with a single woman and former counterrevolutionary, an educated married woman and member of the Communist party, a domestic servant, and a prostitute.

Leo Grande, William M. "Continuity and Change in the Cuban Political Elite." *Cuban Studies/Estudios Cubano* 7 (July 1978): 1–31. Focuses on the leadership of the Central Committee of the Cuban Communist party and its consolidation of power through the mid-1970s.

Matthews, Herbert. *The Cuban Story*. New York: G. Brazilier, 1961. A sympathetic account of the Cuban Revolution by a *New York Times* reporter.

Mesa-Lago, Carmelo. *The Economy of Socialist Cuba: A Two Decade Appraisal*. Albuquerque: University of New Mexico Press, 1981. A critical assessment of the Cuban economy through the late 1970s.

————. *Cuba in the 1970s: Pragmaticism and Institutionalization*. Albuquerque: University of New Mexico Press, 1974. An examination of the revolution's social and economic policies through the 1970s.

Mills, C. Wright. *Listen Yankee: The Revolution in Cuba*. New York: Praeger, 1960. An emotional defense of the revolution and criticism of the United States policy toward Castro.

Moore, Carlos. *Castro, the Blacks and Africa*. Los Angeles: Center for African-American Studies, University of California at Los Angeles, 1988. Argues that despite the rhetoric, discrimination continued to persist in post-revolutionary Cuba.

Padula, Alfred L., Jr. "The Ruin of the Cuban Bourgeoisie, 1959–1961." *SECO-LAS Annals* 14 (March 1980): 5–21. A summary of his dissertation, this essay is a most detailed study of class structure in Cuba.

————. "Financing Castro's Revolution, 1956–1958." *Revista/Review Interamericana* 7 (Summer 1978): 234–46. Argues that the middle sector provided the greatest amount of financial support to the revolutionary cause.

Perez-Stable, Marifeli. "Institutionalization and Workers Response." *Cuban Studies/Estudios Cubano* 6 (July 1976), 31–54. A discussion of labor's response to the process of institutionalization.

Pflaum, Irving P. *Tragic Island: How Communism Came to Cuba*. Englewood Cliffs: Prentice Hall, 1961. A critical analysis that focuses on Castro's betrayal of the ideals of those who fought with him to oust Batista.

Ramos, Marcos A. *Protestantism and Revolution in Cuba*. Miami: Research Institute for Cuban Studies, University of Miami, 1989. Provides a general survey of Protestant missionary activity in Cuba dating back to the mid-nineteenth century.

Roca, Sergio G., ed. *Socialist Cuba: Past Interpretations and Future Challenges*. Boulder and London: Westview Press, 1988. An important collection of essays on Cuban domestic and international affairs during the 1980s.

Short, Margaret I. *Law and Religion in Marxist Cuba*. New Brunswick: Transaction Books, 1993. A critical evaluation of religious freedom within the larger context of human rights conditions.

Special Operations Research Office. *Case Study in Insurgency and Revolutionary Warfare: Cuba, 1953–1959*. Washington, D.C.: Government Printing Office, 1963. An examination of the guerrilla war conducted by the 26th of July Movement and the response by the Cuban military.

Stein, Edwin C. *Cuba, Castro and Communism*. New York: Macfadden-Bartell, Corp., 1962. An early criticism of Castro's policies that deliberately converted the island to a communist country.

Stubbs, Jean. *Cuba: The Test of Time*. London: Latin American Bureau, 1989. A brief and positive interpretation about the accomplishments of the Cuban revolution.

Suchlicki, Jaimie, ed. *The Cuban Military under Castro*. Miami: Institute for Inter-American Studies, University of Miami, 1989. Contains a number of informative essays about the development of the military under Castro.

Suárez, Andrés. *Cuba: Castroism and Communism*. Cambridge, Mass.: MIT Press, 1967. An early but significant discussion of the radicalization of the revolution and its path to socialism.

Thomas, Hugh. "Middle Class Politics and the Cuban Revolution." In Claudio Veliz, ed. *The Politics of Conformity in Latin America*. New York: Oxford University Press, 1967. Disputes the middle-class origins of the Cuban revolution.

Useem, Bert. "Peasant Involvement in the Cuban Revolution." *Journal of Peasant Studies* 5 (October 1977): 99–111. A general overview of the peasantry in the revolutionary war.

Valdés, Nelson P. "Revolution and Institutionalization in Cuba." *Cuban Studies/Estudios Cubano* 6 (January 1976): 1–37. An examination of the process by which the revolutionary leaders seized political power, consolidated control, and institutionalized the revolution to their liking in the 1970s.

Wagner, Eric A. "Sport in Revolutionary Societies: Cuba and Nicaragua." In Joseph L. Arbena, ed., *Sport and Society in Latin America: Diffusion, Dependency, and the Rise of Mass Culture*. Westport: Greenwood Press, 1988. A discussion of the state's use of athletics to attain revolutionary ideals in society.

Wald, Karen. *Children of Che: Child Care and Education in Cuba*. Palo Alto, Calif.: Ramparts Press, 1977. A comprehensive examination of day care and primary education.

Wood, Dennis B. "The Long Revolution: Class Relations and Political Conflict in Cuba, 1868–1968." *Science and Society* 34 (Spring 1970), 1–4. An excellent analytical essay that traces the interplay of social groups over the long haul.

CUBAN AMERICANS

García, María Cristina. *Havana USA: Cuban Exiles and Cuban Americans in South Florida, 1959–1994*. Berkeley: University of California Press, 1996. The first major synthesis of the Cuban-American community in south Florida.

Gonzalez-Pando, Miguel. *The Cuban Americans*. Westport, Conn.: Greenwood Press, 1998. An excellent analysis of the Cuban American community in the United States with an emphasis on south Florida.

Masud-Piloto, Felix. *From Welcome Exiles to Illegal Immigrants: Cuban Migration to the U.S., 1959–1995*. Lanham, Md.: Rowman & Littlefield, 1996.

A brief study of the changing character of the Cubans migrating to the United States since the revolution and U.S. policy regarding them.

Olson, James S., and Judith E. Olson. *Cuban Americans: From Trauma to Triumph.* New York: Twayne Publishers, 1995. A broad synthesis of the secondary literature that traces Cuban migrations from the mid-nineteenth century to the present.

Poyo, Gerald E. "The Cuban Experience in the United States, 1865–1940: Migration, Community and Identity." *Cuban Studies/Estudios Cubano* 21 (July 1991): 24–44. An excellent analysis of the Cuban-American community in the United States.

Ropka, Gerald W. *The Evolving Residential Pattern of the Mexican, Puerto Rican and Cuban Population of the City of Chicago.* New York: Arno Press, 1980. The place Cuban émigrés had among the older Hispanic communities in Chicago is the focus of this study.

CUBA AND INTERNATIONAL AFFAIRS

Belkin, June, and Carmelo Mesa-Lago, eds. *Cuba in Africa.* Pittsburgh: University of Pittsburgh Press, 1982. Cuba's adventures in Angola, Ethiopia, and Eritrea are the subject of this collection of essays.

Benjamin, Jules R. *The United States and the Origins of the Cuban Revolution.* Princeton: Princeton University Press, 1990. Emphasizes the critical decades before the revolution.

———. *The United States and Cuba: Hegemony and Dependent Development.* Pittsburgh: University of Pittsburgh Press, 1977. Emphasis is placed upon the U.S. imperialistic designs.

Blight, James G. et al. *Cuba on the Brink: Castro, The Missile Crisis and the Soviet Collapse.* New York: Pantheon Books, 1993. Despite its title, the volume focuses on the 1962 missile crisis, with transcripts from a Havana conference on the subject that included such key players as Castro and Robert McNamara.

Bonsal, Philip W. *Cuba, Castro and the United States.* Pittsburgh: University of Pittsburgh Press, 1971. An account of Cuban-American relations by the U.S. Ambassador in Havana from 1959 until the embassy's closing in January 1961.

Brune, Lester H. *The Missile Crisis of October 1962: A Review of Issues and References.* Los Angeles: Regina Books, 1985. An overview of the crisis along with an excellent bibliography.

Domínguez, Jorge I. *To Make a World Safe for Revolution: Cuba's Foreign Policy.* Cambridge: Harvard University Press, 1989. An excellent brief analysis of Cuban foreign policy after the revolution.

Duncan, W. Raymond. *The Soviet Union and Cuba: Interests and Influence.* New York: Praeger, 1985. A comprehensive analysis of relations between Moscow and Havana.

Erisman, H. Michael. *Cuba's International Relations: The Anatomy of a Nationalistic Foreign Policy*. Boulder and London: Westview Press, 1985. An excellent brief account and analysis of Castro's foreign policy for the first twenty-five years of the revolution.

Escalante, Fabian. *The Secret War: CIA Covert Operations against Cuba, 1959–1962*. New York: Ocean Press, 1996. An account by the former head of Cuban state security system, relating the story of U.S. efforts to dispose of Castro.

Falk, Pamela. *Cuban Foreign Policy: Caribbean Tempest*. Lexington, Mass.: D.C. Heath, 1986. Contends that Castro pursued a foreign policy independent of the Soviet Union.

Fernández, Damián. *Cuba's Foreign Policy in the Middle East*. Boulder: Westview, 1988. Fills an important void in the literature about Cuba's foreign policy.

Gellman, Irwin F. *Roosevelt and Batista: Good Neighbor Diplomacy in Cuba, 1933–1945*. Albuquerque: University of New Mexico Press, 1973. An excellent account of Washington's relations with Batista.

Hernández, José M. *Cuba and the United States: Intervention and Militarism, 1868–1933*. Austin: University of Texas Press, 1993. Explains that the years before 1898 set the tone for the character of U.S.-Cuban relations after 1902.

Hunt, Howard. *Give Us This Day*. New Rochelle: Arlington House, 1973. A CIA operative involved in the planning and execution of the Bay of Pigs invasion, Hunt tells his side of the story.

Jenks, Leland. *Our Cuban Colony*. New York: Vanguard Press, 1928. A scathing attack upon U.S. businesses, particularly sugar, in Cuba.

Johnson, Haynes E. *The Bay of Pigs*. New York: W. W. Norton, 1964. A contemporary journalistic account of the April 1961 CIA-sponsored invasion of Cuba.

Langley, Lester D. *The Cuban Policy of the United States*. New York: John Wiley, 1968. A brief survey of U.S.-Cuban relations that serves as a good starting point for an understanding of the political relationship.

Levine, Barry, ed. *The New Cuban Presence in the Caribbean*. Boulder: Westview Press, 1983. An important collection of essays regarding Cuba's initiatives in the late 1970s and early 1980s in the Caribbean and Central America.

Mazarr, Michael J. *Semper Fidel: America and Cuba, 1776–1988*. Baltimore: Nautical and Aviation Publishing Co., 1988. Provides a broad overview of relations since the colonial period through the first thirty years of the Cuban revolution.

Montaner, Carlos A., translated by Nelson Duran. *Cuba, Castro and the Caribbean: The Cuban Revolution and the Crisis in the Western Conscience*. New Brunswick, N.J.: Transaction Books, 1985. Traces the historic anti-American sentiments in Cuba that led Castro to challenge U.S. hegemony in the circum-Caribbean region.

Morley, Morris H. *Imperial State: The United States and Revolutionary Cuba, 1952–1986*. London: Cambridge University Press, 1986. An Australian political scientist, Morley argues that U.S. hostility towards the revolution prevents accommodation between Washington and Havana.

Nathan, James A., ed. *The Cuban Missile Crisis Revisited*. New York: St. Martin's Press, 1992. A collection of interpretative essays on various aspects of the crisis.

Paterson, Thomas G. *Contesting Castro: The United States and the Triumph of the Cuban Revolution*. New York: Oxford University Press, 1994. Focuses upon President John F. Kennedy's determination to topple Castro from power.

Pavlov, Yuri. *Soviet-Cuban Alliance, 1959–1991*. Coral Gables, Fla.: North-South Center Press, 1994. The Soviet mistrust of Fidel Castro is the theme pursued by this former Soviet diplomat.

Pérez, Louis A., Jr. *Cuba and the United States: Ties of Singular Intimacy*, 2nd ed. Athens: University of Georgia Press, 1997. An excellent interpretative account that examines the social and cultural aspects of the relationship.

Ratliff, William E. *Castroism and Communism in Latin America, 1959–1976*. Stanford: The Hoover Institution Press, 1976. An analysis of the interaction between the Soviets, the Chinese, and the Cubans in Latin America.

Smith, Earl E. T. *The Fourth Floor: An Account of the Castro Communist Revolution*. New York: Random House, 1962. The former U.S. Ambassador to Havana recalls the last two years of the Batista regime.

Smith, Robert Freeman. *The United States and Cuba: Business and Diplomacy, 1917–1960*. New Haven: Connecticut College and University Press, 1960. Contends that U.S. policy towards Cuba was based upon the protection of business interests.

Smith, Wayne. *Closest of Enemies: A Personal and Diplomatic Account of U.S.-Cuba Relations since 1957*. New York: W. W. Norton, 1987. A personal and critical account of U.S. policy toward revolutionary Cuba by the former head of the U.S. Interests Section in Havana.

Smith, Wayne, and Esteban Morales Domínguez, eds. *Subject to Solution: Problems in Cuban-U.S. Relations*. Boulder: Lynne Rienner Publishers, 1988. A collection of essays that examines the key issues of bilateral relations: the embargo, the Guantánamo naval base, and Cuban relations with Central America and the Soviet Union.

Turner, William W. *The Fish Is Red: The Story of the Secret War against Castro*. New York: Harper and Row, 1981. A study of the U.S. covert operations against Castro and Cuba during the 1960s and 1970s.

Welch, Richard E., Jr. *Response to Revolution: The United States and Cuban Revolution, 1959–1961*. Chapel Hill: University of North Carolina Press, 1985. An excellent scholarly analysis of Washington's response to the evolving revolutionary process in Cuba.

Wright, Thomas C. *Latin America in the Era of the Cuban Revolution*. Westport, Conn.: Praeger, 1991. An examination of the impact of Castro's revolution upon the various communist movements across Latin America.

Wyden, Peter. *The Bay of Pigs Story*. New York: Simon and Schuster, 1979. Remains a standard account of the invasion, especially its planning and execution.

CONTEMPORARY CUBA

Adams, Jan S. *A Foreign Policy in Transition: Moscow's Retreat from Central America and the Caribbean, 1985–1992*. Durham: Duke University Press, 1992. An introductory examination to the meaning of the Soviet withdrawal of support for the entire Caribbean region.

Baloyra, Enrique A., and James A. Morris, eds. *Conflict and Change in Cuba*. Albuquerque: University of New Mexico Press, 1993. A collection of essays dealing with the traditions of the revolution and the reality of the changing world.

Bengelsdorf, Carrolle. *The Problem of Democracy in Cuba: Between Vision and Reality*. New York: Oxford University Press, 1994. An examination of the deepening crisis in Cuba against the larger backdrop of *perestroika* and the collapse of socialism in eastern Europe.

Benjamin, Medea. "Things Fall Apart." *NACLA Report on the Americas* 14 (August 1990): 13–31. An account of the downward spiralling economy and social support network in Cuba.

Cardoso, Eliana, and Ann Helwege. *Cuba after Communism*. Cambridge, Mass.: MIT Press, 1992. A brief analysis that explores the options facing Cuba in light of the successes and failures of the Cuban Revolution and the Cuban animosity toward the United States.

Centeno, Miguel Angle, and Mauricio Font, eds. *Toward a New Cuba: Legacies of a Revolution*. Boulder and London: Lynne Rienner Publishers, 1997. A collection of essays on the impact of the Soviet Union's collapse upon Cuba's internal and external affairs.

Cuban American National Foundation. *Cuba's Transition to Democracy*. Miami: Cuban American National Foundation, 1992. The result of a CANF-sponsored 1991 conference, which includes critical assessments of the impact of the Soviets upon Cuba and CANF's plans for a market economy in a post-Castro Cuba.

Cuban Research Institute at Florida International University. *Transition in Cuba: New Challenges for US Policy*. Miami: Latin American and Caribbean Center, Florida International University, 1993. A thoughtful academic analysis of the possible alternatives facing a post-Castro Cuba and its relations with the United States.

Domínguez, Jorge I., and Rafael Hernández, eds. *U.S.-Cuban Relations in the 1990s*. Boulder: Westview Press, 1990. Another thoughtful collection of essays on the expected course of U.S.-Cuban relations in the 1990s.

Eckstein, Susan E. *Back from the Future: Cuba under Castro*. Princeton: Princeton University Press, 1994. A most cogent analysis of the revolution's thirty-five years and the crisis it now confronts.

Erisman, H. Michael, and John M. Kirk, eds. *Cuban Foreign Policy Confronts a New International Order*. Boulder and London: Lynne Rienner Publishers, 1991. Brings together the expectations of various scholars on how the changing world order will affect Cuba's relations with Russia, East and West Europe, Africa, and the United States.

González, Edward, and David Ronefelt. *Cuba Adrift in a Post-Communist World*. Santa Monica: The Rand Corporation, 1992. A comprehensive examination of the deepening economic, social, and diplomatic crisis of the early 1990s.

Halbesky, Sandor, and John M. Kirk. *Cuba in Transition: Crisis and Transformation*. Boulder and London: Westview Press, 1992. Papers from a 1989 scholarly conference in Halifax, Nova Scotia, that offer important assessments of Cuban political, economic, and everyday life at the time.

Kaplowitz, Donna Rich. *Anatomy of a Failed Embargo: U.S. Sanctions against Cuba*. Boulder: Lynne Rienner Publishers, 1998. A brief analytical volume providing insights into the failure of U.S. policy, even through the most recent times.

————, ed. *Cuba's Ties to a Changing World*. Boulder and London: Lynne Rienner Publishers, 1993. An important collection of essays that presents various perspectives on Cuba's relations with the world following the collapse of the Soviet Union.

Mesa-Lago, Carmelo. *Are Economic Reforms Propelling Cuba to the Market?* Coral Gables, Fla.: North/South Center, University of Miami, 1994. Examines government policies for the post-Soviet Cuban economy.

Miami Herald. *Cuba Watch*. A monthly publication of current events in Cuba. An important news source for contemporary events.

Oppenheimer, Andrés. *Castro's Final Hour: The Secret Story behind the Coming Downfall of Communist Cuba*. New York: Touchstone, 1992. A provocative monograph by a leading Latin American journalist for the *Miami Herald*.

Pérez-López, Jorge F. *Cuba at a Crossroads: Politics and Economics after the Fourth Party Congress*. Gainesville: University Press of Florida, 1994. An analysis of the issues confronting the first communist party congress meeting in Cuba following the loss of Soviet assistance.

Pérez-Stable, Marifeli. *The Cuban Revolution: Origins, Course and Legacy.* New York: Oxford University Press, 1993. Places the contemporary changes in Cuba within their historical context.

Rabkin, Rhoda P. "Cuban Socialism: Ideological Response to the Era of Socialist Crisis." *Cuban Studies* 22 (February 1992): 27–50. An examination of the economic and ideological adjustments in response to the collapse of the Soviet Union.

Tulchin, Joseph S., and Rafael Hernández, eds. *Cuba and the United States: Will the Cold War in the Caribbean End?* Boulder and London: Lynne Rienner Publishers, 1991. A collection of papers from a 1990 conference in Washington, D.C. co-hosted by the Wilson Center and the Center for American Studies in Havana. The papers provide perspectives on how the internal dynamics in each country and the changing international order will affect U.S.-Cuban relations.

NON-PRINT ELECTRONIC SOURCES

Fundación MAPFRE América, Madrid, Spain. In cooperation with the Hispanic Division of the Library of Congress of the United States, *Handbook of Latin American Studies CD-ROM (HLAS/CD)*, Volumes 1–53 (1936–1994). A CD-ROM for DOS 5.0 or higher that contains this annual and most important annotated bibliography.

Latin American Video Archives. New York. Provides Internet access to Latin American videos and films. Access by country and/or subject. Contact: http://www.lavavideo.org

VIDEOS

Castro: The Last Revolutionary. Interview with Dan Rather, CBS News, July 1996. Castro portrays himself as a humanitarian and Cuba the victim of misguided U.S. policy for the last forty years.

Castro's Cuba. Turner Broadcasting System, Atlanta, Georgia, April 1991. James Earl Jones hosts a tour through Havana, talking with Cubans about life in the country.

Changing Tides. The Cinema Guild, New York, 1994. Examines the phenomenon of the Cuban *balseros,* those Cuban citizens who in the summer of 1994 made desperate attempts to reach Florida, only to face an uncertain future.

Che Guevara: A Biography. Arts and Entertainment Television, August 1996. A sympathetic portrayal of a revolutionary idealist confronting problems in Cuba and Bolivia.

Cuba: In the Shadow of Doubt. Seven Leagues Production, 1986. Describes U.S.-Cuban relations from the Spanish-American War in 1898 to 1986.

Cuba Holding Back the Tide. Films for the Humanities and Sciences, Princeton, N.J., 1996. A thirty-minute examination of Cuba's worsening situation in the 1990s.

Cuba in Transition. Cable News Network, Atlanta, Georgia, June 1995. A week-long series that includes interviews with Cuban government officials on the status and future of the Cuban economy.

Cuba Va!: The Challenge of the Next Generation. The Cinema Guild, New York, 1993. Looks at Cuba's future from the perspective of the outspoken youth.

Cuban Missile Crisis. Public Broadcasting Television, 1992. A *Frontline* presentation examines the events surrounding the 1962 crisis.

Cuban Missile Crisis: 30 Years Later. NBC News, Special Report, October 1992. This two-hour documentary includes interviews with policymakers at the time in a detailed retrospective of the crisis.

Dateline: 1961, Cuba. MTI Film and Video, Northbrook, Ill., 1989. Part of the "Eagle and the Bear" Series dealing with the United States-Soviet Cold War confrontation, this brief documentary places Castro in the communist camp.

Dateline: 1962, Cuba. MTI Film and Video, Northbrook, Ill., 1989. Part of the "Eagle and the Bear" Series dealing with the United States-Soviet Cold War confrontation, this brief documentary portrays Cuba as a Soviet client state and the U.S. as forcing the Soviets to back down in the 1962 missile crisis.

Fidel Castro: El Commandante. Arts and Entertainment Biography Series, 1996. A profile of Castro that traces his life from his rebel days in the Sierra Maestra to his decades-long confrontation with the United States.

Fidel Castro: The Last Communist. Public Broadcasting Television, 1992. A portrayal of Castro's ability to stay the course despite the economic and social collapse of Cuba.

Improper Conduct: Castro's Cuba. Films for the Humanities and Sciences, Princeton, N.J., 1996. An hour-long series of interviews with Cuban exiles in the Miami area. They represent all walks of life and offer their perspectives on Castro's impact upon Cuba.

Inside Castro's Cuba. Filmakers Library, New York, 1994. Filming in Cuba for a year, the video presents economic and political conditions in Cuba, and also shows a glimpse of Fidel Castro.

Last Days of the Revolution. University of West Florida, Pensacola, Fla., 1994. Tells the story of the economic and political deterioration in Cuba. Shot primarily in Cuba, it illustrates the hardships of the Cuban people and looks closely at the effects of the U.S. economic embargo.

Latin American and Caribbean Presence in the U.S. From *The Americas* Series. The Annenberg/CPB Collection, 1993. This hour-long program dis-

cusses the various Hispanic communities in the United States, including
    Miami's Cuban Americans.
Miami-Havana. The Cinema Guild, New York, 1992. Examines the human trag-
    edy of families divided as a result of the two-generation conflict between
    Cuba and the United States.

Index

About the Author

THOMAS M. LEONARD is Distinguished Professor of History and Director of the International Studies Program at the University of North Florida. He is the author of seven books on Latin America, including *Guide to Central American Collections in the United States* (Greenwood, 1994). His area of specialization is U.S.–Central American relations.